PENGUIN AFRICAN LIBRARY

Edited by Ronald Segal

Mozambique:
Memoirs of a Rev

John Paul was born in Plymouth, England, in 1928 and
was educated at Winchester College and Edinburgh
University. He trained for the Anglican Ministry at Ely
Theological College, was ordained in 1954 and served
as a curate in a Portsmouth parish for two years. He then
joined the Universities' Mission to Central Africa, from
which he was sent as an assistant priest to Messumba
Mission on the Mozambican shore of Lake Malawi, and
within two years became Superior of all the Anglican work
in northern Mozambique. He was appointed an
Archdeacon in 1965 a few months after Frelimo had
begun military operations against the Portuguese. In 1969
he married Susan Woodhouse, formerly secretary to the
Hon. Garfield Todd. Health forced him to leave
Mozambique in 1970. He is now Rector of the small
Episcopal Church in Castle Douglas, Scotland. He has
been interviewed on B.B.C., Grampian and Portuguese
television and has broadcast on G.D.R. (East German) and
B.B.C. radio. He still maintains his contacts in
Mozambique and other parts of Africa.

JOHN PAUL

Mozambique:
Memoirs of a Revolution

Penguin Books

Penguin Books Ltd,
Harmondsworth, Middlesex, England
Penguin Books Inc.,
7110 Ambassador Road, Baltimore, Maryland 21207, U.S.A.
Penguin Books Australia Ltd,
Ringwood, Victoria, Australia
Penguin Books Canada Ltd,
41 Steelcase Road West, Markham, Ontario, Canada
Penguin Books (N.Z.) Ltd,
182–190 Wairau Road, Auckland 10, New Zealand

First published 1975

Copyright © John Paul, 1975

Made and printed in Great Britain by
Hazell Watson & Viney Ltd,
Aylesbury, Bucks
Set in Linotype Plantin

This book is sold subject to the condition that
it shall not, by way of trade or otherwise, be lent,
re-sold, hired out, or otherwise circulated without
the publisher's prior consent in any form of
binding or cover other than that in which it is
published and without a similar condition
including this condition being imposed on the
subsequent purchaser

Contents

Acknowledgements

Acknowledgement is made to the following for
permission to reproduce material in this book:

Lord Kilbracken and the London *Evening Standard*
The *Church Times*
The United Society for the Propagation
of the Gospel

Introduction

John Paul was working as an Anglican missionary in Mozambique when African rebellion against Portuguese rule there began. And he stayed to continue his work while the ensuing war spread to surround and inevitably involve his Mission.

His book is important and necessary. For here is the character of Portuguese colonial rule drawn not in statutes and statistics, nor in the propaganda of either apology or denunciation, but in the lives of its various victims, white as well as black: administrators and police and soldiers, traders, teachers, peasants and labourers, schoolchildren. Here is recorded the rise of the Frelimo movement, alongside the decline of a régime whose moral nonsense made it rely increasingly on terror to survive, and whose increasing reliance on terror only nourished the challenge to its survival. It is a story that does not always keep a straight face. John Paul has a sharp sense of the ridiculous, and in Portuguese Mozambique horror jostled with farce.

But the book is more than history written in the first person singular. It is the history of a singular personal dedication, which became a battlefield in the clash of armies and ideas. John Paul succeeded at least for a while in having his Mission recognized by both sides as a 'neutral zone'. He never became a neutral zone himself. There is no doubt where his sympathies lay, though his protection of the Mission and of all those who sought a home, a school, a hospital, a haven within it, persuaded him that he should close its doors to the rebellion if he was to keep the régime from closing them altogether. Indeed, this is, above all, a book about a decent human being who gave abundantly of himself.

Ronald Segal

Preface

Since I returned from Mozambique, it has been suggested more than once that I should write of my experiences there. This was not possible while Caetano's Government was in power, as what I have written would not only have jeopardized Messumba's very existence, but would also have got particular persons into trouble.

I have read glowing accounts of Portuguese rule in Africa written by M.P.s and others who had been completely hoodwinked by Portugal's 'public relations', and I have been astonished at their naïvety.

When the Mucumbura massacres coincided with the White Fathers' withdrawal from Mozambique in 1971, I hoped that this might open the eyes of the politicians and the public here to the true state of affairs in that country. But in 1973, England was celebrating her Ancient Alliance with Portugal, and fêting Dr Caetano in London. Her Majesty, 'head' of the Established Church of England, was required to entertain a Prime Minister whose Government was responsible for the oppression of millions of people in Africa. As a British subject and an Anglican, I found this distressing and repugnant.

The then Foreign Secretary and the Archbishop of Canterbury returned bland answers when I addressed to them pleas that at least Her Majesty and the Duke of Edinburgh might be allowed to hold themselves aloof from this political jamboree.

My arguments were subsequently strengthened by the disclosure, through Fr Adrian Hastings and *The Times*, of the Wiriyamu massacres. I was, at that time, frequently asked if I could corroborate the stories. As I had left the country almost three years before these horrifying events, I naturally could not do so. But I could, and did, say that in the light of my experience,

Preface

I found myself able to believe every word that Fr Hastings wrote. The bitter denunciations of Fr Hastings that followed did little credit to his detractors. Following the *coup* of April 1974 in Portugal, there has been ample evidence of the massacres. Predictably, the United Nations' commission investigating the massacres made a statement on 13 June 1974 regretting that Portugal had failed to cooperate.

The *coup* took most people by surprise – myself included – but the character and life of General Spínola do not seem to augur as well for the future as some commentators would have us believe. His vacillations during the months immediately after the *coup* inspire but little confidence in him as a leader of a sincerely liberal Portugal. The recognition of his failures as a military commander in Guinea-Bissau formed the basis of his theory that there is no military solution to the problems of Portugal's overseas 'states'.

The overthrow of the Caetano régime was primarily due to Portugal's problems in Africa, and most particularly in Mozambique.

Castle Douglas, August 1974

1   Introduction to Africa

I can remember no time in my life when I did not want to go to Africa; and when I was old enough to learn about David Livingstone and other great men of the continent, my desire to go there strengthened into determination. Along with this resolve went an ambition to be a doctor, like my maternal grandfather, whose family had a long medical tradition. Only much later did I realize that I really wanted to be a priest. Religion had its place in our lives, and there must have been few Sundays when I have not gone to church. If this smacks too much of piety, let me disclaim it: in fact, there are those among my spiritual superiors who have had occasion to deplore my lack of it.

A cheerful school in Seaford prepared me for Winchester; and owing, I suspect, to wartime difficulties and perhaps a shortage of aspirants, I managed to get a place. As will become obvious, I am no scholar, but I found in Winchester a place to love, a society in which to grow, and a source of almost totally happy experiences and memories. But even Winchester could not teach me to read a book for pleasure – a great loss, I am told.

My school career was pursued with an eye always to medicine, and when I left in 1946 to do my National Service, it was in the knowledge that I had a place waiting for me at Edinburgh University.

In my initial training camp I spent the first months of 1947 being shouted at on the parade ground, and being colder than I had thought possible. The pipes froze solid, and sanitation was limited to a row of buckets in a corridor. Thanks to the rigours of Winchester, I alone remained unperturbed. As I was a prospective medical student, I was drafted into the R.A.M.C., and in due course was sent to Northern Ireland. My education continued: I learned that there was a part of Britain where religious intolerance was carried to such lengths that 'only Catholics' or 'only Protestants' were asked to reply in newspaper advertisements for staff of all kinds. I was more than glad, therefore, to be posted a few weeks later to Africa, though I am never quite sure whether Egypt really is part of Africa.

Within a couple of months I was posted to Kenya (real Africa at last), and, from the moment of my arrival at Mombasa, I knew that this was my continent. As a white private, I now found myself a kind of inferior officer, even to the extent of having an *askari* to look after me and my uniform. The Commanding Officer informed me that I was no use to him until I had learned Swahili, and that I had just three weeks in which to do it. This was alarming to one who had never acquired even adequate schoolboy French. It was left to me to get myself taught, so I worked in the ration store where nothing was spoken but Swahili. In this unlikely place, I made the miraculous discovery that I had an ear for languages, and at the end of my three weeks I could truthfully report that I had a working knowledge of Swahili.

In September 1948, I returned to England and entered the medical faculty of Edinburgh University in October. But I soon discovered that my real ambition was to be a missionary priest in Africa. This change of direction seemed to me a slight one; but it was not so regarded by some members of my family, who took a little time to accept it. I changed to a wide Master of Arts programme on the advice of the board that recommended me for training for the ministry, and in due course I went to Ely Theological College. There I made some lasting friendships. We managed to make life fairly interesting, and certainly we enjoyed it.

From time to time, earnest visiting speakers would alarm us by their lack of humour, or great men inspire us, and when the saintly Bishop Frank Thorne of Nyasaland came seeking recruits to the ranks of his missionaries, I was caught by his enthusiasm, his obvious love for his people, and the equally obvious need. Bishop Frank belonged to the Universities' Mission to Central Africa, an Anglo-Catholic society which had been formed in the 1850s to work among the peoples who lived around the shores of Lake Nyasa. The enormous surge of missionary interest which had resulted from David Livingstone's well-publicized explorations, and from his passionate calls to help the people of darkest Africa beset by the evils of the slave trade, had led to the establishment of many such missionary societies; but the high-church bias of the U.M.C.A., with its band of extraordinarily dedicated priests, nurses, doctors and teachers, had particular appeal for me.

In 1956, two years after my ordination, Bishop Frank visited England again, and I went to see him. He asked me to go, at least at first, to that part of his diocese which lay in Portuguese East Africa (Mozambique), as it was the ideal place to learn Chinyanja, the language which I would need anywhere in his diocese. Officially, I would be resident in Nyasaland.

I knew little about Mozambique, but what I had heard was hardly commendable. My father had visited Beira in 1953, and told me that he had seen African dockers in chains. Such tales of Portuguese brutality weighed heavily on me, especially as I had just read *Naught for Your Comfort*, Trevor Huddleston's book about South Africa, which gave me a horrifying insight into white attitudes.

On 6 December 1956 I left Southampton for Cape Town on the *Winchester Castle*. The voyage took two weeks and was followed by an interminable railway journey north to Salisbury, Rhodesia, and then east to the little border town of Umtali.

The first station in Mozambique was Machipanda, where we went through immigration and customs formalities. There was little to be seen out of the window apart from a few uniformed Portuguese officials, standing about in front of rather dilapidated station buildings. Next morning I awoke to see the Pungwe flats for the first time – with only an occasional house interrupting the desolate, flat and featureless, seemingly unending stretches of swamp.

Twenty miles short of Beira I got out at Dondo, where the diesel train to Nyasaland was waiting. The Portuguese guard told me that there was no room. But I waved my seat reservation at him; and after some argument, he allowed me in. The railway ran through untamed scrub bush country, relieved only by a sandy track that followed the railway line. We stopped at small stations from time to time. One I particularly remember was Inhaminga, which was to find itself in the news some seventeen years later, where we waited for quite a long time, and I was able to watch the activity in the small marshalling yards. Torrential rain was falling, and I felt sorry for some Africans in tattered clothes, loading trucks, who were watched over by a Portuguese official under cover. On we went slowly towards the Zambezi. As we were leaving one small station, our driver put his head out of the cabin window to shout something at the stationmaster, and his cap blew off. We had already reached quite a speed, so he brought the train gradually to a halt and then reversed, climbed out of the cabin and retrieved his cap. It all seemed very un-English. At some of our stops, the stationmaster would climb up into the cabin and have a beer with the guard. We eventually reached the great bridge that spans the Zambezi at Dona Ana: we were already an hour late, but no one, except the non-Portuguese passengers, seemed in the least disturbed.

After Dona Ana, a British driver took over, and we entered Nyasaland, where things were brisker.

The contrast between the first part of the journey in Mozambique and the second part in Nyasaland could not have been more marked. Every European in Mozambique seemed to have a uniform, though Portuguese attitudes were generally cheerful and carefree. In Nyasaland I saw very few Europeans (every stationmaster was an Indian) and those I did see, like the engine-driver, gave an impression of efficiency in spite of their informal appearance. The country in Mozambique was drearily flat; in Nyasaland it was hilly and cultivated. There were few Africans to be seen in Mozambique, and these were normally dressed in rags; Nyasaland seemed to be teeming with Africans, often wearing bright cotton frocks or shirt and shorts.

On arrival at Blantyre I was whisked off to Zomba, forty miles away: a tiny town, but one which surely deserved its reputation as 'the most beautiful capital in the British Empire'. It was

Christmas Eve and I was to take the services there the following day. It was a pleasure, after almost three weeks in boat and train, to sleep in a stationary bed once more, and a joy, after so many years away from Africa, to sleep under a mosquito net, with the fireflies dancing round me and the sound of the crickets outside.

A couple of days after Christmas, Fr Pocklington came to take me back to Blantyre, where he lived. He and his curate looked after the spiritual needs of the largely white Anglican congregations in the area. Pocklington initiated me into the workings of the Diocese of Nyasaland. He seemed to enjoy showing me round Blantyre and advising me about the kit I would need. He was not at all enthusiastic that I was going to Messumba (the Mission to which I was posted) and thought the best that the Bishop could do about the place would be to wind up all the work. When I suggested that this might not be to the liking of the Africans, he replied at once: 'But many would come across the Lake to Nyasaland.' Pocklington had spent about three years at Messumba, but told me that he had had quite enough of the lakeshore. He had little good to say about the Portuguese, under whose Government he had seen Africans in chains.

A few days later, Bishop Frank took me to the diocesan headquarters at Mponda's some 120 miles farther north and just a couple of miles south of Lake Nyasa. Seventy miles after leaving Blantyre and its temperate climate at 4,000 feet, we descended the Rift Valley escarpment; and, although we were still nearly 1,500 feet above sea-level, it was hot and humid. Everywhere there were throngs of people. We arrived at Mponda's after a hot and dusty ride, and the Bishop was obviously thrilled to be home.

I stayed at Mponda's a couple of days, and then we were off to Chipoka, which was to be of such importance to the Portuguese in later years. There we boarded the *Ilala* for Likoma Island, and a voyage lasting some twenty-four hours.

Likoma Island is a remarkable place. It has no rivers; covers only ten square miles; is quite infertile; and yet has some 5,000 inhabitants. This density of population is almost entirely due to the Universities' Mission which chose it as the headquarters for its work among the lakeshore peoples. In February 1882, two young English missionaries reached the eastern shore of Lake Nyasa a few miles north of Messumba, having walked from the Indian Ocean, 500 miles away. By the end of that same month one of them, Charles Janson, was dead, and his grave is to be found at Chia. The other, William Percival Johnson, continued his work up and down the eastern lakeshore, and his memory is revered to this day. The Nyasas make particularly faithful Christians, but the missionaries' work was continually hampered by hostile tribes who lived inland and carried out sporadic raids on the Nyasas. The missionaries therefore asked Chief Chiteje, who lived in what is now Mozambique and in whose area much of the mission work was concentrated, if they might base their work on Likoma Island, which lay a few miles offshore from the Chief's home. He agreed to this, and well into the present century the whole of Likoma Island remained the actual property of the Universities' Mission. A large cathedral was built, complete with cloisters and a library; medical and educational work was developed; and the missionaries, with all those who wished to join them, were able to live in safety from the inland tribes, who were afraid to cross the few miles of water separating the island from the mainland. With the Mission firmly established, individual missionaries regularly visited those groups of Christians who lived on the mainland lakeshore; and, as their work expanded, they built up sizeable Christian communities.

Political difficulties arose when Portugal, by the Treaty of Berlin of 1885* (later ratified by the Anglo-Portuguese Convention of 1891), was given the vast area which came to be called Portuguese East Africa or Mozambique, and which included the southern half of the eastern lakeshore, where most of the work of the Mission lay. Chief Chiteje now found himself in

---

* The first Portuguese official to reach the Lake was a Lieutenant Augusto Cardoso who led an expedition there in 1888. (This fact was commemorated in the mid 1960s by the renaming, after him, of the small lakeshore town of Metangula.)

Portuguese territory, and Likoma Island itself was threatened because it lay only four miles off the Portuguese colony. The Universities' Mission had made unsuccessful representations when Lord Rosebery was Foreign Minister to have a strip of land all the way down the eastern lakeshore declared British (a map was even published claiming this as a sphere of British influence); but at least the waters of Lake Nyasa were declared to be British.

The Portuguese were never to forget what they regarded as the gross impertinence of the Universities' Mission. Tribal warfare was a thing of the past; but now hostility came from the Portuguese, who regarded the Mission, perhaps with some justi-fication, as a 'tool of British imperialism'. The Mission, for its part, was extremely suspicious of the Portuguese because of their involvement in the slave trade (slavery had been officially abolished by Portugal in 1836; but, in fact, the most that she had done to stop it in her African colonies was to turn a blind eye). The Portuguese established an official post (*posto*) at Cóbuè, opposite Likoma, to mark their presence, and relations with the missionaries, who continued to visit their people in what was now Portuguese territory, were sometimes strained. One mis-sionary was shot by a 'Chefe do Posto' at Cóbuè (Kango) in 1911 for interference. It appears that Fr Douglas had com-plained about the Chefe's immorality with several African girls and his frequent flogging of villagers. The Chefe, Senhor Tavira, was brought to trial after a long delay and then imprisoned for one year.

The priest-in-charge (and virtual king) of Likoma when I first arrived there was Fr Gerald Hadow. He was essentially a man of action, as well as being a devoted pastor, and could turn his hand to almost anything practical.

Also living at Likoma at that time was Canon Cox, who had been at Messumba from 1919 until 1949, when Archdeacon Stanley Pickard took over from him. He was a great old man, the very first European priest to live at Messumba; for his first ten years, with no other white person for company. In spite of the drawbacks, it appeared that Messumba had much to commend it. For a start, it was perfectly situated, up and away from the shore, with a cooler climate than most lakeshore places; and, perhaps best of all, it was in the midst of a pleasant people. This was the place I was to go to, and it was an exciting prospect. But the missionaries on Likoma were concerned about my going there: partly because the Portuguese made life difficult for the missionaries; and partly because they were unsure of the reception I would get from Archdeacon Pickard.

Across the water from Likoma I could clearly see several villages on the mainland. Hadow told me that nearly all the people there were Christians, but so inaccessible from Messumba that they were rarely visited by Archdeacon Pickard. He told me, however, of an excellent priest, Fr Juma, who was stationed there. Very clearly visible were some European-style buildings, and these apparently belonged to the Roman Catholic Mission which had been built a few years previously, practically adjoining the house of the Portuguese Chefe do Posto. The priest there, Padre Eugénio Menegon, was a good friend of his, said Hadow, and frequently came to see him at Likoma, where he got many of his supplies. The Chefe do Posto also came over from time to time.

Next morning, Hadow and I boarded the *Paul*, a ten-ton iron sailing boat which had an auxiliary engine. It was an extraordinary craft to most people, but was Hadow's pride and joy. The crew were great characters, with Hadow a firm commander. We collected a few passengers, and there appeared to be no obstacles or formalities involved in leaving Nyasaland (Likoma) and sailing to Mozambique (Messumba).

The journey took about six hours, sailing south along the Mozambican lakeshore. There were very green hills only slightly inland, many sandy bays where the Africans were engaged in mending their nets, overhauling their boats, drying their fish, and generally passing the time with talk and laughter. This was the real Africa; and, forgetting Hadow and myself, one might have been forgiven for thinking that whites did not exist. After a few hours, we ran the *Paul* on to the beach at Chia for some passengers to disembark.

Then with long thick bamboos, we pushed the boat away

from the shore, started up the engine and continued on our way to Messumba. In just a couple of hours we would arrive at the place that was to be my home for the next thirteen years.

2 Introduction to Messumba Mission

Messumba Mission, the headquarters of all the Anglican work in northern Mozambique, was situated on a ridge in the middle of a valley, about a couple of miles from where we beached the *Paul*. As we jumped on to the sand, a little crowd gathered.

The area was thickly populated, and I was immediately struck by how fertile the place seemed. This was clearly no barren island, but well-cultivated countryside. As we walked along the narrow path in single file through the villages and tiny 'fields', we were greeted by the people sitting outside their houses – low, square huts of wattle and daub, or of rough bricks, with grass-thatched roofs. Some of the villagers would get up and shake hands or join our procession. I was not expecting any great welcome. I had been told that missionaries should not go out with the idea that they would immediately become the centre of attraction: 'People must get to know you first.' Hadow bounced along in his customary style, saying '*moni – moni – moni*', the Chinyanja greeting. Soon we started to climb gently; and ahead, on the top of a high ridge, I could see what were obviously the Mission buildings. Most were thatched with grass, but some had tiled roofs (such as I had not seen since we had left Dona Ana), and were whitewashed on the outside. The large, rather long, church was at the centre, and a short distance from it, loosely surrounding an open area, were the houses of the missionaries.

As we approached one of the tiled houses, Archdeacon Pickard came out to greet us. He was clearly surprised to see us, and when Hadow explained who I was, said he wished someone had warned him in advance. However, he took us to the dining-room for tea, and there we were joined by the other missionaries: the sister-in-charge of the hospital, Irene Wheeler, and the teacher, Joan Antcliff.

My house consisted of two rooms – a study and a bedroom. It was built of rough bricks and, unlike the houses at Likoma, was whitewashed inside. It had a stone floor and a grass roof. There was a bare minimum of furniture, but everything was spotlessly clean. A few yards away from the house was an earth closet, consisting of a hole in the ground topped by a box with a hole in it. I found this a very eerie place, and was sometimes appalled to meet snakes there. The Mission had no piped water supply and no electricity. The water was brought twice a day from either the Lake or a well to one's house, where there was a washstand and a tin bath. It was the duty of the 'boy' to heat water every evening for a bath, otherwise one washed in cold water. For light there was generally a hurricane lamp, though there were a couple of pressure lamps in the care of the Archdeacon. At least I had been prepared for such bare essentials, and things were considerably better organized at Messumba than they were at most other missions in the diocese.

I made the acquaintance of the servant assigned to me, Tito; had a lovely bath in my tin tub (which brought back memories of Winchester); and made my way back to the dining-room (which I learned that day to call the *mezane*) as a bell was ringing. This was the dressing-bell, rung to remind us that dinner would be served in half an hour. The U.M.C.A. had its roots firmly in Victorian England. The warning bell made present sense, however, since it usually indicated that the bath water was ready and rapidly cooling.

Drinks were followed by an excellent dinner; and when I remarked on this, Hadow was quick to point out that Messumba not only had a plentiful supply of milk and eggs, but also an outstanding housekeeper in Irene Wheeler. Pickard said that since we had to work in Portuguese territory and were therefore more isolated than any other mission in the diocese, we should have some compensation in the way of a few luxuries.

Soon the church bell rang and we went to Compline, the final service of the day. The church was very large, though not quite of cathedral proportions, and as we entered about a hundred

Africans turned round to look at us. These were the school and college boarders with two or three teachers. Compline was said and sung in Chinyanja, and it was a wonderful experience for a stranger, although I understood not a word, and the singing sounded unmelodious to my ears. We then returned to the *mezane*, but soon after nine it was obvious that it was time for bed. I said good-bye to Hadow, who was returning on the *Paul* to Likoma very early next morning, and Pickard escorted me to my house. He sat and talked, explaining things to me, for some time, and I thought he was pleased that I had come to Messumba. I could understand why others had been a bit doubtful whether we would get on together, but we began that evening to establish those friendly relations which have lasted (almost uninterrupted) for many years.

Nearly all the Africans at Messumba were Christians; most of them could read and write; and almost all seemed healthy. This was entirely due to the Mission, which was the permanent influence on their lives. The first missionaries had arrived in the area in 1882, and since 1919 there had been a resident missionary Superior. Now, in 1957, Pickard was only the second Superior they had ever had. Consequently, the whole atmosphere was steeped in tradition, and there was a strong sense of belonging to a family-which-mattered. There was no industry, and though many men went to other countries to find work, they knew that on their return, Messumba stood as firm as the rock it was built on. When a man came home, he invariably reported back to the Mission. The registers that were kept in the office gave great detail about every family. Benson Caomba had been responsible for keeping them up to date since the 1930s, and still is as I write.

I caught this sense of belonging as soon as I arrived. I had no doubt whatever that this was the job I had come to do, and this absolute certainty of my place in the scheme of things was never to waver, even though in the next decade I was to sustain some considerable shocks.

Irene Wheeler was in her mid forties. She had been a Norland nanny; but soon feeling the call to become a missionary, she trained as a nurse at St Bartholomew's Hospital, London. She was sent by U.M.C.A. first to Tanganyika, and then to Lisbon to learn Portuguese before being posted to Messumba. Life for Irene at Messumba was not easy. She was no linguist, and she did not like having to adapt her Bart's standards to a bush hospital. But she was devoted to her work. As the nurse, she was also housekeeper, and her excellence in this second, unsought, role was famous throughout U.M.C.A.

Joan Antcliff was not much older than myself. She came out to Nyasaland as a teacher in 1952, and she soon proved herself to be not only extremely energetic, but also a good linguist; so she, too, after two years in Lisbon, found her way to Messumba.

Archdeacon Stanley Pickard, in his late forties when I arrived, had originally come out to Nyasaland in 1939; but it was not until ten years later, after a spell in Portugal, that he arrived at Messumba. He spoke Chinyanja very well, but his knowledge of Portuguese was limited, as was his liking for the Portuguese people as a whole. However, he realized the necessity of substituting many Portuguese ways for English ones at Messumba, and this policy, though unpopular with the Africans and some missionaries, reaped a rich reward in the years to come. Like all missionaries, he had plenty of his own ideas; and, like many missionaries, he was a somewhat controversial character.

Two or three days after my arrival, Archdeacon Pickard took me to Metangula to get my passport stamped by the Chefe do Posto there. Metangula is a few miles south of Messumba on the lakeshore, but the journey there and back took the best part of the day. In January the rains are usually heavy; the River Lunho, which rises at Mt Chisindo eighteen miles away and flows into the Lake not far from the Mission, is in spate; and there is no bridge. Pickard and I walked the mile or so down to the river, over which we were carried by some of the Mission workmen. We walked up the slippery bank on the other side, and so on to the only road. Criticism has often been expressed that the Mission is sited on the 'wrong' side of the Lunho, but that was where the population was centred, and in 1919 when Canon Cox arrived, there was no road anyway, and all supplies and missionary personnel came by water from Likoma, as I had done a few days earlier.

A hundred yards or so along the road, there was a shed which housed the Mission land-rover during the rains. Reggie, the driver, was waiting for us. The dirt road to Metangula was quite appalling; and the bamboo bridges over the small streams that flowed into the Lunho were unnerving for anyone using them for the first time. After a couple of miles, at Chiwanga, the road reached the lakeshore which it followed, with hills rising steeply on the left. We passed no cars and for the last five miles no habitation whatever, as there was hardly any flat ground for building. People were walking along the road in both directions; and, almost without exception, they stopped as we passed and saluted us. Pickard explained that the Portuguese authorities were very strict about this, and that not many years previously there had been a Chefe do Posto who, if someone failed to salute him, would either beat him or bundle him into the car and let him out only when his own destination was reached. I had already heard that the Portuguese were harsh, but this shocked me considerably.

Approaching Metangula, the first building I saw was a tiled cattle dip standing rather incongruously in the middle of the bush. Then, after a few hundred yards, we came to a fairly large African village. The Africans looked different because Metangula had a large preponderance of Muslims, and many were dressed in Arab *kanzus*. The Lunho really forms the northern boundary of Islamic influence among the lakeshore Mozambicans. There was a church looked after by a resident catechist, Salathiel Chizuzu, the son of one of our clergy. We passed a group of small tiled and whitewashed buildings on the right which I was told was the Government hospital. Until recently there had been a doctor, but now his Mediterranean-style house was empty. The principal purpose of the medical work at Metangula was to eradicate sleeping sickness, and this had been done successfully. Now, the hospital was in the charge of a trained nurse, an *assimilado*, who came from the south. The amount of work he had to do was slight in comparison with what was done at Messumba, however, as the local population was much smaller, and apparently many people preferred to visit Messumba for treatment.

At the very end of the road stood the house of the Chefe do Posto, Senhor Reis. He greeted us warmly and took us inside. The house looked very grand from a distance, but in fact it was drab and furnished in a spartan manner. There was a small group of people on the back verandah, and off it an office, where sat an African, the official interpreter, trying to get through to somewhere on an old-fashioned telephone.

Reis was very keen to teach me Portuguese, but I only remember his telling me the word for fried potatoes. While we sat sipping drinks and eating small snacks, a young bearded Italian priest came in. This was Padre Inácio Mondine, who had arrived only a few hours previously and was on his way to the Roman Catholic Mission at Cóbuè. When he had gone, Reis made rather scathing comments about Italian priests, and I gathered that non-Portuguese Roman Catholic missionaries were not generally liked in Mozambique. At least we Anglicans made no pretence of being tied to the Portuguese state, and a Portuguese, it seemed, would far rather deal with someone from the north of Europe than with a fellow Latin.

I found that the local Africans liked Reis, for he was easygoing and, as he had no means of transport, hardly ever left Metangula to tour his vast area. Near his house were about half a dozen *cipais* (native police), some of whom were locals. The rest came from Maniamba in the country of the Yao tribe where the Administrador, Reis' immediate superior, had his headquarters. As we came out of the house, the *cipais* jumped to their feet and bowed, and Reggie got out of the land-rover, took off his hat and respectfully greeted the Chefe do Posto, who took no notice. We then visited the store owned by Senhor Cristina of Vila Cabral, but managed by a Senhor Pereira who had lived in Metangula for years and gone native. Metangula was the main Portuguese base on Lake Nyasa, but Reis and Pereira were the only Portuguese people there in 1957. This was all to change dramatically within the next few years.

Pickard wrote down for me a few Portuguese words, but otherwise he was much more concerned that I should learn Chinyanja. Apart from muddling it a little with Swahili, which

27

it resembles, I managed to pick it up fairly quickly, and preached my first sermon in it within two months of my arrival. Pickard taught me quite a lot himself, but every evening Jaime Amanze, the Mission's master-of-works, or Carlos Juma, a teacher, would come and teach me as well.

Our daily programme did not alter much: in church by 6 a.m.; breakfast in the *mezane* at 7.30; start work at 8. At noon there would be prayers in church; then lunch. From 1 until 2.30 was the *sesta*; then afternoon tea; and to church again at 4 for Evensong. After this came my lesson in Chinyanja from Jaime Amanze, and then the dressing-bell would tell us that it was time for the tin bath before supper. Compline with the school boarders in church at 7.30; back to one's house, or maybe to the *mezane*; and bed about 10.

The school consisted of several buildings in various stages of dilapidation. But, judged by examination results, the teaching was excellent. Our school was the only full primary school in the area. The nearest equivalent was the small Government one at Vila Cabral, 75 miles away. The nearest secondary school was at Nampula, 500 miles away. We had a junior primary school at Ngoo, a lakeshore village 15 miles to the north, and the Roman Catholics had three small junior primary schools, but their nearest full primary school was at Massangulo, 140 miles away. The Nyasas were very keen on education, and many sent their children to Nyasaland and other countries for lack of adequate schooling in Mozambique. Our school at Messumba was large, with about five hundred day pupils from the surrounding area, and a further hundred boarders, boys from our distant outstations. When a pupil had completed the course at the primary school, he could, if he was lucky, study for a further three or four years in our college, which, unlike the school, was not officially recognized by the Portuguese Government. During his first year in the college, we attempted to fill some of the gaps left by the out-dated, but rigid, Portuguese primary school syllabus, and also touched on some secondary school subjects. The second and subsequent years at the college were geared to teacher-training.

The school at Messumba was obliged, as were all schools, to

use only Portuguese as a means of instruction, apart from the teaching of religion, and to follow the official syllabus. But in terms of the Concordat and subsequent Missionary Agreements of 1940 and 1941 between the Vatican and Portugal, non-Roman Catholic missions were discriminated against, particularly in regard to education. For example: no African teacher could take charge of a school unless he had attended the Government Normal School. The only one that existed for ordinary Africans was at Manhiça, 1,200 miles away near Lourenço Marques, and, since 1945, it had only admitted Roman Catholics. We were, thus, now effectively prohibited from opening any more schools. The school at Messumba satisfied the authorities because Joan Antcliff had a teaching diploma from Portugal, and our school at Ngoo was able to continue because of Basílio Farahane, the only Manhiça-trained teacher we had left. The teachers at Messumba were merely classed as auxiliaries: an African in our college, however bright, had no hope of rising above the rank of an auxiliary teacher unless he was to 'go over to Rome' or take a course at a predominantly European college in Lourenço Marques. This our Africans felt very bitterly, and they classed Portugal and the R.C.s as one. That was the position when I arrived at Messumba in 1957, and it was not to change much until the late 1960s.

The hospital also consisted of several buildings, though these were in a slightly better state of repair than the school: maternity, out-patients, operating theatre, men's ward and women's ward. There was, of course, no doctor. Irene took people for training provided that they had completed at least one year in the college, and she spared no effort or time in trying to train her staff to Bart's standards. The hospital could accommodate about 35 in-patients, and out-patient attendances averaged about 150 a day. I think the record for a day was somewhere just above 500. The hospital always seemed to be swarming with people, many of whom had come from great distances for treatment. The greater number of out-patients had very minor complaints, but the people had no medicines of any kind at home. The main work, apart from maternity cases, was concerned with tuberculosis, malaria, hookworm, bilharzia, and burns – but crocodile bites were not unheard of, and successful amputations had been performed.

The school and hospital were scenes of constant activity and provided real services to the community, but the Portuguese Government provided neither financial nor material aid for either, though from time to time a cooperative Portuguese doctor or nurse might unofficially slip us a small quantity of medicines. As a 'foreign' (i.e., non-Roman Catholic) mission, our presence was officially tolerated and we had the free use of the land on which the Mission was built, but otherwise we had to be entirely self-supporting.

The Mission covered an area of some thirty-five hectares, and I remember that some years later, when I showed a young and energetic Chefe do Posto round the place, he exclaimed: 'But, Senhor Padre, this is not just a mission, it is a town!' And he never did see the whole place as he dropped out of the tour from exhaustion.

Archdeacon Pickard's house was also the scene of comings and goings all the time. People would wait hours to see him about some seemingly trifling matter, and when I asked why they did not get fed up with all the hanging about, he explained that Africans, unlike Europeans, are a very patient people. In later years I was to appreciate the truth of this remark. I spent a lot of time with Pickard learning the work of the Mission, and every evening we would sit together while he answered my inexhaustible questions. I thought that much of what happened at Messumba Mission was very outdated, and, like so many new people, I was quick to criticize the system. It seemed to me that for Messumba and her devoted missionaries, the Second World War had never occurred and time had stood still since 1939. This was understandable, in a way; for, during the war, many missionaries (including Pickard) had spent their furloughs in South Africa, because of the risks involved in travelling to England. Pickard himself had rarely gone to England during his previous eighteen years in the diocese, even when the opportunity occurred. So neither the missionaries nor the Africans had any desire to see much change in the way that the place was run.

Pickard did his best to dispel suspicions that we were agents of British colonialism by the 'Portugalization' of the Mission wherever possible. This was not easy as, apart from shopping expeditions and rare visits to Reis, his contact with the Portuguese was slight. None visited the Mission during the rains, as it meant crossing the River Lunho; and, as I have said, the two Portuguese at Metangula had no transport. Consequently, Messumba gave the appearance of being a British enclave trying to be Portuguese because it happened to be situated in a Portuguese colony. But Pickard's insistence on Portugalization was right; for, without doubt, if the Mission had remained as it was when he took over in 1949, the Portuguese would have closed the place down within a few years.

Pickard worked extremely hard. This was partly because of his reluctance, common amongst missionaries, to delegate responsibility to others. But it was mainly because he was running one of the largest mission areas in Africa with far too few assistants, very limited financial resources, and no help whatever from Portuguese officialdom. In the area he covered, there were not far short of 25,000 Anglicans and just over sixty outstations dependent upon the head-station at Messumba. Much of his time was concerned with secular activities: the repair of existing buildings and the construction of new ones; the laying and repair of paths and roads on the Mission; care of the vegetable garden; the making of bricks; the building of a temporary bridge over the Lunho when the rains came to an end; and so on. Then there was the paying of wages; the keeping of accounts; the writing of official letters (all in Portuguese); and the filling in of countless forms with which the Mission was bombarded by Portugal's passion for statistics. Then there were all the problems of individual people: troubles maybe with the Portuguese authorities, or with other members of the family (and given the strong family traditions of the Nyasas, these problems could be tortuous and almost insoluble, requiring many hours of consultation). There seemed to be no end to the variety of jobs which Pickard was called upon to do, and I learned with astonishment the wide range of a missionary's activities in Mozambique.

Church services were nearly always in Chinyanja, though there was a school service in Portuguese once a week. Sunday was, of course, the most important day, and just about everyone came to Mass. The church was packed for the two services which were most impressive, once one had come to terms with the music. Afterwards everyone gathered round a flag-pole in the centre of the Mission. Someone would beat the large drum, and everyone would sing the Potuguese National Anthem as the senior boy in the school hoisted the national flag. It seemed to a newcomer rather unusual to hear Africans and British missionaries singing with fervour a completely foreign song in which we identified ourselves with the Portuguese nation. (This became even ironic when one learned that the words about 'taking up arms' had been written at a time when Portugal and Britain were engaged in one of those half-forgotten incidents that were a feature of Africa in the nineteenth century.) But what really shocked me that first Sunday was seeing everyone make the fascist salute, as the National Anthem was sung and the flag raised. Subsequently one accepted it as part of what had to be done, but I refused absolutely to give the Heil Hitler salute myself.

When my three months' visa expired, I went to Likoma for about ten days, and then returned to Messumba for another three months. The missionaries at Likoma were glad that Pickard and I had apparently got on so well, but doubted whether it was wise for me to consider Messumba as a permanent posting because of its remoteness, and its situation in Portuguese territory. For my part, I only wanted to return to Messumba, which seemed to me to have a much happier atmosphere than Likoma, and my return to Messumba after the short break was like coming home. Of course the Africans did not rush up and greet me, but it was clear that they were pleased I was back. Pickard now thought I knew enough about Chinyanja to go to some of the outstations by myself, and he suggested Chicale for my first visit.

Preparations for my first *ulendo* (the local word for a journey) were extensive, as Pickard was anxious that nothing should go wrong. Chicale was among the nearer and less primitive outstations, and the resident catechist, Carlos Messosa, was not only competent but also spoke a little English. So I set out for Chicale with Tito, a cook, and four porters. It took about two hours to get there, walking along narrow paths between the low bushes and tall grass. There was no road, and it was fairly muddy going all the way, as the rains were still not quite over. Here and there were bright touches of colour from some wild flower or shrub, and almost always in my ears rang the sound of the crickets. Along the path we passed Africans from time to time, most of whom looked scared to see me, and saluted nervously until Tito assured them that I was not a Portuguese official. Then most of them came forward and shook hands. On arrival at Chicale, we passed between some grass-roofed African houses and then entered a large clearing with the church on one side, the catechist's house on the other and, straight ahead, the tiny hut in which I was to spend two nights. Carlos Messosa came to greet me. I knew him by sight, as he had visited Pickard a few times to collect his wages and obtain things for the church. Outside his house, I recognized one or two of our Mission teachers (the school being on holiday), and I began to feel less of a stranger. After exchanging greetings with many of the village people, I entered my hut, stooping down to avoid the low lintel. Tito, who had already unpacked my table and chair, was making up the camp bed. The cook had put a pot of tea and a plate of biscuits on the table. This was all clearly part of the established pattern of their work. I found it hard to believe that apart from our missionaries, no white person had probably ever set foot in Chicale. Soon came the ringing of the church bell (most out-stations had only an iron bar). A lot of people had turned up, and children stopped and stared at me through the doorway of the hut. The cook appeared to be bargaining with a vociferous group over produce, and from time to time would pop in for money to pay for a bunch of bananas or a chicken.

I walked over to the church and with the catechist went through various papers that he had for me – lists of people who were to be baptized or approved for confirmation classes; of those who wished to receive communion the following day; of the sick, and so on. Also there was to be a marriage, and a burial. After Evensong, scores of people came to make their confessions. This was all part of the *ulendo* pattern which I was to experience very often: it was as if the circus had come to town, and no one wanted to miss anything.

Near the church was a ruined building which, until a few years previously, had been the school. It had to be closed since there had been no 'qualified' teacher to keep it going.

The next day after Mass I dealt with all the questions, complaints and requests brought to me by individual villagers. Everyone was very friendly, and as they rarely saw a missionary from Messumba they seemed to consider it an honour that one had come to visit them.

In May the rains ended, our workmen built a bamboo bridge over the Lunho, and Reggie brought the land-rover back to the Mission. Pickard suggested that we go to Manda-Mbuzi, about forty-five miles away, where some twenty years previously a missionary had been stationed.

On reaching the road on the far side of the Lunho, instead of turning right for Metangula, we turned left, and some four miles later passed what was then the very small Roman Catholic Mission near Nova Coimbra. Here the main road bore right for Maniamba and beyond, but we went straight on. This road was only passable in the dry season and for several miles ran parallel to the Lunho through fairly thickly populated villages. We passed several Africans working on the road, usually supervised by a *cipai*. Apparently some of them were prisoners, but the majority had been recruited from the surrounding villages, sometimes by force.

Near a large village, Mpochi, there was a ford across the Lunho, and then we climbed to Lucambo village. The view from the escarpment towards the Lake was very fine. We were now in sparsely populated country and the few villages were widely scattered. At Manda-Mbuzi the people were Nyasas and staunch Anglicans. There was a beautiful church and a well-above-average *ulendo* house, though there was seldom anyone to occupy it.

On another occasion, we went to Maniamba which was the administrative headquarters, twenty miles beyond Nova Coimbra. The drive there was even more spectacular than the one to

Manda-Mbuzi, as we climbed to 3,000 feet. The people at Maniamba were of the Yao tribe and were ninety-nine per cent Muslim, so we had no permanent mission work there. The only Europeans at Maniamba were the Administrador, the *secretário*, the *aspirante* and the *enfermeiro*. The Administrador corresponded roughly to a district commissioner in the British colonies; with the Chefes do Posto at Metangula, Cóbuè, and a couple of other places in the interior as his immediate subordinates. The Administrador wielded tremendous power and could do more or less what he liked with anyone. The *secretário* was responsible for the day-to-day paper work. The *aspirante* was a cadet. The *enfermeiro* was the official male nurse and was in charge of the hospital, when, as was usually the case, there was no doctor in residence, and his job was supposed to be the medical welfare of everyone who lived in the Administrador's vast area or *circunscrição*.

There was then no school of any sort at Maniamba, although there was a small Roman Catholic chapel. These chapels were to be found at almost every Portuguese administrative centre, whether or not there were any Christians there. The chapel at Maniamba was mildewed and mouldy, as it was neither used nor looked after. The Africans were few and servile. Whenever I appeared, they jumped to attention, especially if I was accompanied by the Administrador. There was a lot of bowing and scraping which I found most distasteful. Maniamba and Messumba were two different worlds: with different tribes, different religions, different languages, different ways of treating a European – and different ways of treating Africans.

In July 1957, Bishop Frank came to Messumba, and when he asked me if I would like to be there permanently, I had no hesitation in saying yes. He stressed what I knew only too well, that in order to obtain a resident's permit I would have to learn Portuguese. The best place to do this was Portugal itself, and it was agreed that I should go there as soon as my current three-month visitor's visa expired. I offered to share the expenses of this (so that I might be free to make my own arrangements) and within a few days had left Messumba and was on my way to Portugal.

3   Interlude in Portugal

I had never been to southern Europe before and even as the taxi took me from the airport to the hotel in Lisbon, I realized how different a world I was entering. It was Saturday night and there were crowds of people in the streets, just walking and chattering, or clinging on to the trams, while my driver raced through the streets at an alarming speed, blowing his horn constantly like every other driver. From time to time I saw a policeman trying to control the flow, gesticulating and blowing the whistle which seemed part of his face. The next morning, being Sunday, there was less traffic, and drivers seemed even less inhibited about speeding.

At Messumba, I had purposely made no attempt to learn Portuguese, but now in Portugal I was determined to identify myself with the people as much as I could. This was not so easy for an obvious foreigner who was a magnet for every shoe-black in Lisbon. I slipped into the modern church of São João de Deus for Mass, and found it crowded: the women mostly dressed in black from head to toe and seemingly attentive; the men mostly in black suits and white shirts but rather less interested in the service. There was a noticeably casual air about the whole scene. On the steps as we came out there were a few pathetic people asking for alms. I continued my walk, still trailed by men trying with great determination to shine my shoes. My knowledge of Portuguese amounted to little more than the greetings that I had learnt at Messumba, so I was speechless – and helpless. Very few people I met understood English, but by using signs I managed to buy a map of Lisbon and its suburbs, and studied it during a meal at a pavement café. I decided to go to Estoril for the afternoon. The half-hour train journey along the shore of the wide estuary of the Tagus was full of interest, and I had at last shaken off the shoe-blacks. It was strange to see the poorer women walking with loads on their heads, as in Africa, and even stranger to catch a glimpse of some with a pair of slippers on the top of the load as they walked barefoot. I later learnt that people were forbidden to walk barefoot in tourist areas, and carried a pair of slippers in case they saw a policeman.

In Estoril, I sought out a Portuguese couple to whom I had a letter of introduction. I hoped they would help me get accommodation as a paying guest in a Portuguese household. Other missionaries at Messumba had lived in rooms and gone for lessons each day, but I felt I would learn the language more quickly if I lived with a family, as well as taking lessons. They made inquiries for me among their friends, and three weeks later I went to live with the Schrecks at São João do Estoril.

I came to know both Lisbon and Estoril fairly well, and even now can remember the names of all the stations between the two. I avoided my fellow-countrymen so that I would mix as much as possible with the Portuguese people. I may have looked very un-Portuguese but my way of living corresponded much more closely to theirs than it did to that of the many hundreds of British people who lived along the line from Lisbon to Estoril. My mornings were spent usually in Lisbon and my afternoons in Estoril, studying, and then I would go for a walk along the sea front and occasionally for a swim. One of the ways I found helpful in learning Portuguese was to read the papers, each one bearing the censor's stamp. Remembering a little Latin and French, I was able to make out the gist of what was written.

The Schrecks, with whom I lived nearly all the time I was in Portugal, were from the north of the country. He was of German extraction, and looked it, but was Portuguese in every other respect. He was not very keen on having me in the house, I gathered, as he had been pro-German during the war. Mrs Schreck was altogether Portuguese and was a graduate, I think, of Oporto University. They were a youngish middle-class couple with four children ranging in age from five to thirteen, so conversation never flagged. In 1957 the Portuguese middle class had not long emerged as a distinct feature in the social system. The children, like nearly all Portuguese children, went to a state school. It was a modest household, in spite of having a living-in maid, and a part-time cook and gardener. These servants were treated very much as members of the family, though of course they did not sit and eat with the rest of us, and I was shocked that the maid never had a day off, and that there never seemed to be any time when she was off-duty, except after she had washed up the dinner things at night.

Not long after my arrival, the churchwardens of St George's, Lisbon, asked me if I could help them out, as their chaplain had been taken seriously ill in England. So every Saturday evening I would go to Lisbon and spend the night at the vast parsonage in the Rua da Estrela, opposite the barracks of the Guarda Nacional Republicana. Apart from two maids who spoke no English, I had the place to myself, and lived like a member of the Diplomatic Corps. The staff at the British Embassy helped me a great deal in my efforts to obtain a resident's permit for Mozambique. The Counsellor was very interested in what I had to tell him about Lake Nyasa and the Mission, as the British and the Portuguese Governments were in the process of negotiating an agreement whereby half the southern half of the Lake would belong to Portugal, while Likoma Island, although to be within Portuguese waters, was to remain an integral part of Nyasaland. I was rather surprised to find how limited was the British Government's knowledge of Mozambique, even though it was officially classed as a province of Portugal.

While I was in Portugal there was an election. The press made much of it, but otherwise it seemed to be largely ignored. When election day came few voted. The Schrecks did not appear to be at all interested. Their view was 'What is the point of voting? We know who will get in, in any case.' One got the impression that Salazar was very much in control of the country and likely to remain so for the rest of time. When I said to my British friends that Portugal was a dictatorship, that the P.I.D.E. (political police) was modelled on the Gestapo, and that the Mocidade Portuguesa had its origin in the Hitler Youth Movement, the invariable reply was: 'Well, you should have seen the country before Salazar came to power. There were fifty governments in twenty-five years. At least Salazar has given the Portuguese

people a pride in their country, and there is a stable economy.'
(Shades of 'Mussolini, who at least made the trains run on
time'.) I was told that P.I.D.E. had tabs on everyone and that in
every street where a foreigner lived there was an informer. If I
had come to Portugal simply as a tourist, I should not have seen
the pathetic hovels that lay behind the classy residential suburbs,
but as it was I saw more than most foreigners: the rural slums
in which live the *saloios,* and the urban slums behind the
Alcântara. The great joke, when I was there, was that for the
Queen's visit to Lisbon, hundreds of trees were brought into the
capital, to hide the fact that the streets were in a mess from the
building of the underground system. The Portuguese had a saying among themselves *Para o inglês ver* – 'for the English to
see'.

My Portuguese lessons took place at an old-fashioned flat in
Lisbon (near the Saldanha) and consisted almost entirely of
taking dictation, translating short English children's stories into
Portuguese, and reading and translating the Portuguese primary-
school official readers. These readers gave me an insight into
what Portuguese children were expected to know. There were
many stories about Portugal's glorious past and the bravery of
the Christians who crushed the Moorish armies, but above all
emphasis was laid upon the navigators of the fifteenth and sixteenth centuries, with frequent references to Camões' epic poem
Os Lusíadas. I had never heard of Camões before I arrived in
Portugal, which was as incredible to the Portuguese as it was to
me that few of them had ever heard of Shakespeare. There was
an essay in one of the readers, *'Portugal é Grande',* in which it
was explained to the child that Portugal is much bigger than it
seems to be, as it includes not only various islands in the Atlantic
Ocean, but also vast areas of Africa, territories in the Indian sub-
continent, Macau in China and even Timor in the Malay archi-
pelago. Also, Brazil, the largest country in South America, was
founded by Portugal, and the Portuguese language, the most
beautiful in the world, is spoken there too. Whatever may have
been the shortcomings of Portuguese primary schooling, it certainly provided *me* with a mass of ideas that had been lacking
in my own education.

The principal reason for my coming to Portugal had been to learn Portuguese, but I decided I would also take the opportunity of getting an identity card and a driving licence. Obtaining these two documents gave me my first taste of the almost unbelievable, time-consuming pointlessness of the bureaucratic complexities that enmesh life in Portugal.

Before I could begin, I had to have my signature formally registered with a Notary Public. The British Consul was very helpful and asked a Goan colleague to arrange this for me. He and I went to an old building in the 'Baixa' (down-town Lisbon), and there we climbed up many flights of stone steps into a small office. My companion explained our errand to the man there, and a large book was produced. On the line indicated I wrote my full name and my signature. The Goan countersigned this and so did someone else in the office. I paid over a small sum of money and my signature was now formally registered. Thereafter there were many opportunities to make use of the Notary's services, as every time I signed any official document, his verification of my signature was necessary. This procedure had to be followed by everyone, not just foreigners.

Now I could go ahead with the much more complex and expensive procedure of getting a *bilhete de identidade*. For this the following documents, etc., were required:

a) two or three passport-type photographs of myself.

b) the *bilhetes de identidade* of two Portuguese nationals who were prepared to sponsor me.

c) my birth certificate, passport, and a note from the British Consul.

d) a *requerimento*: this is a very formal application written or typed on *papel selado*, which can be bought at authorized shops and kiosks for about ten pence. I signed over, and date-cancelled, the appropriate revenue stamps and took it to my Notary who stamped and countersigned it to the effect that my signature was mine, officially.

I then took all this material to the large and rather grubby building in the Rua de São Paulo which issues identity cards. There I was hand- and finger-printed very thoroughly; various personal details were noted down; and I paid the appropriate

fee. A few weeks later I received my *bilhete de identidade* which
was valid for a number of years. It was a white folded card, and,
apart from a photograph and the finger-print of my right index
finger, there were few details. Every Portuguese person has an
identity card which must be produced on demand.

As I was shortly, I hoped, to be resident in Mozambique, I
decided to get a Portuguese driving licence, which would be
valid in Mozambique (even though in Mozambique one drives
on the the left-hand side of the road, and in Portugal itself on the
right). At Messumba the nearest place I could take a test was
Nampula, 500 miles away. I had been warned that practically
every examiner was connected with the driving schools and the
chances of passing a test were negligible unless I went to a driving school first.

Friends told me that the Automóvel Clube de Portugal ran an
excellent driving school, but this of course meant I would have
to join the Club, before I could apply to have lessons. Joining
the Club presented no problems as I was able to find a proposer
and seconder in St George's congregation. But the Club entrance
fee and subscription added considerably to the cost of the licence.
When I asked about lessons, I found I had to buy a book of
vouchers entitling me to twelve lessons. I only had three lessons,
but my instructor obviously expected the remaining nine
vouchers to be handed to him as a tip, so I did not disappoint
him. We would meet at the Club garage and he would drive at a
tremendous speed to some residential part of the city, where the
lesson would begin. He realized I already knew how to drive, but
kept on saying 'not so fast, not so fast'. Then he would take over
the wheel and return us to the Club, breaking almost every rule
in any Highway Code. When the day came for my test, I asked
a friend to accompany me as interpreter in case I was asked
something I did not understand fully. My test began with four
of us in the car, the examiner, my instructor, my interpreter, and
myself. Off we went and within five minutes, the examiner told
me to pull into the side; he got out and went into a telephone
kiosk. 'What on earth is he doing?' I asked. 'Oh, he's only phon-
ing his wife to tell her he will be home for lunch in good time
today,' replied the instructor. We then drove on somewhere,

where the examiner left us. I asked my instructor if he thought I'd passed: 'Of course you have,' he replied. A few days later, my driving licence arrived but it had cost me, in all, about £15.

At the beginning of January 1958, my teacher told me that she thought I was ready to take the language exam. My grammar was by no means perfect, but I had a good accent and command of the language. The examination meant persuading an official primary-school teacher to sign a declaration that I was fluent in Portuguese. Mrs Schreck told me that the schoolteacher in her children's school would be sure to help me and was to visit the house that afternoon. She advised me to have ready some special paper with thirty-five lines on it, a sheet of *papel selado* and some revenue stamps. The schoolteacher duly came and when she heard what I wanted, there and then wrote out a formal declaration on the *papel selado* that I spoke Portuguese fluently. All I had to do was to take the declaration to her Notary to certify her signature, and I was left with the special-paper-with-thirty-five-lines-on-it!

I now made formal application (on *papel selado*, of course) to be a resident of Mozambique; producing the language declaration and a statement that (among other things) I had never been a member of the Communist Party. As I was not a Roman Catholic, the Missionary Statute Decree-Law No. 31,207 of 5 April 1941 did not apply. Article 16 of this says: 'The foreigners referred to' (i.e., missionaries)

will only be allowed to enter Portuguese overseas territories when they have expressly declared that they renounce the laws and courts of their nationality of origin and submit to the laws and courts of Portugal, which will henceforth be the only ones empowered to rule and judge them.

Although my application had not yet been granted, I was still officially a resident of the Federation of Rhodesia and Nyasaland and so was able to return to Mozambique on a three-month visitor's visa.

When the time came for me to leave Portugal, I wanted to travel by rail right across Africa, and so sailed from Lisbon to Lobito Bay in Angola. Lobito was a ramshackle place but obviously a very busy port, as well as the terminus of the Benguela Railway. The Benguela Railway is owned by Tanganyika Concessions Limited of London, but the only thing remotely English about it was the departure of its trains on time. I had a second-class coupé entirely to myself for the four-day journey to Elizabethville; a piece of luck for which I was very grateful, as most of my fellow passengers were rather tough Belgians on their way to the Katanga copper mines. Soon after leaving the coast, we started to climb, and the views were wide and splendid. Angola is very beautiful; the Belgian Congo and Northern Rhodesia, I thought, less so. The population was sparse and the only large town we passed through was Nova Lisboa high up on the Angolan plateau. Near most stations was a neat cluster of identical houses where the railway gangers lived. At Vila Texeira de Sousa, near the Belgian Congo frontier, we had our passports stamped and an official came into my coupé. To my astonishment he removed everything that was not a permanent fixture – soap, towel, tumbler, carpet, cushions – everything! The dining-car was taken off, and we crossed into the Congo like a ghost train going through no-man's land. At Dilolo, the Congo frontier town, we had a scheduled stop of about eight hours during which another dining-car was attached and my coupé refurnished.

At Elizabethville, I spent the night in a small hotel, and next morning caught the train for Ndola in Northern Rhodesia – a whole day's journey. From there I went to the Victoria Falls which, like every visitor, I particularly wanted to see. I stayed at the hotel for a couple of nights, and then (being weary of trains) got a lift in a car to Bulawayo, sending my heavy luggage on by rail to Blantyre in Nyasaland. On my arrival at Blantyre several days later the luggage was nowhere to be found. It never was. For several months I made inquiries about it, but the Nyasaland Railways blamed its disappearance on the Trans-Zambézia Railway in Mozambique, and the T.Z.R. blamed its disappearance on the Nyasaland Railways. I had learned, the hard way, the truth of the maxim I had heard when I first arrived: 'In Africa, never become separated from your luggage!'

I returned to Messumba via Likoma Island and the *Paul*, but this time Hadow did not accompany me. The Lake was very rough and a short distance from Messumba the engine broke down. We hoisted a sail, but it was far too rough to bring the boat to the shore, so we spent the night at anchor, if not at rest: I was terribly seasick and the little cabin, uncomfortable enough at the best of times, was alive with cockroaches.

4 Missionary Apprentice

Dawn broke on a calm Lake and a beautiful morning, as so often happened after a storm, and we were able to run the *Paul* on to the beach without difficulty. It was a great homecoming. The crowds collected, and I had no difficulty in finding people to carry my things up to the Mission – especially as the school was about to start the day – so we formed a procession about a hundred strong. When we arrived, my fellow missionaries came to greet me, and the Africans roared with laughter at my Portuguese. It was only then that I realized that Mozambique Portuguese was different, and the people found my Lisbon pronunciation almost impossible to understand. The Portuguese spoken in Mozambique is to Lisbon Portuguese as Brooklyn American is to English. Our Africans at Messumba were at a particular disadvantage in this respect, as contact with the Portuguese was practically non-existent, and they learned their Portuguese mainly from English people.

During the morning the teachers came *en masse* to welcome me: not because I had made myself particularly popular, but because in me they realized that the Mission, which they loved, had a more certain prospect of continuity. From the staffing point of view, Messumba's existence had always been precarious, and the Africans knew that if we missionaries were to leave, the Portuguese would almost certainly close the place down or hand it over to the Roman Catholics, and for them R.C.s meant Portugal. It is also important to remember that for 25,000 Africans concentrated in northern Mozambique, the Anglican Mission at Messumba has been the corner-stone of their lives. In later years, the Portuguese were to realize the truth of this.

Archdeacon Pickard had prepared a different house for me this time which was near the church and had three rooms instead of two; otherwise it was much the same. However, Tito had left, and in his place I had Artur Buanacaia to look after me. He stayed with me for the rest of the time I was at Messumba, apart from the three years he spent, untried, in Machava political prison. Buanacaia had been in his second year at the college during my previous stay at Messumba, but had failed to pass the necessary exam to move up into the third year. He was now about nineteen years old and a delightful lad. I knew I was lucky to have such an intelligent and pleasant person to look after me. He had a great sense of humour, a frank and open nature, and he was utterly loyal to me, though I know I was a great trial to him at times. I shall never forget Easter Monday 1958 when he reported for work with a frightful hangover. He did not know what had hit him, so I explained that it was too much drink the night before and he had better take a couple of Alka-Seltzers and go home to bed. He laughed and laughed, thanked me very much and went off to his village.

One of the first things I wanted to do was to revisit Chicale. Pickard was delighted as he did not like *ulendos* very much. This time I spent four days away and visited other outstations in the vicinity. Frequently, before I left a village in the morning, people would come to me with all sorts of ailments to be treated, so I learned to take a bare minimum of medicines and bandages with me. I gave what advice I could, which was usually to go and get properly treated at Messumba hospital. I often visited these near-by villages, and Buanacaia organized everything superbly. Although he was so young, the older men showed him great respect.

I quickly came to realize that in Africa time does not have its European meaning. To me, as to every other British missionary who ever went to Africa, this at first was irritating. For instance, I would be all ready to return to Messumba after a *ulendo*, with everything done, everything packed, only to find that the porters were not to be seen: they had gone off for a meal, or to visit a relative, or to buy some maize from someone. Buanacaia, however, understood that Europeans are impatient, and did all he could to keep an eye on the other men, and see they were there when wanted.

After Easter, Pickard suggested that I should visit the lake-shore villages that were in the care of our African priest at Ngoo. Ngoo was a large, straggling village, about six hours' walk from Messumba. The path went through several other villages, including Chia where Charles Janson's grave* is, and crossed various streams, which flowed into the Lake, including the fairly wide River Fúbuè. Ngoo was our largest outstation and there, besides the impressive brick-built church, was the only other Anglican school in the whole area. This school was in charge of Basílio Farahane, with two assistant teachers. It was a junior primary school of about a hundred pupils, and the brighter ones always received preferential treatment for boarding places at the Messumba school if they passed their exams. Basílio was an Angoni, not a Nyasa, and also a strict disciplinarian, so he was not popular with those who would defy him. But he was the only teacher left of those we had sent to train at Manhiça, and because of him we were allowed to keep our school at Ngoo. The Mission in general, and the people of Ngoo in particular, owed a great deal to Basílio, but I am afraid we sometimes forgot this.

Almost everyone who lived at Ngoo was an Anglican, and apart from Basílio and his assistants, there was the African priest-in-charge and a catechist. In spite of this, the people sometimes felt rather neglected. Few of them had ever seen a Portuguese, and the Government provided nothing for them. They were great fishermen like all the Nyasas, but looked as much to Likoma Island as they did to Messumba.

One quite attractive little house was reserved for any visiting missionary, but this was seldom in use as the only people who ever came to Ngoo were Joan Antcliff or myself. It was a thriving community, which always gave me a great welcome. The actual Mission at Ngoo, unlike Messumba, was close to the lakeshore, which formed a vast sandy bay where the bathing was excellent, and the area was studded with palm trees.

On my first visit to Ngoo, I spent a couple of nights there, and then went north in the direction of Likoma Island. The first place I came to was a very small village where I slept in the church. The following day's walking involved a great deal of

* See p. 18.

climbing over an extensive wooded hill and then down to a fairly large village where there was a *ulendo* house for me to sleep in. The last leg of the *ulendo* was to Mala where we had a retired catechist, Geldart Chisaca, who took prayers each Sunday. At Mala there are plenty of sandy coves, and a clear view of Likoma. I returned to Ngoo from Mala, after my first visit, by canoe, and as we went round Mala point the canoe capsized, and all our things were thrown out. We managed to salvage everything except a case of church articles (vestments, etc.) which went to the bottom. The people who owned the canoe were very frightened and apologetic, but I think Buanacaia was far more annoyed with them than I was.

My next journey was a long one, on foot all the way, visiting our outstations on the Manda Plateau, high up above and behind the Lake. This journey was to take me almost to the Tanganyika border. Eight carriers were necessary, and we asked for volunteers, but people were very reluctant to come forward. The Nyasas are not very happy away from the Lake, unless they are among their own people. They are fisher folk and do not take readily to the 'hill tribes'. *Manda* in Chinyanja means 'grave', and maybe the Manda Plateau derives its name from the days when they were enslaved and taken up to the plateau before being sold to the Arab (or Portuguese) slave dealers. The Nyasas, too, are used to travelling by canoe and not on foot, and find it irksome to carry heavy loads for long distances. Eventually we found eight men, and together with Buanacaia and a cook we set off into the hinterland. We slept that night at Mpochi, and the next day climbed the escarpment to Lucambo, the village of the Angoni Chief, where we had a church and a *ulendo* house. The next three days were spent visiting our outstations in Angoni country.

The Angonis are patrilineal, unlike the Nyasas, and are descendants of the Zulu dispersion of the nineteenth century. However, they now have very little Zulu blood in them, as only men moved north from Zululand, and these married into the tribes they conquered, which, in our area, of course, were the Nyasas. Because they are patrilineal, many of their customs have survived even though their language, Chingoni, is spoken very little. (In African society, the father is rather a remote figure until adolescence, so the children learn to speak from their mothers.) The Angonis, in complete contrast to the Nyasas, are warriors and hunters. During the First World War, a German column from the north invaded Portuguese East Africa and behaved with great brutality to the Angonis. Eventually the Portuguese drove the Germans out and peace was restored. It is for this reason that the Angonis were often regarded as being pro-Portuguese, though, in fact, the Portuguese did little else for them.

Coming from the bustling crowds of Messumba, I was at once struck by the sparse population of Angoni country. The villages were widely separated, and the few people I met on the bush paths appeared to be less sophisticated. Nearly all of them are Christians, and many of them Roman Catholics. Originally they were all Anglicans; but probably due to their remoteness and the concentration of missionary work on the lakeshore, they were, I am afraid, rather abandoned by the Universities' Mission. The dry-weather road from Nova Coimbra to Manda-Mbuzi and Cóbuè passes through Angoni country, and the Roman Catholic missionaries, on their journeys, converted a number of Angonis and established minute schools in the remote bush country. (In terms of the Concordat, the Roman Catholics, unlike ourselves, were allowed an almost free hand in the field of primary education.)

At Lucambo, some of my Nyasa porters decided to return to the Lake, but I had no difficulty in finding replacements from among the Angonis who were used to walking long distances, with heavy loads on their heads. (Here again, the Angonis are very different from the Nyasas, where only women carry loads on their heads; the men carrying them on their shoulders.) My programme at each village varied little. Usually I would spend one night, sometimes sleeping in the church, sometimes in a mud hut. Very occasionally, if two villages were close together, I would sleep a couple of nights in one and go to the other just for the day.

Leaving Angoni country, we walked along the rough road for some five hours to Manda-Mbuzi, which, although on the plateau, is near the Lake, and here we were back in Nyasa country. There I spent about two nights to rest and buy provisions from the villagers before continuing my journey north.

Our route now passed through some remote but very beautiful country. On leaving Manda-Mbuzi there were a number of people to be seen working in their fields, but then we entered primitive bush country, and villages were rare. We walked along the foot of ranges of hills and sometimes the going was pretty rough. I had a large labrador with me and as we entered one cluster of houses a group of teenage girls thought it was a wild animal and nearly fainted with terror. This was too much for Buanacaia's ever ready sense of humour and he became almost hysterical with laughter. After two days we reached Magachi, where we had a catechist. When I told him I was going on to Lipilichi (the Portuguese call it Nova Olivença) he told me I could not possibly take the dog all that way, as not only was it ten hours' walk, but it was through tsetse fly country and the dog might get ill. So I left him there for the next three days. We walked six hours to a tiny church apparently in the middle of nowhere; but miraculously a dozen people turned up from somewhere. I spent the night there. The final stretch of the journey took me within a few miles of the Rovuma River and the Tanganyika frontier. Even if I had wanted to, it was not easy to cross into Tanganyika, as there was no bridge over the Rovuma. Some years previously the district commissioner on the Tanganyikan side, and the Administrador on the Mozambican side, with Pickard as interpreter, had started some correspondence about a bridge; but nothing ever came of it.

On my return to Magachi, Buanacaia became seriously ill, and he could walk no farther. I could not leave him, and we were due to be met by the land-rover at Manda-Mbuzi two days later. I borrowed a bicycle, propped him up on the saddle, and the porters and I took it in turns to push the bicycle with Buanacaia astride it. Eventually we got to Manda-Mbuzi and put him to bed. He was feverish and I feared he would die. When Reggie came we propped Buanacaia up in the front of the land-rover between Reggie and myself. Our carriers were paid off and had to continue their journeys home on foot for lack of room in the land-rover, but at least they were now free of their loads. I had been away from Messumba for nineteen days, and during that unforgettable journey had not seen a European, nor heard a car. We got Buanacaia home and into hospital, where Irene diagnosed relapsing fever, and he soon recovered.

Within three months of my return to Messumba, I was told that my application for a resident's permit had been granted. Such speed was almost unheard of, as the Portuguese did not admit foreigners into Mozambique very readily. I well remember reading of a district commissioner in Tanganyika, whose area extended as far as the Rovuma River, writing something like this '... and there, over that wide river, lay the vast expanse of Portuguese East where no one really knows what happens'. That is just how the Portuguese liked it, and how they wished to keep it. There was no opposition to tourists from South Africa and Rhodesia visiting Lourenço Marques and Beira, but until recently foreigners, except missionaries, were seldom seen anywhere else.

I knew that as a foreign and non-Roman Catholic missionary, I would find it difficult to get a resident's permit, and especially in Mozambique, as, for some reason, Protestant missionaries were even less welcome there than in Angola. I know of no Anglican missionary who had obtained his permit with so little delay. (Some even gave up waiting and went off elsewhere.) I can only assume that it was because I was able to deal with everything on a personal level, and also because I received so much support from the British Embassy in Lisbon. Many people had told me that I would only be able to get the wheels of Portuguese bureaucracy moving if I greased certain official palms, but I never did this, and for most of the time that I was in Mozambique I was courteously treated by the civil authorities.

This was, I am sure, in no small measure due to António Borges de Brito who was now the Administrador at Maniamba and stayed there until 1962. We came to know one another well, and he supported me, even in difficult situations, long after he had left Maniamba, and, indeed, until I finally left the country.

He was a plump, talkative, cheerful fellow and obviously intelligent. He came to love Maniamba and the people in his area almost as much as I came to love Messumba and the people in my area. He made no pretence whatever of being a Christian, and in fact left me in no doubt that he was a convinced atheist. He told me once: 'I shall never get much higher than an Administrador, as I am not a practising Catholic and have no intention of becoming one just to gain promotion.' But he was never arrogant about this and came to have great respect for what we were trying to do at Messumba.

Our nearest town, Vila Cabral, was another fifty miles beyond Maniamba. When I first arrived in the country, Vila Cabral was like something off a Western film set. There were certainly less than fifty Europeans, and a mere handful of Indians; but many Africans, mostly Yaos. We had a small church three miles outside the town with a resident priest-in-charge, and about a dozen outstations in the huge area around, which used to be called Yaoland. In Vila Cabral, Pickard would do our fortnightly shopping. To anyone recently from England this was an unbelievably protracted business. The only big shop was owned by a very fat man, Senhor Cruchinho, but one seldom saw him. His assistant, Joaquim Salvado, was an excellent salesman who took one's order while keeping one's whisky glass full. The shop was divided into two main sections: the larger one for Europeans and the smaller one for Africans, so that while we chatted away with Salvado in our part, Reggie chatted away with the African assistant in the other. There was also quite a good shop owned by an Indian called Shariff, where Pickard used to shop as the proprietor spoke good English, whereas Cruchinho and the others spoke none. When relations between Portugal and India became strained over Goa, it was hinted to Pickard that he might make himself more popular with the authorities if he was to leave Shariff, which he did. Shariff then put up a sign outside his shop saying that he was not an Indian, but a Pakistani. The other shops were very small, and, whether owned by Portuguese or Indians (no African could *own* a shop), really catered almost exclusively for the African trade, and were not above cheating their very poor customers.

There was a small hospital which had a Portuguese doctor; a small Roman Catholic church, served from time to time by Padre Camillo from the Mission at Unango, about fifteen miles away; a small primary school which had one or two Portuguese teachers and whose pupils were almost entirely Portuguese or Indian; a bus station which ran a coach two or three times a week to Nova Freixo, the railhead two hundred miles to the south; a post office; a small barracks with about thirty African soldiers under a European officer; and a police-station with one European sergeant and some African constables. Like Maniamba, there were, of course, an Administrador and his subordinates, but, unlike Maniamba, his area was not called a *circunscrição*, but a *conselho*, which signified that there were slightly more than a mere handful of European settlers. In Vila Cabral there was no hotel, no restaurant, no café, only the grubby Pensão Mira Lago (which in fact had no view of the Lake at all); but this presented no difficulty in those days, as we were always invited to have lunch with someone – maybe Salvado, maybe another. The town was high up on the Niassa plateau, and it could be very cold indeed. It was nearly always windy, which meant a great deal of dust in the dry season as the roads were not tarred. There was no garage, but the Public Works Department and the bus station were friendly, and between them they could usually rustle up a mechanic if necessary for minor repairs. Petrol was bought by the tin or drum from Cruchinho's shop. Vila Cabral was really just a small Portuguese settlement in the middle of the African bush, and the people who lived there were either engaged in civil administration or commerce because there were a few Portuguese farms and estates in the area. The Universities' Mission had had outstations in Yaoland since about 1890, whereas the first Portuguese to settle in the area arrived in about 1930.

Occasionally Pickard would go to Blantyre by road and on one occasion took me with him. I was to go there countless times on my own in the years to come. Blantyre is 325 miles due south of Messumba, the road passing through Vila Cabral, and then, some sixty miles farther on, Massangulo Mission. This was to the Roman Catholics what Messumba was to the Anglicans. It was run by the Consolata Fathers, from Italy, and their local Superior, Padre Calandri, had been in the Niassa Province of Mozambique for many years. The missions at Unango (near Vila Cabral) and Cóbuè (on the lakeshore opposite Likoma Island) were both substations of Massangulo. I always found the missionaries friendly, but they had the reputation, as did so many Roman Catholic missionaries in Mozambique, of being more concerned with making money from what they produced in their fields, than with their work of education, so they were not popular among the Portuguese settler-farmers – or their flock, for that matter. Messumba was rather like an African village, consisting of several small buildings, whereas Massangulo was much more of an institution in that it was composed of a few large brick-and-tile buildings.

The Nyasaland frontier was reached at Mandimba, midway between Messumba and Blantyre. Customs and immigration formalities here were minimal. Only about five vehicles a day crossed the frontier, so that one spent quite a lot of time chatting to the official who usually wanted various things bought for him in Blantyre.

The contrast between Nyasaland and Mozambique was great in almost every way, and it was difficult to believe that the frontier was, in fact, an artificial one. Nyasaland was teeming with people and hundreds of bicycles (and no one dismounted and saluted as you went by); there were petrol pumps and African-owned shops; the road, although not tarred before Zomba, was nearly always in fair condition; people sold things at the roadside; and our land-rover was not the only car in the area. There were scores of other differences, and for me the most striking (and most pleasant) was being no longer in a police-state. After Vila Cabral, Blantyre was a sophisticated metropolis, and goods were delightfully cheap. But Messumba was home, and I was always glad to leave Blantyre and return to the place I had come to love.

Every July, the schoolchildren had to take the Government exams. When I first returned from Lisbon, I was astounded to find that the books which our African children had to study were the very ones I had seen in Portugal. When I asked why this was so, I was told 'Because the province of Mozambique is as much a part of Portugal as is the province of the Algarve, and therefore all children in this pluri-continental nation should study the same books, irrespective of what part of the Portuguese world they happen to live in.' Our children could tell you quite a lot about Portugal – and next to nothing about Mozambique. As I remember it, the final year 'reader' devoted one page to Mozambique and another to Angola; the rest of the book was about Portugal, her towns and cities, rivers and mountains; the differences between people from the Minho and people from the Alentejo; and, of course, there was *'Portugal é Grande'*. It was hardly surprising that one boy at Messumba, when asked what the world consisted of, replied: 'Angola, Metropolitan Portugal, Mozambique, Macau and Timor.' They had to learn the Portuguese railway network, but had no idea that there were any trains in Mozambique. The whole education system was simply not geared to the needs and experience of Mozambicans – and was about thirty years out of date as well. Mental arithmetic was positively discouraged, and every mathematical problem, however simple, had to be worked out on paper. This method of teaching resulted in idiotic delays at any post office where, on being asked for five two-escudo stamps, the counter clerk would solemnly write down $5 \times 2 \cdot 00 = 10 \cdot 00$. Great surprise would be shown when my ten-escudo coin was on the counter before the sum was set down on paper.

One feature of the unique Portuguese educational system was that the place where the final primary exam for our children at Messumba was to be held was not announced until a few days beforehand. Sometimes it was at Vila Cabral, and this produced immense problems for us. In those days we only had a land-rover, and we had usually prepared some thirty candidates for this important exam. We would try to borrow someone's lorry, but on many occasions the bigger boys had to walk the whole seventy-five miles there, while we did a shuttle service for the girls and the smaller boys. At Vila Cabral, our outstation just could not deal with a sudden influx of thirty children; so the poor kids had to sleep where they could in the bitter cold. We also had to take a cook with us and food – in fact, everything.

Most of the children had never been to Vila Cabral previously, or spoken with a Portuguese person, so as well as feeling complete strangers, they particularly dreaded the oral exam. In spite of these great disadvantages, ninety per cent of our candidates passed the exam each year, much to the surprise of the examiner, who not only had fewer pupils from the schools at Massangulo and Vila Cabral, but also had no idea that a Protestant mission *could* produce such results. The oral exam was held in public, and I must admit that the examiners were usually very kind to the children.

If I had never been to Lisbon, I do not think I would have been able to come to terms with the system; but with the experience gained during those five months, I was able (at the risk of displaying some of the arrogance justly attributed to the British 'abroad') to accept it for what it was: simply the way in which a backward European country worked.

Towards the latter half of 1958, Pickard told me that the Archbishop of Cape Town had offered him the Bishopric of Lebombo. This needs a little explanation. In 1893, the Diocese of Lebombo was established, to comprise the southern part of Portuguese East Africa. There were many thousands of Anglicans in that part of southern Africa who had been converted to Christianity while working away from home in the gold mines of the Witwatersrand. The Church naturally wished to follow its converts when they returned to Mozambique, and so work began among the Shangana and others who came from the south of the Portuguese colony. The Anglican Church did not wish to claim any territorial rights and so called the diocese after the range of mountains that separates Mozambique from the Transvaal – the Lebombo.

Pickard was the obvious choice for the vacant bishopric: he spoke Portuguese, already had a resident's permit, was accustomed to life in Mozambique, and had someone to take over from him at Messumba. However, he was convinced that all the Anglican work in the colony should come under one bishop, and one who was resident in the country. I am sure Pickard was right in this. In 1958, the Anglicans in Mozambique were almost equally divided numerically between the then Diocese of Le-

bombo and the Archdeaconry of Messumba in the Diocese of
Nyasaland. There was also a sprinkling of Anglicans in Beira
who were included in the Diocese of Mashonaland (Rhodesia);
and the Dioceses of Northern Rhodesia and Masasi (Tanganyika) geographically covered parts of Mozambique, though they
had no work there.

It was obviously impracticable for our work to straddle political frontiers, even though the people of Messumba were far more
akin to the people of Nyasaland than they were to those who
lived in southern Mozambique. And the Portuguese, who were
increasingly establishing their presence throughout the country,
resented the fact that anyone outside the colony should have any
control over those who lived within its boundaries. Fewer people
at Messumba now could understand English, and more spoke
Portuguese, so that diocesan meetings in Nyasaland were becoming almost impossible for lack of a common language. Our problems in many ways were not those of Nyasaland. We were
unable to transfer our African clergy and teachers to other parts
of the Diocese of Nyasaland, if we wished to do so, as they were
unqualified in almost every way to work there, even if we were
able to persuade the authorities in Mozambique and Nyasaland
to agree to such a move. Sentiment apart, there seemed no good
reason for us at Messumba to continue within the Diocese of
Nyasaland, and every reason why we should join with our fellow
Anglicans in the south of Mozambique.

After Pickard's appointment as Bishop, there was very little
time for him to hand over to me his many and varied responsi-
bilities at Messumba. He had always been reluctant to delegate
authority, with the result that I knew very little about the inner
workings of the Mission. Now, each evening, we went through
the files and sorted out the masses of papers that had accumu-
lated over the past ten years, and even during Canon Cox's time.
During the day, while he packed, I tried to deal with the day-to-
day running of the Mission, and was thankful to be able to refer
many problems to him. My command of Chinyanja was still
poor in comparison with his, and I had no experience of writing
official letters in Portuguese or of filling up the innumerable and
complicated statistical returns that were required by the authori-

ties. In fact, I had little experience of anything and no more time in which to gain it.

Late in October 1958, Pickard left Messumba and, as I stood on the hill and watched the land-rover disappear in a cloud of dust, my mind was almost dazed with bewilderment at the task that lay ahead: the running, with less than two years experience as a missionary, of one of the largest and most remote missions in Africa.

5   Portugalization

My first reaction after Archdeacon Pickard's departure was a feeling of utter loneliness. In spite of minor disagreements, we had become good friends and now I was on my own. Irene Wheeler and Joan Antcliff obviously understood my state of mind and were extremely helpful.

The Nyasas dislike change of any sort. Pickard had had difficulties when he took over from Canon Cox; and now I, as a younger and very much more inexperienced priest-in-charge, was bound to encounter difficulties. Bishop Frank had suggested that Fr Juma become Archdeacon and I priest-in-charge of Messumba, but Pickard had told him that such a move would not have commended itself to the Portuguese: not only was Juma a black and not even an *assimilado*; but also, like all our African staff, he had little more than primary education. His command of Portuguese was now very rusty, since he had spent so many years as priest-in-charge at some of the outstations. He was then at Chigoma, the village of Chief Chiteje (one of whose predecessors had given Likoma Island to the Universities' Mission), and I was determined to visit Fr Juma there as often as I could because I realized some of their feelings of neglect. Chigoma was one of the few outstations one could reach in the dry season in a four-wheel-drive vehicle. Now that I was in charge of all the Anglican work in this vast area, walking *ulendos*, that took many days, were clearly out of the question.

To reach Chigoma, I took the dry-weather road that passed through Lucambo and Manda-Mbuzi to Cóbuè, where there was a Chefe do Posto and a Roman Catholic Mission. Some miles after Manda-Mbuzi, a track branches off to the right for Magachi and Lipilichi, with Cóbuè lying ahead, at the foot of the escarpment. I know of no place where the views are so spectacular, with the Lake, Likoma, the Mozambique coast reaching right up to Tanganyika, and away in the blue distance the coast of Nyasaland on the other side of the Lake. No one lived on the escarpment, but I frequently saw people trudging up to Manda-Mbuzi, and there was an occasional gazelle or other animal to be seen. The hairpin bends were quite terrifying, and many times in subsequent years I have come to within an inch of plunging over the side.

At the foot there was a small concrete bridge and, within a very short distance, Cóbuè itself. My first duty was to make the customary 'courtesy call' on the Chefe do Posto (something I was always careful to do when visiting anywhere in my area, as the Portuguese were very sensitive about due respect being paid to their position). He greeted me warmly and insisted that I lunch with him. I was offered Rhodesian cigarettes, which he told me he bought on his occasional visits to Likoma, clearly visible from there. It appeared that at least half his supplies came from across the water; hardly surprising as during six months of the year the road was impassable, and he only had a tiny boat which might, in ideal conditions, have got him to Metangula. He relied almost entirely on the *Paul* and the Roman Catholic Mission. Here we were in Mozambique, but the only sign of the Portuguese presence for hundreds of square miles was this one man in his Mediterranean-style house – and he was dependent upon the Anglican Mission in Nyasaland for much of his supplies. The lad who waited on us at table was João Farahane, a nephew of Basílio, and when I asked the Chefe, 'Why him?', he replied: 'When one of his relations left Mozambique to work elsewhere, he was in arrears with his taxes, so I took João to work here until the taxes are paid.' When I said this seemed a trifle unfair, the Chefe replied: 'These people are very family conscious, so if a member fails in his obligations, they quite understand that another member should fulfil them for him.'

The Roman Catholic Mission was only a few hundred yards from the Chefe's house, and there I met the Superior, Padre Eugénio Menegon (of whom Hadow had spoken well) and Padre Inácio Mondine (whom I had met briefly at Metangula the previous year). Both were Italian Consolata Fathers. Their Mission was quite unlike ours at Messumba, and more like Massangulo, though on a smaller scale, and they were building a Portuguese-style church. Many years previously the Diocese of Nyasaland had had its teacher-training college at Cóbuè, but this had been moved to Nyasaland because of the obvious practical difficulties that resulted from its being in Portuguese territory. The name of the college had been St Michael's, and when the Roman Catholics started their mission at Cóbuè, with Padre Calandri as the Superior, they called it St Michael's Mission. The founding of a Roman Catholic mission at Cóbuè was a clear case of 'poaching' Anglicans, which had been encouraged by the Portuguese, for many of whom 'being Portuguese and being Catholic are one and the same thing' (Eduardo Mondlane, *The Struggle for Mozambique*). One might add that for the Portuguese Government 'being English and being Anglican are one and the same thing', too. The Portuguese, therefore, resented the obvious and far-reaching Anglican presence, especially in a diplomatically sensitive area, and, in addition, they deplored what seemed to them to be the 'denationalizing effect of Protestantism' (Adrian Hastings, *Wiriyamu*). (In 1964 the President of Portugal, Américo Tomás, presented Padre Calandri with a decoration for his work in Niassa. But when I congratulated him, he replied: 'It should have been Canon Cox who received this, for it was he, much more than myself, who spread the Gospel here – I was only sent to poach his Anglicans.')

The Mission at Cóbuè, in fact, had very little influence on the Africans who lived in the villages near by. There was no medical work; the primary school was small and did not take its pupils beyond the third grade. Any who wished to complete their primary education had either to become Roman Catholic and go to Massangulo nearly two hundred miles away, or try for a place at our school at Messumba, or go across the water to Likoma.

Padre Menegon was very civil to me on my first visit to Cóbuè, as he was on my subsequent visits, but I felt he was ill-at-ease in my presence. He was not to me, as he was to Hadow, 'a good friend', but then Cóbuè was his base, and he was dependent upon Hadow for many of his supplies, which were openly smuggled across the few miles of water that separate Cóbuè from Likoma Island. The Mission had a small shop and also a flour mill, both of which attracted quite a number of Africans to the place, even if not to join the flock.

Chigoma is about twelve miles beyond Cóbuè. At that time there were countless villages spread along the shore, and at all the larger ones we had a thriving church. Whereas Messumba was about ninety-five per cent Anglican, these villages were about ninety-nine per cent Anglican, though the area was not so densely populated. Fr Juma had about twelve outstations under him, most of them with a resident catechist. His area stretched from Cóbuè to Wikihi on the Tanganyika border, a distance of at least fifty miles. The track was impassable for any vehicle after Chigoma, and so he visited his many churches occasionally by bicycle or canoe, but mostly on foot – and he was by no means a young man. Likoma Island was clearly visible from every village, and Likomans themselves were constantly coming across to buy firewood, milk, grass for thatching their houses, bamboos, poles, and practically everything they needed, which the barren island could not produce. Many Likomans even had their own fields in the Chigoma area, which, apart from the presence of the Chefe do Posto at Cóbuè, might not have been in Portuguese territory at all. The only shop in the area was at the Mission, so many people either went to Likoma to do their shopping, or to Tanganyika if they lived close enough to the frontier. Although there was no industry or other employment, the people in the Chigoma area were not as poor as one might have expected. They were excellent fishermen and sailed across to Likoma where they were able to sell large quantities of fish, especially on the days when the *Ilala* called. Like every village in our part of Mozambique, money was brought in by the scores of men who went to other countries to earn a living.

There is no doubt that our Christians in the Cóbuè–Chigoma area felt a great sense of abandonment. If the area could have been worked from Likoma, it would have been much easier for them; but as it was, they were in Mozambique, and Messumba, where all our work was centred, was more than sixty miles away, along a road, little more than a track really, that, because of the heavy rains, was impassable for six months of the year. We at

Messumba had no boat, and it was impossible to walk from Messumba to Chigoma in under two days. In spite of their feeling of isolation, however, and the presence of the Roman Catholic Mission at Cóbuè, the people remained staunchly Anglican.

One of the many anachronisms that I inherited was the Likoma messenger. He lived at Messumba and his job was to walk to Cóbuè almost every week, leaving wage packets, letters, and supplies at the various outstations he passed through. At Cóbuè he was supposed to report to the Chefe do Posto, after which he would hitch a ride to Likoma in someone's canoe and there report to Hadow. The messenger, armed with a long spear, was a fearsome-looking man, especially when he arrived, unexpectedly, late at night or early in the morning. He was a vital link between Messumba and the larger outstations like Chia, Ngoo, Manda-Mbuzi, and Cóbuè. I rarely had any reason to send him to Likoma, but when I suggested he should not go there and only visit our outstations, I met with great opposition. Many people, including my fellow-missionaries, often had their letters addressed to them at Likoma, and not at Messumba; or wanted their letters to be posted in Likoma rather than in Vila Cabral; not because the contents were subversive, but because there was an old-established prejudice (sometimes justified) that the Portuguese post was unreliable. I continued Pickard's policy of discouraging people from sending their letters via Likoma, but nothing I could do would deter people from other countries sending letters to us in this way. It was a practice which got us into a great deal of trouble with the Portuguese a few years later.

Our nearest post office was in Vila Cabral, and if I missed going to Vila Cabral any week, the post office would send the letters by the weekly bus to Metangula. My office acted as an unofficial sub post office, and Benson Caomba sold stamps, sorted letters, and dealt with the considerable sums of money that were sent to individuals via either Likoma or Vila Cabral. Nearly all the registered letters and parcels were addressed to me, with a letter inside saying something like 'Dear Father, Please give my nephew Carlos Mtambo £10 for him to buy a cow. Your beloved son, John Waite.' Sometimes the instructions were very involved, and sometimes the sender forgot to enclose any at all. The money might come in almost any form, but usually in cash: Mozambican escudos, Tanganyikan shillings, but more often South African or Rhodesian pounds. This multiplicity of currencies caused endless confusion, and headaches for the Mission Superior. The confusion was confounded by the fact that there was, until the mid 1960s, very little Portuguese money in circulation at all. Occasionally, people in the outstations refused escudos in payment for something I had bought while on *ulendo*. Sometimes I have received requests from catechists in some outstations for their wages to be paid in non-Portuguese currency.

Shortly after Pickard left, Reis at Metangula was replaced by a young and energetic Chefe do Posto, Ferreira de Silva, who was extremely friendly to us at Messumba. He and the Administrador, Borges de Brito, were determined to develop the area, and they recognized that the Anglican missionaries at Messumba were the most influential people in the *circunscrição*, so that our cooperation was vital. What they did or said behind our backs I do not know, but I could not have wished for a better relationship between us. They were determined to get to know the area well and to listen to all complaints; in complete contrast to most of their predecessors, who had often been posted to northern Mozambique as a punishment, and were content, as had been Reis, simply to stay put and do little, apart from, every so often, seizing people and forcing them to work on the road, or sending them away to places like Beira for work in the docks.

Now, and for about the first time, we had an educated Administrador at Maniamba and an educated Chefe do Posto at Metangula. They made no secret of the fact that the Portuguese administration in Niassa had been a disgrace, and that they meant to stay some years and do properly the job which they had been sent to do. They were both fully aware of what the first popular reactions would be and were prepared to face them with firmness, tempered by some understanding. They spent a great deal of time holding *banjas* (open-air meetings) in the villages, explaining that they would do all they could to develop the area, and often frankly admitting that the only practical aid the people had received had come from Messumba. The Portuguese

Government now was going to help, too, but it would require the cooperation of the villagers. Borges de Brito was no Salazarist and was fully aware that corruption in Government circles was widespread. He knew that the few Portuguese store-keepers in the *circunscrição* were out to make their fortunes at whatever cost to the Africans. He quickly discovered that the Roman Catholic Missions in his *circunscrição* at Cóbuè and Unango were also to some extent making commercial profits at the expense of their African people. Thus Borges de Brito, both an atheist and an admirer of Messumba, soon incurred the displeasure of Padre Menegon at Cóbuè and Padre Camillo at Unango; and within a few months of his arrival, word reached the Bishop of Nampula, Dom Manuel Madeiros, whose vast diocese then included the whole of the far north of Mozambique, that the new Administrador of Maniamba was anti-Catholic. This, for a Portuguese official, was tantamount to saying he was a traitor.

Borges de Brito had told me that he had a small group of Messumba Anglicans working for him at Maniamba, and that I could use the little chapel there to minister to them. I was very grateful for his thoughtfulness but told him that I did not think the Bishop of Nampula would approve. 'It's nothing to do with him,' he replied, 'these chapels belong to the Government.' When a few weeks later, I stopped at Maniamba on my way to Vila Cabral, I saw, to my surprise, that Borges de Brito was dressed in his official uniform. He explained that the Bishop had gone to visit the Mission at Cóbuè and was due at any moment to pass through Maniamba on his return journey to Nampula. 'I'll just give him the obligatory salute, and hope he doesn't stay too long.' He had just spoken, when a car pulled up outside the secretariat, and out got the Bishop. Everyone rushed to pay their respects. The Administrador saluted and then led the Bishop in my direction to introduce me, but Dom Manuel ignored me completely and went into the secretariat. I was rather relieved, since not only was I not dressed as smartly as the Bishop would expect on such an occasion, but I knew his rather unfriendly reputation even amongst his own clergy, most of whom were, of course, non-Portuguese. He was very much of the 'old school', a Salazarist moulded in the tradition of Cardinals Cerejeira of Lisbon and Teodósio de Gouveia of Lourenço Marques.

On my return that evening I dined with Borges de Brito, as I often did, and he was full of apologies for the Bishop's behaviour. He also told me that he had been reprimanded by him for favouring Messumba while 'harassing' the Missions at Cóbuè and Unango, which, even though they were run by Italians, were fully integrated into the Portuguese missionary organization; an organization concerned as much with making the 'natives' good Portuguese as it was with making them good Catholics. Borges de Brito reported that during their conversation he had brought up the matter of my using the Maniamba chapel. The Bishop apparently had been very displeased. He had made it quite clear that the chapel was ecclesiastically part of Fr Camillo's Mission at Unango, and that I was on no account to use it for any purpose whatsoever.

According to the Concordat and Missionary Agreements signed in 1940 and 1941, the Bishop was within his rights. Diocesan Bishops are on a par with District Governors, both in regard to status and *Government* salary, and the Administrador was therefore of lower rank. Additionally, article 82 of the Missionary Statute Decree-Law of 1941 states:

The Authorities and public services shall give all the help and support, in the exercise of their functions, that the development and progress of Catholic missionary action necessitates, in harmony with their national and civilizing aim.

Luckily for us all, Nampula was a long way off, and the Bishop revisited our area only once after that. In 1963 the Diocese of Vila Cabral was carved out of the Diocese of Nampula, and the attitude of the Roman Catholic Church towards us changed dramatically with the arrival of Dom Eurico Nogueira as first Bishop of the new diocese, and the Second Vatican Council under Pope John.

The possession of a *caderneta indígena* was a legal necessity for all adult Africans who were not *assimilados*; these, being 'honorary whites', possessed a *bilhete de identidade*. As far as I know, there were no Nyasa *assimilados* in 1958 in the Messumba area, though there were two or three who came from other parts of Mozambique. All our clergy, teachers, hospital staff and catechists, of course, possessed *cadernetas*, but very few of the village people did. Now, with the new Administrador and the new Chefe do Posto, things were to be regularized, and this caused no small stir, as *cadernetas* and tax payments went together. It was all right for those who lived at Messumba and near other places where employment could be found, but for those who lived in distant villages this brought great problems. Borges de Brito and Ferreira de Silva gave the people some genuinely helpful answers at the *banjas*: 'Catch more fish, and we'll sell it for you in Vila Cabral and elsewhere; we'll give you seeds to plant and then you can sell part of your harvest; come and work for us in the *circunscrição*, maybe in the secretariat, or on the roads which we intend to improve greatly; ask Fr Paul to give you work on the Mission; what about joining the army or becoming a *cipai*, because then you won't have to pay any tax at all; what about offering to work on the railways, or in the docks at Beira.' And, finally: 'You know perfectly well that many of you have relations working in other countries who can easily send you the hundred escudos that you need to pay your annual tax.' Borges de Brito's jovial manner largely won over his audiences, encouraging them to ask questions. His attitude was one of benign paternalism, and, though he would not subscribe to the belief that the best way for an African to absorb Portuguese culture was by becoming a Roman Catholic, he was in many respects a disciple of Dr Adriano Moreira, the fairly 'liberal' (by Portuguese standards) Under-Secretary of State for Overseas Administration. In common with virtually all Portuguese officials, he made no effort whatever to learn any African language, so that his personal contact with the village African was entirely through an interpreter.

Nearly every African in the *circunscrição* existed on subsistence farming or fishing, and this, according to Portuguese native legislation, was a 'state of idleness'. It was the duty of the State, together with the Church, to teach (by force, if necessary) 'the native' the 'dignity of work'. This, in fact, meant that the authorities could seize anyone, at any time, and force him to work for them or for some middle-man. This Borges de Brito wanted to avoid, and his appeals for people voluntarily to come forward and sell their services or their surplus crops and fish met with a measure of success. Clearly he had been given considerably more financial help than his predecessors, and he seemed to be honest. On nearly every journey to Vila Cabral, when I stopped at Maniamba, I would come across yet more Messumba people working in the secretariat, some of whom were later sent as interpreters and clerks to the Chefes do Posto at Metangula, Cóbuè and elsewhere. We were, after all, turning out annually from our school some thirty-five comparatively well-educated young men and women. Previously, we had been unable to find jobs for more than a very small proportion of them. We simply did not have the money to employ any more teachers or other professional staff.

Borges de Brito encouraged Portuguese traders to open more stores and shops in the area, and this meant more jobs for the Africans. He even allowed a few Africans to open their own small stores. A watch was kept on fair trading, and sometimes I was warned by him of bad employers who might ask me for people from Messumba, and this I appreciated enormously. He was rightly one of the Administradors best liked by the Africans – and one of the most actively disliked by the Europeans. On one occasion, when he went with me to Vila Cabral, he asked me to stop at Unango Mission, where he collected two lads who had been assaulted by Padre Camillo, against whom he later brought a case. The Unango Mission was one of the worst examples of a mission involving itself in commerce. It was situated in very fertile country, and the pupils at the school spent as much time working in the Mission's fields as they did in the classrooms. This brought Padre Camillo into almost immediate conflict not only with Borges de Brito, but also with the local Portuguese farmers, who did not have unlimited free labour at their disposal; and who could not afford, as could the Mission, to sell things in their shops at such low prices. (In terms of the Concordat, the Church was not liable for customs duties on many things, especially if the cases contained 'images', which a customs officer friend told me many of them purported to do.) The Unango Mission made great material profits, but the number of Christians in the area was very small, as the people, being of the Yao tribe, were mainly Muslims. It may be significant that Unango was the only Mission in the whole area to be attacked by Frelimo guerrillas some years later.

At Messumba we employed about thirty manual labourers who signed on at the beginning of each month and were paid by the day. Once people realized that they had to pay taxes, the space outside my house was crowded by work-seekers on the first day of each month. There was certainly plenty of work to be done but not the money to pay for it. It was heartbreaking having to turn scores of people away every month. I would suggest that they ask Ferreira de Silva at Metangula to give them work on the roads, but they would not, from choice, work under the hated Portuguese Government, even though conditions were now much better than they had been.

Our teachers and nurses and others had already been asking for an increase in their wages, as their colleagues across the Lake in Nyasaland were being paid, by the Government, wages which far exceeded what we could pay. Now they were asking for still bigger increases to pay the taxes demanded. The African 'extended family' system bore hard on a wage-earner, as he could not refuse to pay the taxes of the less fortunate members of his family. My own position as the intermediary between the Administrador and the people was becoming more difficult. The people agreed that with Borges de Brito as Administrador and Ferreira de Silva as Chefe do Posto there was more justice than before; people were no longer beaten indiscriminately and rounded up for forced labour on the roads in quite the same way as they had been; but they could not see any justice in their being asked to pay taxes when they received nothing in return. 'What do the Portuguese do for the people?' they would ask. The Administrador would explain patiently, but unconvincingly, to the people that the inhabitants of every land pay taxes for the running of the country, and that he was trying to improve the lot of the people in his *circunscrição*: the road was better, and there was a regular bus service between Vila Cabral and Met-angula; there were more shops; the Government was giving people more employment; but things could not all be completed in an instant. 'All right,' said the teachers, 'we agree with that; but why should the people who live at Ngoo and Cóbuè pay taxes? They receive nothing from the Government, and we here at Messumba are in a privileged position in comparison with them.' There was no answer to these objections. Borges de Brito did persuade one Portuguese trader to open a shop at Ngoo, and promised to do what he could about providing some regular transport on the Lake, but this came to nothing. So the question-ing and the feeling of injustice grew among the people.

Increasingly our teachers and others at the Mission had radios; and with the constant traffic between Messumba and other places, people were not unaware of what was going on in the outside world. Our people, being Nyasas, were particularly interested in what was happening in Nyasaland: first with the return of Dr Banda, and then his arrest and transfer to detention at Gwelo, Rhodesia. They knew about the 'troubles' in Nyasa-land. They knew, too, that Tanganyika was on the road to inde-pendence. The Administrador at Maniamba and the Chefe do Posto at Metangula were above the average of officials, but what went on in the *circunscrição* of Maniamba was not typical of what went on elsewhere in Mozambique. Our people did not trust the Portuguese (any more than I did) and knew that Portugal herself was an under-developed country. It was natural for them to think that if Britain and other colonial powers were in the process of negotiating the independence of their former colonies, there was all the more reason that Portugal should do the same.

A doctor from the Diocese of Nyasaland stayed with us once, and on his return I drove him to Blantyre. He was greatly struck by the unexpected kindness of Borges de Brito and said that he thought the Portuguese were perhaps not as bad as they were made out to be, though it was obvious they had done nothing much to develop the country. But when we reached Vila Cabral we saw, both of us for the first time, Africans walking through the streets in chains. There must have been about twenty of them, under the charge of a *cipai*. No one, apart from us, seemed to be in the least bit disturbed by the dreadful noise of the clanking chains. I recalled hearing my father speak of this on a visit to Beira in 1953; I remembered what had so disgusted Pocklington about the Portuguese; I remembered Bishop Frank telling me about visiting one of our catechists many years previously in Vila Cabral prison and finding him chained. Reggie told me that though I had never seen it before, it was an everyday occurrence, as the prisoners were taken to and from the prison.

While Borges de Brito was establishing the Portuguese presence in his *circunscrição* of Maniamba, the Portuguese presence was being established in a different way in the *conselho* of Vila Cabral. Administrador Cunha of Vila Cabral was popular among whites, but tyrannized over the blacks. He was always accompanied by several *cipais* armed with truncheons, and kept a *palmatório* (a perforated flat piece of wood used for beating the palms of the hands) and a *chicote* (a whip made out of a strip of hippopotamus hide) in his car. Vila Cabral grew rapidly during his time there, and he himself did well financially, coming to own one of the principal buildings.

As remarked earlier, we had some outstations in the *conselho* of Vila Cabral which were under the care of one of our African clergy. But the Anglicans were vastly outnumbered by Muslims, and slightly outnumbered by Roman Catholics. In spite of this strong Muslim influence, some of the Chiefs, like the Paramount Chief of Vila Cabral itself, were Anglicans. In the early 1960s, an unsuccessful attempt was made by the authorities to close down all our work in the area, and confine it to the *circunscrição* of Maniamba. But we protested vigorously; and, happily for us, the matter was soon forgotten. Our presence in the *conselho* was of little influence in comparison with what it was in the *circunscrição* of Maniamba.

In July 1960, I went to Nampula, in a lorry we had recently acquired, to buy some roofing material. As the lorry would be going there empty, Borges de Brito asked if he could come with me. On the long journey he told me that things were very serious in Cabo Delgado. I was very surprised, as I had heard nothing, so I asked him what he meant. He told me that less than a month previously 'hundreds' of Africans of the Maconde tribe had been shot at Mueda when the Administrador or some-one had lost his nerve during a demonstration. The Government were trying to keep it quiet, but he felt that the incident, the exact details of which he was rather vague about, would be only a beginning of trouble. The Macondes, unlike the Nyasas, are a war-like tribe, and the area in which they live straddles the Rovuma River. Borges de Brito told me that there had been quite a lot of trouble recently with the Macondes and that the Governor from Porto Amélia had gone to Mueda, the principal town on the Maconde Plateau, to investigate things. Now people were wondering what would happen next. The incident could have wide implications, as many of the Africans in the Portuguese army in Mozambique were Macondes. He was obviously very disturbed; but apart from what he told me, and what people in Vila Cabral let fall from time to time, nothing was ever said officially about the events at Mueda on 16 June that year. One day, while we were both still in Nampula, we had lunch with a friend of his who, I gathered, had been the Administrador at Mueda, and had been removed rather quickly after the mas-sacre. But they did not say much in front of me, naturally. At the time, our attentions at Messumba were focused far more closely upon the situation in Nyasaland, especially as Henry Chipembele (at that time, one of Banda's chief lieutenants) had his original family home at Messumba.

Nampula was much larger than Vila Cabral, with wide, tree-lined streets and pavement cafés. It was very much in the style of a town in southern Europe but with very little traffic. In spite of being 500 miles from Messumba, here was our nearest bank and our nearest airfield (literally a field). It was not until the mid 1960s that the various Government departments all opened offices in Vila Cabral. I was a complete stranger in Nampula, as we had no work in the area at all. The Africans are of the Macua tribe – a short dark people – and the few that were not heathen were Roman Catholics. I was to visit Nampula many times when Borges de Brito became Mayor of it in the late 1960s, and saw its transformation into a busy army headquarters: all military operations in the north of Mozambique were planned there.

The roads from Messumba to Nampula and Blantyre branch off at Mandimba, and the only town of any size one passes through on the way to Nampula is Nova Freixo. This was the railhead, and a railway bus took passengers the two hundred miles from there to Vila Cabral. The railway line from Nova Freixo to Vila Cabral was being constructed during the whole of my twelve and a half years in Mozambique and was completed in 1969. Between Mandimba and Nova Freixo, the road and the path prepared for the railway line crossed each other countless times, and signposts were almost non-existent; so that on one occasion I set out from Mandimba to go to Nova Freixo only to return to Mandimba several hours later, having followed the track prepared for the railway. Nova Freixo was larger than Vila Cabral, partly because it was the railhead, and partly because there were a number of Portuguese farmers in the area. The railway was being built almost entirely by forced labour – Africans 'recruited' from all over the northern part of the country by the local Administradors and Chefes do Posto and sent, like prisoners, to work on its construction. They were housed in the most primitive conditions and paid a minute wage, and after nine months or so would return home knowing that they would not be officially liable for further forced labour for approximately six months. To my knowledge, Borges de Brito did not recruit anyone from the immediate area of Messumba, but I heard later that he had encouraged people from other parts of his *circunscrição* to help on the railway. The son of Cruchinho was the Government (and only) doctor in Nova Freixo when I went to Nampula with Borges de Brito in 1960, and he told us of his anxiety over the health problems of the railway labourers.

As I drove through Macua country, I passed centres where cotton was collected. In the Vila Cabral and Maniamba areas, there had been no cultivation of cotton for some years, but here the Macuas were forced to grow cotton and sell it, for almost nothing, to the Portuguese. At each of these centres were weighing machines, often presided over by a Portuguese with attendent *cipais*, and long queues of people waiting to have their cotton weighed. The Macuas in this area were very poorly clothed, and obviously far worse off materially than our Nyasas. There were few missions and little foreign influence, but at Nawela, there was a mission run by the South Africa General Mission, who had inherited it from the Church of Scotland many years earlier. The Portuguese simply did not understand their evangelical type of religion and trusted them even less than they did us, whose religious practices at least bore some resemblance to Roman Catholicism. Nawela was in the midst of the cotton-growing area, and very near to the tea-growing area slightly to the south, where 'forced' labour was freely used. The Mission had absolutely nothing to commend itself to the Portuguese, and they regarded it with the greatest suspicion. So I was not altogether surprised, if saddened, when, within a very few years of my arrival at Messumba, the Portuguese forced it to close.

6 Black in Pluri-Continental Portugal

Some months after Pickard had been consecrated Bishop of Lebombo, he came back to Messumba to collect his belongings, and I returned with him to Lourenço Marques for a short visit.

Mozambique was once described to me by a Portuguese Governor as being like a large segment of an upturned saucer, with all the major rivers flowing east from the westward highlands into the Indian Ocean, so that lines of communication from north to south were virtually non-existent. It was almost impossible to travel from Messumba to Lourenço Marques – a distance of more than 1,200 miles – without passing through other countries.

The road took us first to Nyasaland, where we spent a night in Blantyre. The next day we re-entered Mozambique at Zóbuè, and there was no doubt that we were back in Portuguese territory: few people, no African-owned shops, and those subservient salutes. We crossed the Zambezi on the terrifying ferry and entered the small town of Tete. First reached by the Portuguese in the sixteenth century, Tete was no modern town when I first saw it, though it has grown enormously in succeeding years, when both the war and the Cabora Bassa Dam have given it great importance. On to Changara, where we cleared Portuguese customs and, thirty miles on, entered Rhodesia, but it was another sixty miles to the official entry point, Mtoko, where we spent the second night. We drove on, along good roads, through Rhodesia, then through the Transvaal, and finally re-entered Mozambique at Ressano Garcia. We reached Lourenço Marques after driving for one night and nearly five days.

I told Pickard on my first visit, as I told him many times later, that Messumba was too big a job for me, with only Irene and

Joan as my colleagues, and he promised to try to find more staff.* However, he felt that the proper solution was to enable some of our most promising teachers to obtain secondary education, so that they might not only relieve Joan of some work in the school but also be better able to help me with administrative work on the Mission. In northern Mozambique it would have been quite impossible for our students to receive any secondary education (the Escola Técnica in Vila Cabral was not opened until 1963); but with Pickard living in a large house in Lourenço Marques, they might live there and attend night school. At Messumba, we also had half a dozen ordination candidates, and it was agreed that they should study at Maciene, the principal mission station in the Diocese of Lebombo. Money, of course, was the great problem, but supporters of the diocese generously helped us with these plans.

Thus, on my return to Messumba, one of my first jobs was to make the necessary travel arrangements for our ordination candidates to get to Maciene. As they were all *indigenas*, this was incredibly complicated. First of all, their *cadernetas* had to be in order, and their taxes for the current year paid to the Chefe do Posto at Metangula. (The taxes were not officially required to be paid until the end of the year; but as administrative officials received a one-per-cent bonus from all taxes they collected, no Chefe do Posto would allow anyone to leave his area without having first paid taxes to him!) The men were then authorized to leave Metangula and report to the Administrador at Maniamba, who wrote in their *cadernetas* that they were authorized to go to Lourenço Marques. I took them in our lorry to Vila Cabral, where the Administrador of the *conselho* stamped in their *cadernetas* that they had duly presented themselves, and I then put them on the bus for Nova Freixo, where they would get the train to Nampula. So far, it had all been fairly simple. They were with me and I could speak for them, so they were not shouted at or kept hanging around. None of these men had probably ever seen

* Canon John Kingsnorth wrote of my situation at that time: 'Fr Paul, the overworked priest at Messumba, had twelve curates and sixty churches under his care at one time.' *Supplement to the History of the Universities' Mission to Central Africa.*

a train before let alone the sea; they were totally unused to such things as buying tickets for trains and boats, and, although they all spoke Portuguese, they found it hard to understand most Portuguese who spoke to them. At Nampula, they had to present themselves to the administrative headquarters and then catch another train to Lumbo on the coast, where they awaited a ship to take them the twelve-day journey to Lourenço Marques. They had to fend for themselves entirely in completely strange surroundings and amongst Africans whose language they did not understand. Even if it had been possible in Vila Cabral to book them tickets for the boat, it would not have been practicable. No one knew how long they would be kept hanging about all the various offices they were required to visit, and the cargo boats that plied up and down the Mozambique coast followed an extremely elastic timetable, depending upon how much cargo there was to load and unload at each port. I only hoped that they would not be robbed of the money and the official papers and my letters. They reached Lourenço Marques safely, where they were met by Bishop Pickard, but here again they had to present themselves to the authorities, who authorized them to go to Maciene. On arrival at Maciene they presented themselves to the Chefe at the nearest administrative *posto*. I give all this laborious detail to show the enormous difficulties put in the way of a Mozambican African wishing to travel on a legitimate journey from *one end of his own country to the other*. Seven administrative offices had to be visited: Metangula, Maniamba, Vila Cabral, Nampula, Lumbo, Lourenço Marques, and the one near Maciene. And it must be remembered that each visit they made on their own might entail a day's wait or more before the official would see them.

The immediate answer to Messumba's problems, however, was Fabião Mahetane, who held a secondary-school diploma. I liked Fabião from the first, and he seemed the ideal person to send to Messumba, particularly as Joan Antcliff was due for furlough soon, and his qualifications fulfilled (more or less) Government minimum requirements. Fabião was a member of the Chopi tribe, about my age, and an *assimilado*. His stay at Messumba made history. He was the first *assimilado* and the first southerner to come, and it was a pleasant surprise to us

77

all how well he fitted in, and how much the people came to like him. The only other *assimilados* in the area were the Government nurse at Metangula, and a couple of hunters who lived a few miles away; none was an Anglican. As an *assimilado*, Fabião did not possess a *caderneta*, but a *bilhete de identidade* similar to my own. Although he was married, he was classed as a bachelor, because his wife was still an *indígena* and he had not had his marriage officially registered in a civil ceremony, which would have given her status as a 'legal wife'. When she bore him a child, he failed to register the birth within the prescribed time, and when he did, the child was registered as if it were the result of a casual affair with some village woman. The status of an *assimilado* could be revoked at any time, and in such cases the *assimilado* would revert to being an *indígena*.

I took Fabião with me to Vila Cabral on several occasions; and wherever we went, I made a point of introducing him as I would a fellow missionary. This caused most Portuguese a good deal of surprise, until I explained that he was an *assimilado*, and then they would rather unwillingly shake hands with him. (At that time, there were probably less than a thousand *assimilados* in the whole of Mozambique, and most of them lived in Lourenço Marques and Beira.) On more than one occasion, when he was with me in Vila Cabral, and I was invited out to lunch, I would ask that Fabião be invited, too. Often as we left, our hosts would patronizingly remark on his good manners. In fact, his table-manners were infinitely better than those of most of the Portuguese people living in and around the town. At Maniamba, Borges de Brito was always very friendly to him but never invited him into his house, in spite of the fact that he was officially classed as a loyal Portuguese citizen. Borges de Brito tried to persuade Reggie and a few others to become *assimilados*, but they saw no point in going to all the trouble that was involved, particularly when they saw what a hollow thing it was. In Fabião's case it had been quite different, as it was well-nigh impossible to get any secondary-school education without being an *assimilado*. For a village African, there were more difficulties in being an *assimilado* than there were in being an *indígena*, and only one distinct advantage – exemption from forced labour.

The next batch of students to go to Lourenço Marques, where they lived with Bishop Pickard and attended night-school, included Amós Sumane, one of our senior teachers; Jaime Farahane (the eldest son of Basílio) and Carlos Juma (the eldest son of Fr Juma), both of whom were exceptionally intelligent, and the latter a person of particular charm. These three men had to study very hard. We needed them back at Messumba as soon as possible, since we were desperate for teachers with some secondary education. And in less than two years' part-time study, they completed *segundo ciclo*.*

The year after Messumba had been incorporated into the Diocese of Lebombo, the Archbishop of Cape Town, Jooste de Blank, came to visit us. This caused a great stir, not only among the Portuguese, who knew of his outspoken views on apartheid, but also among our Africans. Never before had an Archbishop visited Messumba. An airfield had just been made at Vila Cabral, and once or twice a week a small plane flew up from Lourenço Marques (with numerous stops on the way). As the Archbishop was accompanied by his chaplain and much baggage (and I had, as usual, many purchases to make in Vila Cabral), I borrowed a VW 'beetle' from a Portuguese friend and drove up to meet him, with Reggie driving the land-rover and Barnabé Njawala, a nephew of Henry Chipembele, driving our small lorry. Most of the Portuguese officials in Vila Cabral displayed a total lack of interest; but those who were friendly towards us came to greet the Archbishop, and at Maniamba, Borges de Brito, smart in his best uniform, came out to greet him. The Archbishop was interested in everything we could show him and tell him at the Mission and, realizing we worked against great odds, promised to do all he could to make our needs known to the outside world. This he did, and within a couple of years we were able to put in a piped water supply and electric light. He never lost his interest in what we were trying to do and encouraged many people to

---

* Secondary education was divided into *primeiro ciclo* (two years); *segundo ciclo* (three years) and *terceiro ciclo* (two years), this last for those preparing to enter a university, though there was none such in Mozambique until 1964.

visit us, as a Mission trying to be faithful to great traditions in difficult circumstances.

During the three days he was with us, I took the Archbishop to Manda-Mbuzi for a night, and that evening, Fr Juma, Basílio Farahane and some other employees dined with us in the little *ulendo* house. While we were eating, the Chefe do Posto of Cóbuè suddenly arrived and sat down with us. When he had gone, the Archbishop expressed his great surprise at this friendly visit. He said that if a Government official in South Africa had come across such an inter-racial party, he would have been furious. There was, of course, much talk of the problems both countries shared, and he asked me to explain the *assimilado* system, for which the Portuguese were well known in South Africa. When I had explained this as best I could, he replied that it might sound all right at first hearing, but he doubted that one could morally justify the premise that everyone who lived in Mozambique must become a Portuguese in order to be acceptable – and acceptable to whom? He did not feel that the Portuguese system was any better than the South African one. They might be very different superficially, but in practice they were equally bad, as they insisted on the superiority of one race over another.*

About this time, other visitors to our area were some members of the Missão Hidrográfica, a nautical survey team. The British and the Portuguese had recently concluded the agreement about the transfer to Portuguese jurisdiction of a large section of Lake Nyasa facing Mozambique, which I had heard about when I was in Lisbon in 1957. The coming of the Missão Hidrográfica was the first real step in the enormous development which was to take place at Metangula during the 1960s.

*Jooste de Blank was succeeded in 1964 as Archbishop of Cape Town by Robert Selby Taylor, a former Bishop of Northern Rhodesia.

7 Portugal and World Opinion

1961 was a traumatic year for Portugal. It started with the hijacking, off the coast of Brazil, of the Portuguese luxury liner, *Santa Maria*, by Henrique Galvão, which drew world attention to internal oppression in Portugal and her colonies, and ended with the Indian invasion of Goa. For almost the first time in her recent history, Portugal could not escape the glare of international publicity, nor continue to present herself to the world as a country without serious problems.

That year, I was due for furlough, and Messumba was fortunate to have in my place Fr Charles Wright, who had recently arrived in Mozambique. After years as a public-school master, and later with the British Council in Brazil, he was ordained in 1949 and worked in parishes in and around London until, with his valuable ability to speak Portuguese, he came to Lebombo. He was then in his fifties, an unusual age for a newcomer to the mission field, and such a remote corner of that field as well. His energy, his interest in everything, his sense of humour, and his unpredictability and eccentricities soon gave rise to countless good stories about him, even before I had left. His first *ulendo* to Chicale upset all the long-held *ulendo* traditions. Everything was ready at 10 a.m. but he finally left on his bicycle at 6 p.m. As it got dark, he got lost, but luckily someone met him and put him on the right path. He arrived about 10 p.m. and, as far as I can make out, heard confessions all night.

As Charles had been a schoolmaster, I asked him to take the religious classes in the college, and this he readily agreed to do; though quite how he managed to give twelve lectures on Melchizedek, I shall never know. What I do know is that the students thereafter substituted for *lentamente* (slowly) a new word, '*melchizedekamente*'! He had no idea of time and did not pos-

sess a watch, but this was not too disastrous, as bells were rung
to call people to church, or to meals, or to school.

Within a few weeks of my arrival in England I applied to the
Portuguese Tourist Office in Lower Regent Street, London, for
a part-time job, which might not only help the months pass until
I could return to Messumba, but would also keep up my Portuguese and probably improve it. I received a very civil reply from
the manager, Jorge Dias,* and went to see him. While I was
waiting to be shown into his office, I noticed two men looking
down at me through the glass of the mezzanine floor. The manager greeted me pleasantly and told me how interested he was to
meet someone who had just arrived from Mozambique, and
asked me how I had found things there. We chatted briefly about
this, and then I explained that I had come to inquire whether
he could offer me a part-time job during my furlough. At that
moment in came a fat man whom I recognized as one of the two
I had seen through the glass of the mezzanine floor while waiting for my appointment. Now it was his turn to ask questions:
what did I think about the lies that were being spread around
about Angola? I said I knew nothing about Angola apart from
what I read in the papers, as I had only been there once, in tran-
sit. I had, of course, heard about the uprising on 15 March of
that year, but had no first-hand experience of conditions there,
and really I'd rather talk about the possibility of a job with 'Casa
de Portugal'. To my surprise he replied: 'The best job you can
do for us is to refute these lies that Protestant missionaries and
others are telling about the Portuguese administration in Angola.
Have you seen these papers? You haven't? Well just read them.
Have you ever heard such untruths? And to think such people
call themselves Christians!'

The interview was proceeding along lines I did not like, and I
told them that I really could not enter into the argument at all,
even if I had wanted to do so, as I came from Mozambique, not
from Angola. The manager replied: 'But Mozambique and Angola are both integral parts of Portugal, so if the administration
is brutal in Angola, it must also be so in Mozambique.' I could

* Jorge Dias and other senior members of the Portuguese Tourist Office
were 'suspended' in December 1974.

only repeat that I was too ill-informed about Angola to comment. But the manager and the fat man persisted: 'Look, we will let you have all the material we can, and we will pay you for your efforts on behalf of Portugal. You should have seen the meeting that was held at the Central Hall, Westminster, a short time ago as people, one after the other, made false accusations against Portugal, and when we tried to get up and speak we were pushed down. Call this a democratic country!' As I got up to go, Dias said more calmly: 'The only work I can give you is what I have explained. Please think it over. And for your kindness in coming here, I've asked the receptionist to make up a parcel of some bottles of Dão wine.' I left 'Casa de Portugal' with the wine and a sense of relief – and have never been back. Later I heard that the fat man had a cover job with the Portuguese Embassy in London, but was really a member of P.I.D.E., whose principal job was to keep an eye on Portuguese dissidents in London.

But the two Portuguese men had certainly aroused my interest, and I went straight off to a bookstall in Piccadilly and bought all the papers I could find which might contain some news about Angola. Only as I read them did I realize that, until then, all my energies and interest had been bound up with Messumba and keeping it going. When I had read or heard things about other parts of 'pluri-continental' Portugal, I had not paid much attention to them. But now my horizon had been widened. During the rest of my furlough, the Portuguese sent me regular monthly bulletins with press-cuttings, which were very helpful. One I particularly remember was a letter to the *Church Times* by the late Lord Selborne (a leading Church of England layman) in which he praised Portugal and her administration of her colonies. Clearly he had no real first-hand knowledge of them, and I was shocked by his uninformed views.

With the publicity she was receiving on account of the *Santa Maria* and the troubles in Angola, Portugal realized that she could no longer keep herself to herself. Nearly all information that had been published had come from foreign sources, as Portugal gave little information herself to the outside world, particularly with regard to her colonies. Now she looked for help to various public relations firms, prominent among which were Selvage and Lee of the United States, and the E. D. O'Brien Organisation of London. During the next few years they took M.P.s, journalists, and diplomats on conducted tours in Mozambique, and they did a truly impressive job of making the Portuguese system look philanthropic, and unique in the field of race relations. It was particularly galling to see British M.P.s, like Stephen Hastings, being trotted around Vila Cabral by a member of the O'Brien Organisation, sublimely ignorant of the Portuguese saying *Para o inglês ver* (for the Englishman to see), while my Portuguese friends chuckled over the cleverness of the Portuguese – and the gullibility of the English.

In September I flew to Lisbon with a friend for three weeks' holiday, and as we had a car I was able to see a great deal more of Portugal than I had when I was living there. Every hotel and *pensão* we stayed at had a booklet in English prominently displayed about the 'pirate' Galvão and the *Santa Maria*. At the main tourist office at the Restauradores in central Lisbon, there was a well-publicized exhibition of the atrocities committed by Africans against the Portuguese in Angola. I heard about the sudden flight of several Angolan students in Lisbon to France and other countries, which had been partly attributed to an English Protestant pastor living in Lisbon. (He was deported a few weeks after his arrest.) There was certainly a good deal of orchestrated feeling against Britain and the United States because of their lack of support for Portugal over Angola, and the Indian claims to Goa and the other Portuguese-occupied territories in India. (Frequently expressed was the view that it was all Britain's fault for having handed over India to Nehru.) Also publicity was being given in Britain and America to the Casablanca Conference's call for unity against Portuguese Colonialism – C.O.N.C.P.

In November I returned to Mozambique by sea and arrived at Lourenço Marques towards the end of the month. Here I stayed for a few weeks while the chaplain to the 'English' church was on leave. I did not like having to postpone my return to Messumba, but these weeks gave me an opportunity to see something of the city and the life of the people. Lourenço Marques was very different from other cities in southern Africa because of its continental-style pavement cafés and noise. Traffic raced through the streets regardless of speed limits, and people (of all colours) shouted to one another across the street, or walked along with transistor radios blaring. It all seemed happy-go-lucky on the surface. The iniquity of the 'pass laws' in South Africa has become quite well known outside that country; here in Lourenço Marques I learned about the Portuguese version of these laws. Africans were supposed to be off the streets by 9 p.m. unless they had a special pass. Every African – *assimilado*, pass-holder, and law-breaker alike – was constantly stopped and questioned by the police if on the streets after that hour. Often when I have visited the Costa de Sol Restaurant, a few miles out of the city, some of the African waiters have asked me to drive them home in order to escape harassment by the police after 9 p.m.

All African servants were officially 'contracted' with their employers, which meant, in effect, that they were tied to them until dismissed. Both parties signed the form of contract: the employer agreeing to pay the employee a certain wage, house him and feed him; the employee agreeing to give due service to his master until such time as he decided to leave, in which case he would have to give the statutory notice. Any breach of the contract by either party would involve a fine. This whole system was constantly abused by the employers. An employee who had incurred the displeasure of his employer could be sent to the police-station with a note saying something like: 'My "boy" has been very rude to me, please punish him.' The unfortunate man would probably be given some *palmatoadas* (beatings on the hand) and sent back to his employer. I knew some English-speaking people who quite openly told me that they did this from time to time. An African servant was a paid slave, and the wage was often practically nothing, as the cost of any breakages was deducted.

At the beginning of December 1961 I was free to return to Messumba and set off from Lourenço Marques on the long hot journey by car through South Africa, Rhodesia and Nyasaland. When I got to Vila Cabral, I found that Salvado, who had started off as an assistant in Cruchinho's shop, now had a shop of his own which was, in time, to make him the most important trader in the town. He also became a deputy in the legislative assembly of Mozambique. He had little more than primary education but great ability and ambition. He was particularly pleased to see me, as I had so recently seen his family in Portugal. We remained good friends during the whole of my time in Mozambique, despite the Portuguese dislike of having their bills paid, and the sore trial to my patience of the incredible length of time it took to do the shopping (though this was due as much to his Portuguese assistants as it was to him). We bought goods in large quantities as we lived so far away and never took less than a full load. I always wanted to pay cash, but the shopkeepers were reluctant for me to do this, not only because it took so long to work out my large bill, but also because there was intensive rivalry amongst the ever-increasing number of shopkeepers for one's custom. If they gave you credit, they felt that this gave them a hold over you. Their book-keeping methods have caused cleverer men than I to despair.

There was nothing remarkable about my return to Messumba, as people knew that I was now a permanent part of the Mission, but we missed Charles Wright when he left a few weeks later for the Mission near Inhambane – midway between Lourenço Marques and Beira. He was to return to Messumba some three years later under very different circumstances.

Ferreira de Silva had, unfortunately, been transferred from Metangula; and, in his place, we had Figueiredo, who was not at all helpful to the Mission. In theory, Figueiredo's superior was Borges de Brito, whose superior in turn was the Governor at Vila Cabral, then a Senhor Veloso. However, in practice a Chefe do Posto could do pretty well what he liked within his own area. Borges de Brito was still at Maniamba and continued to be friendly towards us, though there was some strain, caused in part by the anti-British and anti-American feeling that had been stirred up, and in part by the fact that his *circunscrição* now contained many more Portuguese people. But he shared our dislike of Figueiredo.

Anti-British feelings were particularly intense because of

Portugal and World Opinion

Britain's refusal to come to the aid of Portugal when India invaded Goa; a refusal that was seen as an open breach of the Ancient Alliance between the two countries. It is difficult to stress adequately the enormous significance that Goa had for Portugal. The original Portuguese forts on the coast of East Africa had been established almost entirely as staging posts for Goa; and, right up until this century, Mozambique, ecclesiastically, was linked to Goa. One of my more enlightened friends in Vila Cabral said, however, that he thought it quite a good thing Portugal had been forced to abandon Goa, since the millions of escudos that had been poured into the place to keep it going for the sake of Portugal's prestige could now be diverted to the more worthy cause of developing Portugal and her overseas territories in Africa.

Now that Britain had granted independence to Tanganyika (Tanzania) and was obviously preparing to grant independence to Nyasaland (Malawi), Portugal felt increasingly beleaguered. She had been defeated in the United Nations, where, when it came to a vote on Portuguese colonialism, Britain, even if she did not vote against Portugal, usually abstained. We at Messumba were very much affected in our relations with the Portuguese by the British Government's actions, as we were always suspected of being financially and morally supported by Westminster in the same way that the Roman Catholic missions were supported by the Vatican. Further, because the Portuguese had laid the blame for the troubles in Angola largely on the Protestant missions there, Messumba itself was 'suspect'. Many a time I was asked by Portuguese visitors to the Mission if we taught English in the school, and always they were disbelieving when I assured them that we stuck rigidly to the official Portuguese primary-school syllabus. On one occasion, when I was speaking to an African in Chinyanja, a Portuguese visitor asked in a most offensive way what language I was speaking, and why I didn't speak in Portuguese. On another occasion the new *secretário* at Maniamba, António Marques, showed me a copy of Duffy's *Portugal in Africa* and asked me how I thought he had obtained so much *accurate* information.

When the new naval base at Metangula was completed, Irene

87

Wheeler and I were invited to its official opening. Never before had so many Portuguese been seen on the lakeshore. The ceremonial was elaborate; the speeches fervent and patriotic. First of all came the dedication of the base, by Padre Machado, the vicar-general of the Diocese of Nampula, in the absence of the Bishop. (Vila Cabral had not yet been given a bishop.) Padre Machado was well known for his intolerance of anything foreign, and his sermon delivered alongside the flag-pole was unique in my experience. It went something like this: 'Here we are in a remote, though true part of Portugal. Christ led our people to plant His cross in this place many centuries ago, and now with the national flag about to be raised no doubt can remain among those who have wished to deprive the Portuguese of their divinely chosen role in this part of Africa. Viva Portugal!' He then blessed the flag, which was reverently hoisted. Afterwards, Padre Menegon introduced me to Padre Machado, who, having dealt with us foreigners politically, now proceeded to deal with us theologically: 'Yes, I've heard about your Mission in this part of Portugal. It is such a pity that your sect does not have the apostolic succession. I know of course that the Bishop of Nyasaland tried very hard to get it by having a Greek Bishop present at his so-called consecration on Likoma Island. Such a pity the Greek Church is heretical.' Padre Menegon was extremely embarrassed by Padre Machado's impertinence and apologized profusely.

After a sumptuous buffet lunch, a historian who had come from Lisbon specially for the occasion spoke about the historical place of Portugal on the shores of Lake Nyasa. He told us how Portugal had been in Mozambique for nearly five hundred years, and that the Portuguese Catholic traders had reached the lakeshore hundreds of years ago (see note on page 18). Then foreigners, particularly Protestant missionaries like David Livingstone, had challenged Portugal's rightful claim to the Lake. Now at last Portugal's presence was re-established in the area by international agreement. Irene and I sat there in the crowded little room feeling a trifle out of place, though our friends did not seem to think that *we* had anything to do with those frightful missionaries of the past. I am sure that neither

Padre Machado nor the historian had prior knowledge that we would be present.

This new Chefe do Posto, Figueiredo, was a staunch supporter of the Roman Catholic Church and not only distrusted, but actively disliked, our work at Messumba. The Mission was non-Roman Catholic and therefore anti-Portuguese. There seemed to be little that Borges de Brito could do about Figueiredo, except to say how unfortunate it was that so much of the better understanding that he had tried to establish between the Portuguese administration and the people was being destroyed. The people were constantly being called in to Metangula on some minor pretext; our teachers and other Mission employees would be summoned without warning. When we complained that this disrupted the smooth running of the Mission, difficult enough at the best of times, our protest was ignored. Fabião was sometimes summoned, and was supposed to appear often on his own accord. Being an *assimilado*, he was expected to be a loyal Portuguese person, duty-bound to support all that the administration did. Fortunately for Fabião, he was transferred back to Maciene soon afterwards; and, unfortunately for me, Borges de Brito, after four years at Maniamba, was transferred to Inhambane at about the same time. We were, however, to see a lot more of each other three years later.

The *Paul* passed Messumba from time to time on its way between Likoma and Mponda's. Strictly speaking it was supposed to report at Metangula every time it came to Messumba or even passed by. However, the crew tended to be very lax about this, partly because they were often late; partly because when they did report no one took any notice; and partly because they could not get into the habit of regarding any part of the Lake as belonging to any other country than Nyasaland (Malawi). Figueiredo was constantly complaining to me about this. It was difficult for me to do anything, as the crew were employed by the Diocese of Nyasaland, and I belonged to the Diocese of Lebombo. Beyond imploring the *Paul*'s crew always to report to Metangula, however pointless it might seem, I was helpless. Sometimes, the *Paul* came as far as Messumba, but the weather would be bad, and all the crew wanted to do was to turn round and get back to Likoma, without having to sail on an additional few miles to Metangula. The *Paul* visited Cóbuè frequently, and the Chefe do Posto there made use of it, as did the Roman Catholics, to smuggle in their supplies; so naturally at Cóbuè there were no problems at all, and the crew could not see why I was making such a fuss about formalities at Metangula.

In June 1962, the materials for the installation of our long-awaited water supply and electric-light plant were ready to be collected from Chipoka. The simplest way of transporting the material to Messumba was to hire the *Paul*, as she could take all the material in one load. One evening, some people came to tell me that the *Paul* had just offloaded everything on to the beach at Mónduè, two miles beyond the Mission, and that the Chefe do Posto was there, too. By the time I got there, it was getting dark. Figueiredo was there checking the weighbill; but luckily for me, this time the *Paul had* called at Metangula. When Figueiredo found I was going to leave the stuff on the beach all night (as it was far too late to transport it all up to the Mission, and anyway our labourers had finished work for the day) he replied: 'You realize that with all these steel pipes lying around, it would be easy for hostile Africans to take them to make rifles and guns. It will be your fault if they are stolen!' The idea was so improbable that I was speechless at his stupidity.

A few days later, I went to the department of Customs and Excise in Vila Cabral and paid over the necessary duty. The Chief Customs Officer had been an air-force officer, but for various reasons had been demoted and now found himself where he was. He was an exceptionally pleasant person, but I was very taken aback one Sunday afternoon a few weeks later to see him, his assistant and a policeman appear outside my house, followed closely by Figueiredo. 'Whatever's brought you here all the way from Vila Cabral on a Sunday afternoon? Come on in, let's have a drink.' Without further courtesies, Figueiredo chipped in: 'Padre Paul, show the Customs Officer what else you received off the *Paul*, and be quick about it as they don't want to waste time.' So I showed them: two large biscuit tins of Communion wafers, and a dozen or so steel desk frames made out of scrap iron. The

Customs Officer was furious with Figueiredo for having made him undertake a journey of 150 miles on a Sunday afternoon, because of anything so paltry, and told him in fairly strong terms that in future he should ask me, if he wanted to, about what came off the *Paul*. The Customs Officer and I became even firmer friends after this, and when he later became Chief Customs Officer at Beira airport, he was most helpful and often had me into his office for a chat if there was time. Happily for us all, Figueiredo did not stay very long at Metangula, but during the short time he was there, he managed to destroy any goodwill that Borges de Brito and Ferreira de Silva had created between the administration and practically everyone else. Towards the end of his time at Metangula there was a slight reconciliation between him and the Mission, for his wife was obliged to make use of Irene Wheeler's services as a midwife when their first child was born.

A few months before my return to Messumba at the end of 1961, the Estatuto dos Indígenas of 1954 had been repealed, and overnight all Africans became full Portuguese citizens with equal rights before the Law.* For those who had any desire to become a Portuguese citizen, such 'reforms' might have appeared to be great steps forward, but in fact they barely touched most Africans, and what looked, on paper, to be spectacular changes of policy made little or no difference. An *indigena* was now called an *autóctone*; and the *caderneta indigena* had to be exchanged for a *cartão de identidade*. This caused great confusion in places like Metangula as no *cartões de identidade* were available until months afterwards, and then supplies kept on running out. A *cartão* was practically identical to a *caderneta*, and there remained the same distinction between those who held a *bilhete de identidade* (i.e., whites and *assimilados*) and those who did not. Officially, the use of the *palmatório* was now illegal, but in fact every Administrador and Chefe do Posto continued to have one in his office, though it was used slightly less frequently. The one obvious result was the tightening of Portuguese control over

* Various other 'reforms' took place – in 1962 the publication of a new 'labour code' and in 1963 the publication of the New Overseas Organic Law.

the African population by necessitating their re-registration in order to obtain a *cartão de identidade*.

Now, as a result, our schoolchildren had to produce a *cartão de identidade* when they took the final primary-school exam, though until they were adults they did not have to pay taxes. This caused us immense trouble, as at least half of the boarders came from the Cóbuè and Vila Cabral areas and were supposed to present themselves, with their parents and local village headman, at their own local administrative secretariat. Additionally, fourteen was the maximum age for a child to enter for the final exam, and nearly all our candidates would be sixteen or seventeen years old. This was not because they lacked intelligence, but because all teaching had to be done in Portuguese. Thus, the first two years at least of any African's education were spent in his learning the language, before he could even begin the official four-year primary course. The whole system was geared to Portuguese children and not to Africans at all. (Portuguese and other European languages were spelt with an initial capital letter, while Chinyanja, for instance, was classed as a dialect and spelt with a small one.) Becoming a Portuguese citizen added emphasis to Portugal's desire to force the Portuguese language and culture on Africans, and to eradicate the African languages and cultures, or at best relegate them to the status of museum curiosities.

As part of the process of deliberate Portugalization, posters were printed and distributed which, I was told, were the brainchild of the Governor-General of Mozambique, Sarmento Rodrigues. They consisted of a map of Mozambique, divided into the main ethnic groups, with the words above and below the map: '*Moçambique só é Moçambique porque é Portugal*' ('Mozambique is only Mozambique because it is Portugal'). I was also given several photographs of President Américo Tomás and Prime Minister Salazar and told to have them framed and put up in my office, in the hospital and in as many classrooms as possible. Portugal being a dictatorship, and all Africans in Mozambique being citizens of Portugal, meant that the mildest criticism of anything any Portuguese official did or said was tantamount to treason. The theory was that Portugal had bestowed a great privilege on the 'uncivilized masses' of Mozambicans, and whatever went on in other countries could not possibly break the unity of the Portuguese nation. However, it was obvious to those of us who lived amongst the Africans that they knew very clearly what was going on elsewhere, and that they resented Portugal's blind refusal to recognize their own identity.

8 The First Arrests

Major Costa Matos was the second Governor of Niassa District. About the same time as he took up his appointment in Vila Cabral, Dom Eurico Nogueira was appointed first Bishop of the newly-created Diocese of Vila Cabral, which had been carved out of the enormous Diocese of Nampula. Costa Matos and Dom Eurico were to play an important part in the Niassa scene for the next few years. Apart from both being Portuguese, the only thing that the two men seemed to have in common was a guarded respect for our work at Messumba. Costa Matos was a whole-hearted militarist who stood no nonsense from anyone. He was not very popular with the civilian population, which he regarded with suspicion, or with the Roman Catholic missionaries, whom he thought dishonest. His private secretary was a dapper-looking man, who had previously been a somewhat unscrupulous Chefe do Posto not far from Maciene. Dom Eurico, who had been on the staff of Coimbra University before being made a bishop, was fat and rather unctuous; but he was also a compassionate man, and clearly shocked by the way that Africans were treated in Mozambique. With the creation of the Diocese of Vila Cabral, Dom Eurico had been able to add some Portuguese priests to his largely Italian staff. The first Portuguese priest, Padre Piquito, arrived about a couple of years before the creation of the new diocese, and it was really he who established the separate parish of Vila Cabral, and began the enlargement of the small church that was to become the cathedral. After the Second Vatican Council of 1962, and the arrival of Dom Eurico in 1963, relations between the Roman Catholics and Anglicans improved dramatically.

At the same time, the Portuguese opened schools at most of the administrative centres in the area, including Maniamba, where

the neglected little chapel came into its own as a classroom.
These were very small schools, with maybe twenty pupils each,
and usually the wife of someone in the civil administration was
the teacher. Very few of them attempted to do more than teach
the children the three R's. One important advance in education,
however, was the establishment of the Escola Técnica in Vila
Cabral. This was not strictly a technical college, but it did
attempt to provide some secondary education.

We were able to send to the Escola Técnica a number of our
own college students, including Matias Juma (younger son of Fr
Juma), Matias Chissancho, and Jaime Amanze (younger son of
our master-of-works, my former Chinyanja teacher). Sending
students there was not without its problems, however. We
lacked proper facilities to house them in Vila Cabral; and, besides, we could ill-afford the fees. But here Costa Matos proved
his opinion of Messumba by recommending that we be given
some bursaries. In all my years in Niassa, the only really worth-
while thing that the Portuguese did was to open the Escola
Técnica. Matias Chissancho and Matias Juma later worked for
Frelimo, and Jaime Amanze went to Malawi, where he is now a
priest.

At Messumba, we were often criticized for taking children
through the primary syllabus and then not teaching them a trade.
The reasons for our failure to do this were simple: we were not
allowed to increase our missionary staff, and we lacked the necessary facilities, financial and material. When we were able to
employ an excellent carpenter, I started a small carpentry course,
in an attempt to offset some of the criticism, but for various
reasons this had to be abandoned within a year.

At about this time, we opened a clinic at Ngoo, and Susan
Andrew was transferred from Maciene to run it. Susan had been
at Maciene for almost as long as Irene had been at Messumba
and she was the ideal person for Ngoo, since she preferred living
on her own. The people there were delighted that we were taking
more notice of them, and built the clinic themselves. The pre-
paration for all this, and the building of a pleasant little house
for Susan, necessitated frequent journeys for me: six hours on
foot, or about two hours on a bicycle. Sometimes I would leave

a work-force there for a week or ten days, as the people at Ngoo
could not supply much in the way of skilled labour. As soon as
we got Susan properly established there, she was able to employ about six orderlies and helpers, and treated as many as a
hundred patients a day. Anyone needing prolonged treatment
was sent to Messumba, as there were no facilities at Ngoo for in-
patients, and she did no maternity work except in emergency.
The mission area at Ngoo had become quite important with a
clinic as well as a school, and it was not long before a Portuguese
man opened a store there on the lakeshore. But he sold goods at
such inflated prices that many villagers preferred to walk the
twenty miles to Metangula to do their shopping. I had a rough
track made from Ngoo to Manda-Mbuzi, a distance of about
seven miles up the steep escarpment, which could be used by a
land-rover.

Our first employee to get into trouble was our catechist in
Vila Cabral, João Massanche. I was told that he had been drink-
ing in a bar and been heard to say that the Portuguese should
follow other European countries and get out of Africa. People in
the bar had reportedly taken fright at what he was saying and
quickly left him. He was picked up by the police and taken to
the prison, where he was locked up for several days inside a small
cupboard, without room even to squat. I did not hear anything
of this until the day he was released, however, and by that time
he did not want to talk about it at all.

I heard about the cupboard from one of the African prison
warders, but I took no action, as the warder would have got into
trouble, and João would probably have been forced to say that
he had been treated well in prison. Also I did not think it wise
to draw any more attention to what he had said when drunk.
However, I made it plain back at Messumba that the Portuguese
would show no mercy to anyone who 'talked politics'. Those who
wanted to do so, should wait until they were away from the
Mission, as we knew only too well what had happened to the
Protestant missions of Angola in 1961. Looking back, I sometimes think that I should have spoken out more forcefully than
I did about the gross injustices in Mozambique. But I am certain

that if I had done so, I would have been expelled; our work would have been stopped; and even more extreme forms of repression, especially against the 25,000 Anglicans, would have resulted. As it was, I decided that my job was to consolidate our position and continue our historical role as the guardians of the Nyasa people against all who would seek to oppress them. The vast majority of our people looked to Messumba as the one continuing influence for good upon their whole lives.

But I also knew that Amós Sumane, recently returned from studying in Lourenço Marques, had collected a number of thinking people around him, including some of our students, to listen to broadcasts from Radio Tanzania.

The second half of 1962 had seen the formation in Tanzania of the Mozambique Liberation Front (Frelimo), and naturally these young men were vitally interested in its activities. As far as I was concerned, what they did in their own time and in their own houses was their own business, so long as they did not involve the Mission, as such, in what the Portuguese would consider 'subversive activities'. Radio reception from Lourenço Marques was very bad, and no programme was broadcast in Chinyanja until the late 1960s, so that it was natural our people should listen to Radio Tanzania and broadcasts from Nyasaland – shortly to become independent Malawi.

In August 1963, I attended the Anglican World Congress in Canada, as the sole representative of the Diocese of Lebombo, since lack of money prevented our sending the usual three delegates. I was away from Messumba for exactly a month, and on my return to the Mission, I was told that a few teachers (including Amós Sumane), and some of the hospital staff and students had not returned from their holidays. We assumed that they had joined Frelimo, and I was naturally more than a little worried about how this would affect the official attitude to Messumba. A few days later, I went to Metangula. Quite by chance, my visit coincided with that of the new Administrador at Maniamba, Simões Carneiro, and I told him about the absentees. To have failed to do so would have cast suspicion on the Mission, but I found he already knew. He told me that many people from all over Mozambique had joined Frelimo. He added that he was glad I had spoken about it; since if I had not, people would have thought that I was implicated.

Some weeks later, Bishop Pickard came on a visit, and this coincided with an official visit that Brian Heddy, the British Consul-General, was paying to Vila Cabral. On Pickard's arrival, we were both asked to a small reception that Costa Matos was holding in Heddy's honour. Costa Matos took us aside and advised us at Messumba to keep a close watch on our employees so as to prevent more desertions to Frelimo. But he was quite pleasant about it, since we were by no means the only mission involved in this situation.

A few weeks later, when I was in Vila Cabral, a Portuguese acquaintance said to me: '*I* trust you, but many do not, and they think it is you who are responsible for sending Amós Sumane and the others to Tanzania.'

A couple of days before Christmas that year, I was awakened by a European policeman at my door: 'I'm so sorry to wake you up, but Administrador Simões Carneiro told me I had better come to you. I have orders to arrest one of your teachers, António Chizoma. Would you please tell me where his house is, as I don't want to disturb the whole Mission.' Chizoma was arrested. The following day I drove to Maniamba to ask the Administrador what had happened. This was his story: 'As you know, several people went to Tanzania in July and August. Some, like Amós, stayed; others were sent back to Mozambique to spread Frelimo propaganda, and one of the leaders of this latter group was António Chizoma. He was extremely clever about it, and I have had quite a job to catch him. He has been selling Frelimo membership cards for 17·50 escudos each. I told one of my informers to go and buy one of these cards, but Chizoma was suspicious, and it was not until the third attempt that the card was given to him. Here it is, and you will see Chizoma's signature.' The Administrador went on: 'I also had arrested last night some other people, and they include your catechist at Metangula, Salathiel Chizuzu, though I'm not sure to what extent he is implicated. Two others are from Chigoma, but are not your employees. They have had something to do with sending lists of people Chizoma had recruited to Dar-es-Salaam.' Those arrested had apparently spent a few hours at Maniamba early that morning before being sent on to Vila Cabral, where they would be questioned by P.I.D.E. agents sent there for that purpose.

I returned to Messumba and tried to comfort the wives of the arrested men. Everyone was very tense and frightened. One of our African priests, Fr João Sululu, Chizoma's uncle, said that he wanted to visit his nephew in Vila Cabral prison. On his return a few days later he told me, much to my surprise, that he had been allowed to speak to his nephew. Chizoma had apparently made a full confession of almost everything. But when the police had searched his house, they had missed some documents that he had hidden. Among these was Fr Paulo Litumbi's membership card, which he had not yet had an opportunity to give him. He had told his interrogators nothing about these documents, and asked his uncle to collect them in case they should be found later. Fr Sululu then handed them to me, saying that if his nephew was kept in prison, he would tell the authorities that Fr Litumbi had been the ring-leader. I was now in an extremely difficult position. I knew that the two priests disliked one another and I had no doubt that Fr Sululu meant what he said. In addition to Fr Litumbi's membership card, there were a few others, together with some forms. But worst of all, there were the minutes of a couple of meetings which had been held in Fr Litumbi's house (a hundred yards from my own on the Mission). He had been the chairman of both meetings, and it was he who had encouraged people to do everything they could to liberate their country from the Portuguese colonialists. I was angry and perturbed to find that the meetings had taken place on the Mission itself, in spite of my warning. My only grain of comfort was that I had been away at the time.

I locked the documents in the safe and drove to Maniamba to see Simões Carneiro. He told me that Chizoma had confessed everything and had already been taken to Lourenço Marques. Then he showed me a list of all the people who had bought Frelimo membership cards from Chizoma. This included nearly all our teachers, some of the hospital staff, a few catechists, but, to my relief, none of the clergy. Altogether there were about two hundred names, many of whom were ordinary villagers from places as far away as Ngoo. Again to my relief, the names of Reggie and Buanacaia (the people closest to me) were absent. As Chizoma had gone to Lourenço Marques, I felt I had no alternative but to tell Simões Carneiro the full story as I now knew it. He did not think it would make much difference, as he felt that Chizoma, having been arrested, would by now have confessed the full story. If P.I.D.E. had wanted to act further on the information they had, they would have done so already.

I then drove on to Vila Cabral where I asked the Governor for permission to visit Salathiel Chizuzu in prison. Permission was readily granted after agreement from the Chief of Police (the P.I.D.E. people had by then left the place). This man was nicknamed by the local Portuguese residents *o mainato do governador*, the Governor's lackey, as this was exactly how he was treated – and he even seemed to enjoy it. I was allowed to speak to Salathiel alone in the open courtyard of the prison, but was not allowed inside the buildings. He told me that as the P.I.D.E. people had now left, he expected to be released soon. I chatted to him in general terms as I did not want to run the risk of his getting into further trouble for giving away any secrets. He was released a few days later, and it was not long before he made his way to Malawi to live in self-imposed exile.

In January 1964, Bishop Pickard paid a visit to Messumba and was disturbed to hear what had happened. He told me he had heard that many people in the south had fled, via Swaziland, to Tanzania to join Frelimo, but did not think that any of the diocesan staff there had been involved. Simões Carneiro had a friendly talk with us and said that he would like to speak to all our employees within the next few weeks. The administration would pay for travelling expenses – a unique experience. However, when Costa Matos asked to see us, he was rather offensive to Bishop Pickard, lecturing him on the evils of missions that harboured political agitators, and hinting that Messumba was following in the steps of the Protestant missions in Angola.

Simões Carneiro duly came, and all our employees were assembled at Messumba; the *banja* being held in one of the school classrooms. Only about a half of the people present had any idea why António Chizoma had been arrested so not all of them could have guessed the reason for the great meeting, as the subject had never been discussed. Simões Carneiro led into his subject very subtly. He told the people that Portugal did not tolerate opposition of any sort, either in Europe or in Africa, and therefore anyone, of whatever colour, who dared to criticize the régime, however mildly, did so at his own risk. P.I.D.E. was not exactly a very merciful organization. Although Britain and France were giving independence to their African territories, Portugal would never do such a thing; she had, after all, been in Africa for close on five hundred years, and everyone now in her African 'provinces' was a full Portuguese citizen – Britain and other European nations had never granted a similar privilege to their African peoples. He admitted that there was much to be done, and that Portugal had often failed in the past to live up to her calling both in Europe and in Africa. Now, however, things were different. There were real signs of progress: more schools, more medical facilities, more Africans participating in government, etc., etc. Unfortunately, he said, there was a minority of people, even among those employed by the Mission, who had been deceived into joining anti-Portuguese activities, and it was for this reason that one of our teachers had been arrested. He now looked to those in responsible positions at the Mission to make sure that people were not led astray by men like Chizoma. He had a list of everyone who had bought Frelimo membership cards and he suggested that they be destroyed or handed over to him. As far as he was concerned, the matter was now closed.

Most people were stunned into silence, but there were a few questions, and protestations from some that they had no idea this had been going on. There was no doubt that Simões Carneiro had won the day. From those who had been implicated, there was a sigh of relief; while those who had previously known nothing, were clearly shocked at what they had learned.

As the Administrador left, various teachers handed him their membership cards, and I remember vividly Jaime Farahane (recently returned from Lourenço Marques) running after the car so that he might hand his over at the end of that long morning. The Administrador said he thought I ought to transfer Fr Litumbi elsewhere as soon as possible. I returned to my house greatly relieved that all had apparently been forgiven. I felt that, whatever might go on in the villages, those who were employed by the Mission would not again use our buildings for political meetings if they wished to preserve Messumba, which meant so much to them. I am quite sure that no more Frelimo cells were formed on the Mission itself after that day. Within a month Fr Litumbi was transferred to our outstation at Vila Cabral. The only repercussions from this whole episode came from certain Portuguese in the Vila Cabral area, who were now more than ever convinced that Messumba Mission was a breeding ground for anti-Portuguese activities. Some people could not believe that I had been ignorant of what had been going on. I tried to explain that our Mission did not consist of buildings surrounding a courtyard, but was a widely scattered community with many houses; that I did not go snooping around our employees to see what they were up to; and, lastly, that the meetings had taken place during times when I was away. The local African Chiefs were extremely worried about what had happened, since officially, they were part of the Portuguese administration. A Chief had a thankless task, as he was directly responsible to the Chefe do Posto for everything that went on in his area: the collection of taxes; provision of labour for the roads and elsewhere; and, above all, for ensuring the Portuguese presence in the area. When someone in his area did something that was not approved of, it was the Chief who got the blame and probably received the punishment. The Chiefs had little or no education, and were entirely at the mercy of the Chefe do Posto or Administrador.

The next person to fall foul of the authorities was the Likoma messenger. With the existing state of things, I had been even more insistent that he should report to the Chefe do Posto every time he passed through Cóbuè on his journeys to and from Likoma. But one day, just as a new Chefe do Posto had arrived, he did not do this, and as a punishment was set to work on the road for a few days. The mailbag was seized and sent to Mani-amba, where Simões Carneiro opened it, finding several letters which had come from Tanzania. He opened them, read their contents, and then stuck the envelopes down again. One of the letter-writers was Mateus Mazula, who had been in the school and was now at the Frelimo military camp at Bagamoyo, not far from Dar-es-Salaam. Simões Carneiro realized that the Likoma messenger was being used as a means of communication between those who had joined up with Frelimo and their friends and relations at Messumba. Once again, I found myself in an extremely embarrassing position. Simões Carneiro, not surprisingly, now insisted that the Likoma messenger should have his mail-bag inspected at Cóbuè, when all letters from Tanzania would be removed and sent to him at Maniamba. Having read them, he would re-seal them. No one seemed to realize what was going on until one day Mateus Mazula himself came with his father to my house asking to be reinstated in the school. I said this was impossible until he had cleared himself with the Administrador, who knew, as I did, that he had been at Bagamoyo.* He was clearly frightened, but I said that I was sure the Administrador would be only too pleased to know he had given up training as a Frelimo soldier. I took Mateus and his father to Maniamba; and, as I had predicted, Simões Carneiro was delighted. So back into school came Mateus.

However, a few days later, Costa Matos told me that he had heard about Mateus Mazula's return. Would I please bring him to Vila Cabral on my next visit as he would like to meet him? Both Mateus and I were worried about this summons, but there was no way out of it. I went with Mateus to the Governor's office, but was told to wait outside. I heard the Governor's angry shouting, and then he came out to tell me that the boy needed to be taught to grow up a bit and would therefore be sent to Meponda (Porto Arroio) to work for a couple of months: 'Not as a prisoner, you understand, as he will be paid,' added Costa Matos. When I told him that Mateus had brought nothing with him, since I had understood he would be returning with me that evening, he assured me he would arrange for him to be given some blankets and some clothes. I felt I deserved the dirty look that Mateus gave me as he was escorted to another car, and I returned to Messumba dreading the inevitable interview with his parents. But, good people, they bore me no grudge; it was the

* Among the innumerable and pestilential forms that we were obliged to fill in regularly were returns of school pupils.

sort of thing to expect from the Portuguese. Happily, Costa Matos kept his word, and Mateus returned to Messumba a couple of months later, none the worse for his time at Meponda.

After the Frelimo membership card incident, everyone at Messumba was very law-abiding and peace-loving; so much so that when, later that same year, the President of Portugal, Américo Tomás, visited Mozambique, Fr Litumbi said we must do something special when he visited Vila Cabral, in order to reinstate the Mission in the eyes of the authorities. In fact, I had already been told that we were expected to send a token contingent from Messumba and had been wondering how to go about this. Now Fr Litumbi had solved my problem. When the day came, about fifty of us set off for Vila Cabral airport in our lorry, the land-rover and a new Peugeot truck. Everyone was given a Portuguese paper flag to wave, and the teachers had made a banner 'Messumba Welcomes Your Excellency'. As we approached the airport, we passed crowds of Africans, also with the same paper flags, walking along the road. They had no option but to go and greet him, as they lived within a few miles of the town, and many groups were accompanied by *cipais* who acted as 'cheer leaders.' There were about twelve old Dakotas on the tarmac which had brought newspaper correspondents and others from Portugal, Malawi, Rhodesia, and South Africa. I stood next to a group of Canadian journalists who were most impressed by this massive expression of loyalty to Portugal, until I told them that everyone had been obliged to turn up whether they wanted to or not. The President was greeted with loud applause as police held back the crowds. It was a wonderful display of stage-managed enthusiasm, and no one could fail to be impressed by the sham. We drove to the Palácio do Governo (Administrative Headquarters) where various people, including Padre Calandri, were given decorations, and then we lined up to shake hands with the President. Of course, only whites and a token number of Africans got into the Palácio. The rest, including the contingent from Messumba, stayed outside. In the afternoon, we all went to Meponda (Porto Arroio) on the lakeshore about thirty-five miles from Vila Cabral. This was a sort of holiday resort, which Mateus Mazula, so recently, had helped to build. There was already a handful of tourists there. The President's car was almost mobbed by the local Africans, all waving those paper flags. The President boarded a small boat, which had been sent from the naval base at Metangula specially for the occasion, and for the first time a 'President of the Portuguese Republic sailed on the Portuguese waters of Lago Niassa'.

Vila Cabral was always full of rumours, but in late August 1964 I heard one story that I had cause to remember. I was told that a Dutch missionary priest had been killed in Cabo Delgado by some Africans. It struck me as rather odd, but the attitude of my Portuguese friends was: 'Well, you know what some of these Catholic priests are like; he probably only got what he had asked for.' I thought nothing further about the subject, but, years later, I discovered to my surprise that the Portuguese press cited 24 August 1964 as the day on which Frelimo began its armed uprising. We all knew perfectly well that the uprising began on 25 September, and that no missionaries were killed. (In August 1967, when our recently consecrated Portuguese Anglican Bishop, Dom Daniel de Pina Cabral, visited Messumba for the first time, he asked me: 'What is this we always hear about Frelimo killing that Dutch priest? That was nothing to do with Frelimo, was it?' I told him that I certainly had never had that impression, and was always surprised when the press made much of 'the beginning of the Frelimo uprising' each August.)

At the beginning of September every year school resumed, and one of my little problems was to arrange for the journeys of the various teachers whose real homes were situated in the Cóbuè lakeshore area. The simplest method was to hire the *Paul*. In 1964 I decided to combine the hiring of the *Paul* with a pastoral visit to Wikihi (Lipoche), a mile or so south of the Tanzanian border, where we had many Christians. I took Buanacaia with me and we drove to Cóbuè, where we boarded the *Paul* for Wikihi. This was quite a long journey, but we managed it in a day and the people gave us a wonderful welcome. On our return, the *Paul* called at a village to pick up one of our teachers, Alexandre Ncalamba. Our next stop was Cóbuè, where more teachers got on, and I got off for the return journey to Messumba by car.

The teachers went on in the *Paul,* and we all met again at Messumba.

Next day I was told that a lot of anti-Portuguese pamphlets had been found on the road between Messumba and Metangula, but that the Chefe do Posto had come and collected them all. I thought no more about the subject, but a few days later, when I was at Salvado's shop in Vila Cabral, someone came up to me and told me that Reggie and Mário Chaomba (one of our labourers) had just been taken off to the police-station. I immediately went there and was told that it was just a routine check and that I should call back in the afternoon. I happened to meet Costa Matos' private secretary, who was in a rare taking: 'Your Mission at Messumba has still not learnt its lesson. Why did you allow people to bring those anti-Portuguese pamphlets to Vila Cabral this morning. Have you no control over your people?' I said I had no idea that anyone had brought any pamphlets to Vila Cabral, but presumably it was this suspicion that had caused the arrest of Reggie and Mário. 'Of course it is,' he replied. 'Don't you check what your passengers bring with them in your vehicles?' I told him that I most certainly did not. This, of course, made him even more angry: 'So you are just anti-Portuguese?' It is useless to argue when Portuguese start talking like that, so I left. When I was ready to return to Messumba, I went to the police-station and saw the Chief of Police. He was surprised to see me and asked me what I wanted, so I told him that I wanted to know what had happened to Reggie and Mário. 'Oh, I'm afraid they'll have to stay here for a while. We've got to make some investigations, so you'd better return to Messumba without them.' I told him that I was quite sure neither of them had anything to do with the pamphlets that had appeared in Vila Cabral. 'I cannot say anything more,' he said. 'We shall just have to find out.' Once again I returned to Messumba with a heavy heart, and a couple of days later returned to Vila Cabral with Reggie's wife. As I went towards the prison, the Chief of Police was coming out. When I asked if I could see Reggie and Mário, I was curtly told: 'No you can't, they are incomunicado.' I left Reggie's wife outside the prison gates and returned home.

A week later, Reggie and Mário turned up at Messumba. They

had walked the whole way from Vila Cabral after their release from prison and were in a terrible state. Reggie's eyes were so terribly swollen that he could barely see out of one of them, and he was very angry indeed. Apparently while I was shopping, they had both suddenly been surrounded by police and marched off to the police-station. After they had been identified, they were taken to the prison and put in solitary confinement. They had no idea what crime they were supposed to have committed. That evening three European policemen came into their cells and beat them indiscriminately all over their bodies, shouting: 'Tell us about the pamphlets that you brought up with you from Messumba today.' They said that they knew nothing about any pamphlets brought up to Vila Cabral. The police went on beating them; and when they blacked out under the blows, they were revived with buckets of cold water, and the brutality continued. After an hour or so of this, the police left and never returned. Reggie, who must have been about fifty years old, had received a much worse beating-up than Mário, who was almost thirty years younger. Later, another European guard, when he saw what his colleagues had done to Reggie and Mário, told Reggie that he was very ashamed of what they had done to two people who were so obviously innocent. He arranged that the food which Reggie's wife cooked and then brought to the prison should reach them hot. He also offered to arrange for Reggie to see a doctor about his eye, but Reggie was so angry that he refused all help, and said he would rather die than receive medical attention from a Portuguese doctor.

This was only the first of the terrible stories I had to hear. I begged them to realize that not all Europeans were so evil, and gave them a few days' leave. I now knew what the Chief of Police had meant when he said that Reggie was 'incomunicado', and a year later I understood why Mário became a Frelimo soldier.

While Reggie and Mário were in prison, Alexandre Ncalamba, the teacher we had picked up on our return journey from Wikihi to Cóbuè, was arrested. I was told that it was he who had brought the anti-Portuguese pamphlets with him on the *Paul*, had scattered some on the road between Messumba and Metangula, and had arranged for the rest to be taken by someone on a bicycle to Vila Cabral. Unfortunately for Reggie and Mário, the pamphlets were found in Vila Cabral on the day of our visit. Alexandre was later taken to Lourenço Marques and was not released until February 1971. According to the written testimony he submitted to the United Nations' Commission on Human Rights on 11 August 1972 in Dar-es-Salaam, he was never brought to trial. I heard that on his release from prison, he only spent a week or so at Messumba before fleeing over the border to Tanzania.

I was very angry about the treatment that Reggie and Mário had received and on my next visit to Vila Cabral requested an interview with Costa Matos. I told him bluntly that if the Portuguese wanted the people to hate them more than they already did, they were going the right way about it. I emphasized that Reggie had been employed by the Mission for more than thirty years and that he was a respected member of the community. Neither his name nor Mário's had appeared on that damned list of people to whom Chizoma had sold Frelimo membership cards. The men had been unjustly arrested and then cruelly beaten, and now, with Alexandre Ncalamba in prison, the authorities must obviously realize that a mistake had been made. Costa Matos said that he must see the Chief of Police, and asked me to call back and see him in a few hours' time. When I did so, he said he hoped I was now more satisfied. 'What about?' I asked. 'But hasn't the Chief of Police yet spoken to your driver?' 'No,' I said. 'Well, just wait a minute downstairs.' The Mission lorry with Reggie and Mário was outside, and in a few moments I saw Reggie being summoned by the Chief of Police; he then returned to the lorry, so I asked what had happened. He told me that the Chief admitted a mistake had been made, and had given him about 250 escudos. Mário received nothing, not even an apology.

9 War

On the night of Friday, 25 September 1964, I lay in bed wondering if I would get any sleep at all as there was a great deal of noise coming from a wedding feast which was being held not very far below my house. But I must have dropped off for I was suddenly awakened by shots being fired. My first thought was that some Portuguese soldiers had turned up at the feast, since from time to time during the previous few months small groups of soldiers had carried out patrols in the neighbourhood and not infrequently became rather undisciplined. I got out of bed to investigate and, when I opened my front door, found our night-watchman huddled in terror on the verandah. We could see shots being fired into the air down by the school, and then there was absolute silence. I asked him what had happened, and he told me that five or six soldiers, coming from the direction of the feast, had walked by the kitchen where he had been sleeping, and then had started firing single shots just outside my house. I told him that he had better come and sleep in the house, and decided that the following morning I would complain to the Chefe do Posto. I knew that the Mission was unpopular, but I thought this was carrying things rather far.

When the dawn came and I left my house, I was surprised to see that the flag-pole had been knocked down and I thought that the soldiers must have got very drunk at the wedding feast to have done that. So I wrote a strongly-worded letter to the Chefe do Posto at Metangula and dispatched it by Jaime Amanze, my late Chinyanja teacher and the Mission's master-of-works. While I was arranging work for the day, someone told me that there was a bullet hole in the Peugeot truck. I went to the garage and there was a small round hole in the bonnet of the truck, and on the ground the bullet itself. We later found the expended cartridge case a few yards away. By now, I was beginning to wonder if they were Frelimo soldiers who had come the previous night. We had not heard that they had begun military operations, but if so they had got well into Mozambique, as Messumba is at least eighty miles south of the Tanzanian border (as the crow flies), and we had heard no reports of any action elsewhere.

Later that morning Susan Andrew arrived from Ngoo, and I told her what had happened during the night. 'That's funny,' she said, 'because at Chia, I suddenly came across five or six soldiers. One of them was Mateus Malipa, whom we all thought had joined Frelimo.' My suspicions were now confirmed, as I knew perfectly well that Malipa, a former teacher at Messumba, was one of those who had gone off with Amós Sumane in 1963. I told her that the soldiers she had met at Chia must, without doubt, have come from Frelimo. She then admitted that they had been rather unwilling to let her come, but that she had managed to persuade them. Then they had said that the African with her could not come on to Messumba. She had explained that she would never be able to carry her bicycle across the River Fúbuè by herself, and they had very reluctantly then agreed to let both of them go.

I waited for Jaime Amanze's return, but he took so long that I became rather worried, and with a couple of volunteers, drove towards Metangula. On the way we met Amanze, and I asked him if he had a letter for me from the Chefe do Posto. 'No,' he said, 'but the people who fired the shots were Frelimo soldiers, as one of the boats at Metangula naval base was also fired upon.' As we were already halfway to Metangula, I decided to continue, but very shortly we came to a barrier of small boulders that had been put across the road. We jumped out, moved some of them, and managed to pass without difficulty. The Chefe do Posto, who was rather a morose man, seemed a bit confused. He was not particularly interested in what had happened at Messumba, and contented himself with telling me that Metangula and Cóbuè had also been attacked. There seemed to be nothing more I could do, so I returned to the Mission.

At about 6 p.m., a land-rover bristling with armed policemen turned up, together with the Chefe do Posto. The land-rover was

in radio contact with Vila Cabral. One of the policemen asked me
what had happened, and was not exactly pleased when I told
him that my first impression had been that our disturbing visitors were drunk Portuguese soldiers. He wanted to know details
of Susan Andrew's meeting with the soldiers, and I said that I
would ask Susan to come and tell him. Typically, he was not
going to discuss important things with a mere woman, so the
story he got was that which Susan had told me. He came over to
the garage, looked at the bullet hole, and then at me, and said,
'Well, let that be a warning to you.' (Actually, I thought the shot
at the car was a blessing: it might possibly make the Portuguese
a little more just in their dealings with the Mission. It didn't.)
The policeman then said that he was going to Cóbuè. I told him
that I thought this would be very unwise with Frelimo soldiers
in the area. It was getting dark; he did not know the road, which
was in bad condition; and it would take him three hours if he
was lucky. But off he went, radioing to Vila Cabral that he was
leaving Messumba for Cóbuè. He did not seem to be in the least
concerned about what had happened at Messumba. Cóbuè was
his real concern. Off they went and our life resumed its normal
course, except that in the middle of the following night I was
once more awakened, this time by a small group of Portuguese
soldiers. Their officer asked me where Ngoo was, and was rather
taken aback when I told him that it was six hours' walk away –
and there was no road. 'Thanks very much, Senhor Padre, sorry
to have disturbed you,' he said, as they all trooped off in the
direction of Ngoo. But they got there too late – that is, if they got
there at all.

Apparently Mateus Malipa (whose home village was Ngoo)
and his men spent their weekend there, while Susan Andrew was
spending her weekend at Messumba. Unfortunately, as the Frelimo group were idly chatting with one or two of Susan's staff,
they were spotted by some *cipais*, on their way from Cóbuè to
Metangula. On arrival at Metangula, these *cipais* were asked if
they had seen any soldiers on the way, and when they said yes,
they were asked if such soldiers had been seen in company with
anyone. Three teenage members of Susan's staff were arrested
a few days later. This news only reached me some weeks after-

wards, and when I made inquiries as to their whereabouts, I was told that P.I.D.E. had taken them off to Nampula or somewhere. I heard, years later, that two of them were at Mabalane prison camp, and that the third had died on a boat which was transporting prisoners from Lumbo to Lourenço Marques. I shall have more to say about Mabalane and that boat later.

I think it is important to stress here the extreme ruthlessness displayed by the Portuguese Government in Mozambique. For those who have been brought up in a reasonably democratic society under the protection of the rule of law, it is very hard to imagine the dilemma in which a missionary in Mozambique finds himself. If you are prepared to act consistently as an informer for the Portuguese, then you will earn the praise of the Government. If you are not prepared to do so, you will be constantly under suspicion, even if you do not incur their overt hostility. The third course is to come out openly against the Portuguese, in which case you will be thrown out, and your Mission will be closed, and the people you came to serve will have absolutely no one to help them. I chose the second course because of the particular situation I inherited at Messumba. Many people were protected by this action; others, such as Buanacaia, suffered for it. If one spends all one's time complaining to the authorities, then one is clearly anti-Portuguese, and one will not be able to fill the mediatory role, which I believe belongs to the vocation of the priest. In 1971, the White Fathers, faced with this dilemma, voluntarily withdrew from Mozambique, and, I think, acted rightly. But if the Anglican missionaries had done this, it would have made no impact whatsoever, beyond confirming the Portuguese in their suspicion that non-Roman Catholic equalled anti-Portuguese. I hope that by the time the reader has come to the end of this book, he will consider that I was justified in the stand I took.

Some days later I heard about the Frelimo attack at Cóbuè. The Chefe do Posto's house had been riddled with machine-gun fire; but, as at Metangula, there were no casualties. The small group of attackers was under the command of Daniel Polela, who had been at Messumba school and then joined the Portuguese army. Some time later, I spoke to a Portuguese man who had been in the same unit as Polela. He told me he was not at all surprised that Polela had joined Frelimo on leaving the army, because on one occasion he had been brutally beaten with the *palmatório* for some minor breach of orders.

The Roman Catholic Mission at Cóbuè was, at the time, in charge of Padre Mário Teodore, an Italian Consolata Father, for Padre Menegon had been transferred to Vila Cabral. On Sundays, the schoolchildren from the Mission used to go to the secretariat after Mass to be present at the ceremonial raising of the Portuguese flag. On Sunday 27 September, they did not turn up, because an extra Mass had been arranged, but the Portuguese took their absence to mean that Padre Teodore had been harbouring the Frelimo attackers. Costa Matos turned up a week later at the Chefe do Posto's house and called the Padre to him. He was extremely insulting, calling him a traitor, and saying that he had no right to be in charge of a mission as he was not a Christian at all. This all came as a complete surprise to Padre Teodore, since he had no previous knowledge of the Frelimo attack, and the fact that his pupils had not turned up that Sunday to salute the flag had been purely coincidental. In spite of his protestations, Padre Teodore was transferred to Unango Mission a few weeks later, and he returned to Italy after another year or so, whether of his own choice or not, I do not know. I was indeed thankful that Messumba had not been built adjacent to a *posto*.

After Costa Matos had visited Cóbuè, he made use of our rough track from Manda-Mbuzi to Ngoo, and then paid his first and only visit to Messumba. Everyone was rather frightened as we knew that we were not popular in official circles. We took some pains to greet him as a Portuguese Governor would expect to be greeted, and it all went off splendidly.

Some days later when I was in Vila Cabral, Salvado told me that he had accompanied Costa Matos on much of his recent trip, though he had not been with him when he visited Messumba. He told me that Padre Teodore definitely knew (I am still quite sure that he did not) about the forthcoming attack on

Cóbuè, but Salvado felt the excuse for not turning up to salute the flag on the Sunday was a genuine one. Salvado did admit, however, that he had been shocked by the severity of Costa Matos' attitude to the Padre. A message then arrived from Costa Matos requesting me to see him. The Governor surprised me very much by saying that he thought our work at Messumba and at Ngoo was excellent. He had enjoyed his trip to Ngoo, down the rough track from Manda-Mbuzi, very much. But he felt that in the circumstances we should remove Susan Andrew. I told him that I would speak to Bishop Pickard about this, but felt sure she would want to stay on. He replied that even if Frelimo did not attack her, things would be very awkward, should Portuguese troops discover that Frelimo was operating in the area while she was still there. (We had no option, and Susan left Ngoo a few weeks later.) Costa Matos went on to say that he did not know how safe we might be at Messumba itself, and felt it was his duty to protect us. There were certainly no troops to spare, but, to my horror, he handed me an automatic pistol and a sub-machine gun. When I said I could not possibly take them, he told me it was an order. So I reluctantly accepted them and said that I would inform the British Consul-General in Lourenço Marques. I took them to Messumba in a box, locked them up and a few weeks later flew to Lourenço Marques. The British Consul, Alan Morgan, told me to hand them back as soon as possible, since, quite apart from my position as a priest, many missions in Kenya had been attacked by Mau Mau for the simple reason that they were known to have been issued with arms. When I got home, I thankfully returned the weapons to Costa Matos, telling him that I had been ordered to do so by the British Consul, and he implied that he washed his hands of us.

Nothing much of note happened at Messumba for the rest of 1964, though I kept on hearing that '*Wa-tengo*', the Chinyanja name for Frelimo soldiers, were infiltrating the more remote areas. Occasionally there were skirmishes with Portuguese troops, after which the near-by villagers would suffer. This, in turn, resulted in their flight to Tanzania or Malawi, or their joining forces with Frelimo. It still was mostly rumour from far-away places.

Shortly afterwards, I went to Malawi in the Peugeot truck, and everyone was amazed to see the bullet hole in the bonnet. I then went to Rhodesia for a couple of weeks, and while there I visited the offices of the *Rhodesia Herald* to see what, if anything, had been reported about the situation in Mozambique. I read that in September, five groups had crossed into the country from Tanzania; three groups which had entered Cabo Delgado had been eliminated; and two groups which entered Niassa had subsequently fled back to Tanzania. The Portuguese were treating the incidents purely as a police matter. I have no first-hand knowledge about the groups that crossed into Cabo Delgado province. But Mateus Malipa's and Daniel Polela's groups had accomplished exactly what they set out to do; namely, to warn the Portuguese of their presence and force them to send massive troop reinforcements to the area. Meanwhile, Frelimo was secretly sending men and materials into the country.

Shortly after my return to Messumba, our head teacher at Ngoo, Basílio Farahane, was shot by Frelimo soldiers. Apparently, they had come to his house one night and told him to go with them a few hundred yards. There they shot him and left him for dead. But Basílio was not dead. He was carried to Messumba, where he received emergency treatment, and then flown from Metangula to Vila Cabral where, remarkably, he recovered. Frelimo had justification for thinking that he had been an informer, though I am convinced he was not. He was an Angoni, a senior teacher, and a strict disciplinarian, so he was not popular, and certainly many people had reasons for disliking him. He did not really like the Nyasas, and because of this the Portuguese had regarded him as a loyal Portuguese citizen. My own feeling is that Frelimo suspected him of being the one who informed the authorities about Malipa's group at Ngoo; whereas it had been the *cipais*. Basílio Farahane did not return to Nyasa country and was later given a job in Vila Cabral, where he was regarded as a hero by the Portuguese.

All this caused a great deal of uncertainty at Ngoo. Susan Andrew had left; Basílio Farahane had left; and everyone was bewildered. I was determined to go ahead with our work there, so we sent Carlos Catatula, a teacher a few years younger than myself, to replace Basílio. He and I cycled to Ngoo, and I formally introduced him as headmaster of the school. Catatula had great charm but his completely literal mind could be very exasperating. Already at Ngoo, we had two other teachers (Afonso Messosa and a student-teacher), a catechist (Bernardo Goigoi, an Angoni), a priest (Fr Chizuzu, the father of Salathiel), and a medical orderly (Jacinto Mizaia, a great friend of Buanacaia's).

One evening some Portuguese soldiers arrived at Ngoo and asked Fr Chizuzu if they could sleep in the church. He agreed and gave them reed mats to sleep on. Next morning they left, and after some ten miles ran into a Frelimo ambush. That evening the troops returned to Ngoo, extremely angry. They went to Afonso Messosa's house, but he heard them coming and escaped through the back door. They went on to Carlos Catatula's house and, when he answered the door, shot him dead. They rounded up the other Mission employees and brought them to Fr Chizuzu's house. There they cuffed and insulted everyone, and, before their eyes, cut off Catatula's head. They kicked it about 'as if it was a football', and then left. The whole village fled into the mountains, except for Fr Chizuzu, Jacinto Mizaia and the student-teacher, who came to Messumba and told me the story. They were in a state of great shock, so I spoke to each one on his own. But they all had the same story to tell. Next day I cycled to Ngoo, where I found twenty-six cartridge cases outside Carlos Catatula's house, and saw bloodstains on the door. This was a clear case of deliberate murder and mutilation. Carlos had made no attempt to run away, but had come to answer a knock on his door. Bernardo Goigoi had returned briefly from the mountains the following morning, and hurriedly dug a grave for Carlos' mutilated body, so that I was at least spared the grim sight.

I was appalled by the senseless brutality of what the Portuguese had done and went straight to see Costa Matos at Vila Cabral. He was sympathetic, but explained that when Portuguese soldiers were ambushed, for them the only good African was a dead one. I should try to understand how they felt. I replied that to kill someone who had not been involved in the ambush in any way and had not even tried to run away from them, by pumping twenty-six bullets into his body and then cutting his head off and playing with it, was a most terrible crime. Costa Matos said that he would do what he could to investigate what had happened. But nothing more was ever heard. Fr Chizuzu, Afonso Messosa and Jacinto Mizaia are now in Malawi. Bernardo Goigoi joined Frelimo.

The people who murdered Carlos Catatula were almost certainly the *fusileiros* stationed at Metangula. Ever since its establishment, the naval base at Metangula was constantly being enlarged, and its complement of personnel increased. Also stationed at the base, but forming quite a separate establishment from the sailors, were the *fusileiros* (marine commandos), and their job was the security of the lakeshore. They would arrive at or near a village and then ruthlessly seek out Frelimo *bandidos*. They very seldom caught any, but terrorized the local villagers to such an extent that by mid 1965 almost the entire population to the north of Messumba had fled to Tanzania, Likoma Island, or into the hills where they sought the protection of Frelimo. The *fusileiros*, unlike Sérgio Zilhão, the Naval Commander, who was friendly towards us, felt that the Anglican Mission was responsible for bringing the war to the Lake. Their suspicions appeared to be confirmed when, in nearly every village, they found an Anglican church, and learned that everyone who could read had been to school either at Messumba or at Ngoo.

Shortly after Carlos Catatula's murder, I borrowed a boat that belonged to the Roman Catholic Mission at Cóbuè and went to Ngoo. Here I loaded it with as much of the valuable equipment as I could: church plate, microscopes, medicines, school books, and so on, which I brought to Messumba. For lack of room, I had to leave all the furniture, such as desks, tables and chairs, and all this was in due course appropriated by the *fusileiros*, for their sub-base at Cóbuè. In spite of my repeated requests to have our property sent back to us at Messumba, nothing was ever returned.

I had no alternative but to evacuate Ngoo, as all the people had fled into the mountains near by. Some were hiding close to the village, so that they might tend their fields from time to time, and enough of these turned up to help me load the boat. That day, just as we were about to leave for Messumba, a storm arose, and so I returned to Messumba by bicycle with one African companion, leaving the boat to follow when the storm had abated. It was an eerie ride through the burnt-out remains of what had once been happy villages. The only houses still inhabited were those in places which the *fusileiros* had not yet visited. As we approached the wide River Fúbuè, I could hear voices whispering together in the tall reeds, so I hurried on. Certain I might be that it was a meeting of Frelimo soldiers, but I was not at all certain, then, how they would receive me.

A similar terrorization of villagers was being conducted on the Manda Plateau by army units stationed at Nova Coimbra and at Cóbuè. Fr Odala was the priest at Manda-Mbuzi and he told me how troops had come and burnt down fourteen houses. They visited him and asked if he had seen any *bandidos*. He said that he had not; though, like everyone else, he knew that Frelimo units were hiding in the hills. They then entered the lovely church and helped themselves to various things like candlesticks, crosses and church plate, as well as taking some of Odala's chickens and personal belongings. He was forced to accompany them and spent the night under one of the trucks, where he was cuffed or kicked from time to time. He was lucky: they released him in the morning, and he came to Messumba to tell me what had happened. I took him straight to Maniamba where Simões Carneiro asked him to write out a list of all that the troops had stolen. The Administrador said that he would take the matter up with the military authorities immediately; but, once again, nothing more was heard.

Fr Odala wanted to return to Manda-Mbuzi, as there were still people living there. I said that I would come to see him in two day's time; for I wanted to tell Simões Carneiro that I had seen for myself what the troops had done. I supposed that the journey would be difficult, not only because I might run into a skirmish on the way, but also because the River Lunho at Mpochi would only just be passable, and I arranged for three volunteers to accompany me. We loaded up the land-rover at 5 a.m. one morning and were ready to set off when I found that

I had forgotten the ignition key. I went back to the house for it and as I was returning to the garage, saw a man come panting up the hill. He handed me a note from Fr Odala: 'Please don't come as you will find danger on the way.' The man had walked all night from Manda-Mbuzi to give me this note; and if I had not forgotten the key, I would never have received it. Fr Odala fled with his people into the hills and after two months crossed to Likoma Island. He is now working in Malawi.

At Cóbuè, a new Chefe do Posto called Morais had just arrived. Padre Piquito (the Portuguese priest from Vila Cabral) had replaced Padre Teodore as the Superior and he had a small military detachment billeted on the Mission. Morais had come from near Massangulo, where the missionaries had found him fairly helpful; but, at Cóbuè, he regarded every villager with great suspicion. One of his informers was apparently murdered by Frelimo forces near by, and this naturally angered him.

One day some troops went to Mala, about seven miles from Cóbuè. Shots were fired at them on the way, but they continued their journey. Then, when they reached Mala, they began setting fire to houses. Those who could fled for their lives. But about half a dozen people, including our retired catechist Geldart Chisaca, were arrested. These were marched off towards Cóbuè, but on the way were told to get into the Lake and clap their hands. They were then machine-gunned. This story was told me by one of the *cipais* at Cóbuè who, as was often the case, had been sent to accompany the troops. Meanwhile, Morais caught someone at Cóbuè whom he thought was a Frelimo agent; and, calling the whole village together, including one of our retired priests, Fr Polela (the father of Daniel, who had led the original attack on Cóbuè), had the man shot dead. That night the whole population of Cóbuè, including Fr Polela and most of Morais' *cipais*, fled to Likoma Island. Padre Piquito sailed to Metangula in the Mission boat, stopping to see me on the way. He told me something of Morais' atrocities, heartily disgusted by what his own countrymen had done. He said that he was a missionary and not a chaplain to the forces, and as there were no villagers left, he too was leaving. There has not been a resident priest at Cóbuè since.

Of course, I had not seen these atrocities myself. The Portuguese were not so stupid as to perform them in front of a British missionary. But I did see the results: Reggie's face when he was released from prison; Carlos Catatula's grave, the expended cartridge cases and the blood-stained door; burnt-out villages; and worst of all, the terrible burns on people who fled to Messumba after bombing raids on Chia and other villages. Irene Wheeler told me that some of these injuries surpassed anything she had seen in the London blitz. The Bishop of Malawi, Donald Arden, writing in a circular letter, said that when he visited Likoma Island, the sight of the bombed lakeshore villages in Mozambique reminded him of the bombing of British cities during the war. I have no proof that napalm was used; but from what I have heard about the effects of napalm, I have little doubt that it was. I complained constantly to the authorities, civil and military, but the reply was always: 'Pity our poor soldiers, rather. You complain, and this makes it look to them as if you are on the side of Frelimo.'

If the Portuguese had killed only Frelimo soldiers, that would have been understandable. But so many victims were ordinary villagers: elderly men and women and young children. The first killing of a Frelimo soldier that I knew of occurred eighteen months after hostilities began. The Portuguese indulged in indiscriminate killings. Frelimo killed only those whom it had reason to suspect; and, as far as I know, did so without torture or other brutality.

One day, around this time, I was visiting Metangula and on my return to Messumba gave a lift to Matias Chissancho, who had been one of our bright students at the Escola Técnica in Vila Cabral. He told me that he had been ordered to report in a couple of days for service in the Portuguese army. 'What shall I do? I hate war, and I cannot fight against my own people. Look what the Portuguese have done to nearly all the villages north of here.' I told him that he had only two choices: to join up, or flee to the mountains. He chose the latter course and eventually joined Frelimo.

An unexpected return was that of António Chizoma, after barely a year in prison. I was very surprised to see him, now very fat, walking towards my house. He told me that almost immediately after his arrest he had been taken from Vila Cabral to Lourenço Marques, and been kept in one of the cells below a respectable house in Avenida Afonso de Albuquerque, the street in which Bishop Pickard lived. I had been to this place many times, but, although I knew it was occupied by P.I.D.E., thought it dealt solely with passports and the renewal of residence permits. When I asked him how he had become so fat, he said that it was because he had had plenty of food and no exercise. The food had come from the kitchens of the Hotel Polana, the luxury hotel which is very close to where he had been held. I had my doubts about the truth of this statement, but he certainly looked fat and well. I asked him if he had been ill-treated, and he replied that it had not been too bad. But then it was very difficult to get any information from Chizoma, as he seemed unwilling to say anything. My first thought was that he had been sent back as an informer; and this suspicion was confirmed, since more than once Portuguese officials said to me that he should be re-arrested because he never gave them any information. A few months after his return, he fled to the mountains, but he returned to Messumba later. He had never been very popular among the other teachers, as he was so cocky. Now, they disliked him more than ever and distrusted him because he was the one who had started the Frelimo cell on the Mission. He was not re-employed as a teacher, but we were able to find various administrative jobs for him.

By the end of term in July 1965, there was no doubt that Frelimo militants were in our area, though I myself never saw any. As usual, I took our dozen Yao boarders back to their homes in the Vila Cabral area. When we reached Maniamba, I was told that Frelimo had been active there. We went on, and I saw that one of Cristina's shops had been burnt down. A few miles farther, we came to a bridge, and found this partially destroyed. On the other side was a very angry Cristina. He said that if the *bandidos* wanted to play the fool like this, they would pay for it. I told him that his shop near by had been burnt down, but was able to assure him that those at Metangula and Nova Coimbra were unharmed. I managed to get the lorry over what remained of the bridge and we reached Vila Cabral without further difficulty, though it was obvious that Portuguese troops, too, had been active. Vila Cabral was fast assuming the aspect of a garrison town, with troops everywhere. Morale among the Portuguese was high: if the *bandidos* wanted trouble they would get it in a big way; the armed forces would make a clean sweep of everyone they found. I pointed out that this policy was quite pointless: what use was the country if all the inhabitants had been wiped out? Some Africans I met in the town told me that Frelimo was everywhere; a small unit had even come, unobserved, into Vila Cabral one night.

By now, almost the whole area to the north of Messumba was deserted, and this meant that those of our teachers who came from the Ngoo and Cóbuè areas were unable to return home for the school holidays and had to remain at Messumba. One by one, they were called into Metangula by the authorities and did not return; or if they did, would be summoned a second time and detained. I went in, time after time, to complain; but the Chefe do Posto said that he could do nothing: a couple of P.I.D.E. agents had come from Nampula and they were responsible for all this. When I saw them and asked what had happened to one or other person, I was told with a shrug that he had been taken to Vila Cabral 'for questioning'. On my return to Messumba, I had to pass this news on to their wives, who were naturally in great anxiety and distress. (I do not know which interview I dreaded most.) I had thought, after Administrador Simões Carneiro's visit in January of the previous year, that we would have no more trouble, even though he himself had, by now, been transferred elsewhere; and I was almost certain that the teachers had not re-started the Frelimo cell on the Mission, especially as, when called into Metangula, they obeyed and did not run away to the mountains instead. It was hopeless trying to fight the Portuguese system, and in the face of it, one was helpless. As it was holidays, I could not even complain that classes were being disrupted. From time to time, word would reach me that one of our catechists on an outstation had been taken by the Portuguese, or had fled to goodness-knows-where. A few even fled to Messumba.

The *Church Times* of 17 September 1965 carried a front-page headline 'Crisis threatens Anglican work in Mozambique – Priests and Catechists are forced to flee.' The article was written by a correspondent in Malawi and, though written some two or three months after the events it described, gave a fairly accurate picture:

... the censorship imposed by the Portuguese in Mozambique is so complete that little is known in the outside world about the reign of terror that has overtaken a territory regarded by Portugal not as a colony but as a province of the motherland ... methods of unsurpassed brutality are being employed . . . In some places the executions have been completely indiscriminate, and some of the Church's own teachers have been shot. Whole villages have been bombed, strafed with machine-gun bullets and burned to the ground. Infringement of the night curfew results in instant death.

And then the article continued, quoting from a Lebombo Diocesan Newsletter:

Whole areas of our work have ceased to exist, and at the moment we do not know the whereabouts of our clergy and of quite a number of our catechists, apart from many hundreds of Christians.

The article also quoted Bishop Pickard:

We are all beginning to wonder how much longer we can continue with our work, and how much longer it will be possible to leave European staff at Messumba.

10 Terrorization

To those of us who were at Messumba on 24 July 1965, it has become known as Black Saturday. At about dawn there was sporadic shooting, but we were not particularly alarmed as we knew the troops well enough by now to realize that they enjoyed playing about with their guns. However, when the Mission workmen were due, as usual, to report at 6 o'clock, very few turned up. Those who did told me that troops had surrounded the Mission and were arresting every man moving in that direction.

At 7 o'clock, a local middle-aged man was brought into the hospital shot in the head. He had gone out of his house to fulfil the demands of nature and was shot while squatting in the long grass. By noon, in spite of everything that Irene and her staff could do, he was dead.

Reports continually came to me: 'So-and-so has just been taken by the soldiers.' When I went down the hill behind my house to where some of our men should have been working, I found the place deserted, with their tools left lying on the ground. As I returned to my house, I saw for the first time a party of Portuguese, some in camouflaged uniforms, whom I recognized as P.I.D.E. officials. The corpulent man in charge was Inspector Campos from Nampula. He hoped, he said, that we were not being put to any bother, as the troops had strict instructions not to disturb the work of the Mission. I replied that although I had so far seen no troops, our work was practically at a standstill. Few men had been allowed to report for work; and some of those who had turned up, had been arrested on the Mission. Campos just shrugged his shoulders and walked away.

Then two of the P.I.D.E. agents returned and said that they wanted to see the teachers' houses. (One of these agents, called Rosa, I had occasionally seen at Vila Cabral. I think it was he who had been in charge of the investigations during which so many people, especially teachers, had been called into Metangula.) I accompanied the P.I.D.E. agents, as the wives and families of the arrested teachers were still in their houses, and I wanted to do what I could to see that they were not abused or bullied in any way. As we went round the houses, a couple of military aircraft flew above us, threateningly low. In the first group of houses, all the teachers had already been arrested, except for Matias Juma, who had only recently completed his course at the Escola Técnica, and, ironically enough, was soon to join Frelimo. The two agents did not search any of these houses; and as we came to the second and larger group of houses, it was clear that they were really only concerned with arresting the two teachers who were still living there. I will never forget the look on the face of one of those teachers as he was told to 'come with us'. He obviously regarded me as a traitor, and that was exactly what I felt myself to be. I protested to Rosa, but he said that he only wanted to ask them a few questions at Metangula. In the event, one did not return to the Mission till three and a half years later; the other, till some seven years later. They were both senior teachers, and must have been nearly fifty years old.

Rosa then asked me the whereabouts of one teacher who was still free; and I told him that, as he was a local man, he lived in his own village. 'How far is that?' asked Rosa. I replied that it was almost an hour's walk away and that I absolutely refused to accompany them any further. (Later, they went to his village; but, happily, by then he had escaped into the mountains.)

By lunchtime, we seemed to have been left alone. But when Reggie returned from Vila Cabral, where he had gone the day before to collect supplies, he told me that there were hundreds of people surrounded by troops at the side of the road about two miles from the Mission, and that the whole area seemed to be alive with soldiers. I was extremely thankful that he had been allowed to pass. P.I.D.E. had that morning arrested something like 350 people, including some from the Roman Catholic Mission at Nova Coimbra whose Superior was now Padre Inácio Mondine. Those arrested were taken to Metangula where approximately fifty were released as being unlikely to be either *bandidos*, or capable of giving active support to them – the very young, the old, the halt, the maimed or the blind.

I was particularly worried about Buanacaia, who had not appeared all day, so I went to his village, Móndueè, on the lake-shore. There seemed to be quite a number of people standing around in bewilderment, so I asked how it was that they had not been arrested. They told me that when they saw the soldiers waiting for them, most of them had stayed in their homes. But Buanacaia had said that he had had nothing whatever to do with Frelimo and had set out with a clear conscience for my house. The soldiers had seized him as they had seized everyone else on the move. (In some other villages, the soldiers took everyone.) I I did not see him again for more than three years.

Some months before Black Saturday, Fr Charles Wright had returned to Messumba, and he stayed with us until he left Mozambique for good in June 1966. He was now a man of sixty and was of enormous help to us. He had an air of authority about him, born of his experience and fearless nature, and even the most offensive Portuguese person could not fail to respect him. The following day he went to Metangula to try to see the 'prisoners', but Rosa was completely uncooperative. Charles told me that the three hundred prisoners were kept in the open air (and in July on the lakeshore it can be bitterly cold at night) surrounded by a hastily constructed wire fence which was guarded by armed soldiers. He was not allowed to go anywhere near them either that day or on several subsequent visits.

Joan Antcliff, as head of the school, was particularly distressed by the arrest of nearly all the male teachers. Unless they were released before September, it looked as if the school would be unable to continue. She was due for local leave during the holidays and had planned to stay with friends in Malawi. I was very concerned that she should have the leave she needed after a very trying school year, and I wanted to visit Malawi myself, so that I could tell various people what had been going on in Niassa during the previous six months. We therefore left Messumba almost immediately after Black Saturday, leaving Irene and Charles on the Mission, and I dropped Joan with her friends before going on to Zomba. There I went to see a man who was in charge of the Portuguese section of the Malawi Special Branch. During our lengthy interview I asked him what they did when they found Frelimo soldiers in Malawi; for since the country runs deep into Mozambique, I was sure that Frelimo forces must cross it from time to time. He replied: 'If we find arms on them, we arrest them, put them in prison for a couple of weeks to satisfy the Portuguese, and then, to satisfy Black Africa, we put them on a bus to Tanzania, telling them not to return to Malawi!' He asked me if he was right in thinking that Amós Sumane had once been a teacher at Messumba. I told him that he had been, until 1963, and was surprised to learn that Sumane had arrived the previous day at Blantyre airport from Ghana, and was being watched. Malawi had nothing against him, but naturally they did not want to run the risk of his doing anything in Malawi which might upset the Portuguese. In Blantyre I saw the Assistant British High Commissioner, who, although interested in what I had to tell him, explained that his job was solely concerned with Malawi. But if we missionaries at Messumba had to leave, he would do all he could to help us, should we come to Malawi. I also saw a journalist who had written a very non-committal article in the *Nyasaland Times* about Mozambican refugees on Likoma Island, and who explained that the paper's policy was naturally governed by the need for Malawi to maintain friendly relations with Portugal. I wrote a few letters which I did not dare send through the Mozambique post for fear of their being opened, and returned home within four days, as I did not wish to be away from Messumba for longer than was necessary.

On arrival at Vila Cabral, I was pleasantly surprised to meet Borges de Brito once more after an interval of more than three years. He told me that he had been sent by the Governor-General, Costa Almeida, to see if he could do anything to recover the situation in the Cóbuè area, and persuade the people to return to their homes. He had told the Governor-General that he could do nothing without my help, and that he would also like to have the support of Padre Menegon who had been at Cóbuè for a number of years. The Governor-General had agreed to his proposal, and so he had sought Bishop Pickard's permission for me to pay a visit to Likoma Island, where many of the refugees were now living. We decided that he should visit us at Messumba the following week so as to make the necessary arrangements.

I was relieved to learn that, as yet, there had been no incident in the Vila Cabral area similar to that of Black Saturday at Messumba, and that Fr Paulo Litumbi was still living on our outstation just outside the town. It was, however, very worrying to hear that the prisoners who had been held at Metangula were now being interrogated in the prison at Vila Cabral. I went along there, but of course was not allowed to see them. On my return to Messumba from Vila Cabral we passed a convoy near Mani-amba, and the troops favoured me with a very unfriendly look as I sped by : they had run into a Frelimo ambush, the Adminis-trador at Maniamba told me. Nearer home, I met another convoy, and again the troops were obviously very angry with me : I learned later that one or two of their vehicles had hit landmines at Chiwanga, a large village only about three miles from Messumba itself.

We were glad to have a visit from Borges de Brito once again, but he had very sobering news for us. He said that he was ex-tremely worried about the way the troops were viewing the Mission. 'You can have no idea how much they dislike you and everything about Messumba. When I said that I was coming here for lunch, they said that being a Wednesday the road would be quite safe, since that was the day on which Padre Paul usually went to Vila Cabral and so Frelimo do not mine the roads on Wednesdays.' It had never struck me that for the past few months I had happened to find Wednesday the most convenient day to visit Vila Cabral; and I had never even met any Frelimo soldiers, let alone reached some agreement with them about not mining the roads. He went on to say that relations between the troops and the Chefe do Posto were very strained too, and the events of Black Saturday had taken place without any proper reference to the civil authorities. He doubted if he would be able to do any-thing; but at least we were now to get a new Chefe do Posto at Metangula, Soares de Cruz, who used to be at Cóbuè and whom he liked.

We then discussed the visit to Likoma. Borges de Brito told us that he would not come with us, but would like Padre Menegon and myself to go to Likoma Island, at the Government's expense, to make contact with the refugees on the Island and see if we could persuade them to return to Cóbuè. We replied that we did not think there would be much chance of this, especially as Morais was still there as Chefe do Posto. Borges de Brito said he thought he would be able to keep Morais in order, since he had been sent by the Governor-General himself, but he confessed his doubts that he could accomplish the task he had been given.

We spoke of the war all around us, and I learned that, from the Portuguese point of view, apparently, the situation was far more serious in Niassa than in Cabo Delgado. They had been expecting more trouble from the Macondes for some time, and so were better prepared there. Here in sparsely populated Niassa, though, Frelimo units had penetrated much deeper into the country, which, being less developed, was more difficult for Portugal to control. I asked him to what extent he thought that Russia and China were involved, and to my surprise he said that though the bulk of Frelimo's support in money and materials obviously came from Communist countries, he thought that the C.I.A. was involved to some degree: 'In the game of international politics, as soon as America thinks that an organization like Frelimo is being assisted by the Communists, she usually steps in as well, so as to offset the danger that another part of the world might be coming under the influence of the Eastern bloc.' I knew, of course, that Eduardo Mondlane, the President of Frelimo, had taught in the United States and that several Mozambicans who had joined Frelimo had been attending the African-American Institute in Dar-es-Salaam which ran a school for southern African studies. Borges de Brito, however, was not hinting that the C.I.A. had had anything to do with Mondlane's training.

We had just finished lunch when we saw clouds of dense smoke in the direction of Chiwanga, and realized that the village was on fire: grass huts burn easily in the dry season. We got into our land-rovers and sped towards the village; but by the time we got there, the troops had left. We found the people sitting completely stunned outside the charred remains of their homes, with pathetic heaps beside them of possessions that they had had time to salvage. Outside one smouldering ruin, Barnabé Njawala, now a Government driver, stood weeping furiously: 'Why have they burnt down my village? That is where my house was, and I work for the Portuguese Government!' Borges de Brito tried to comfort the distraught man, but his private comment to me was: 'If I was Barnabé, I would join Frelimo today. I should not say so as a member of the Portuguese administration, but that is how I would feel.' Borges de Brito was driven back to Metangula by a sobbing Barnabé, and Frelimo must have gained at least two hundred recruits that night from Chiwanga.

I drove with great haste back to the Mission, and then Charles Wright and I returned to Chiwanga with our two lorries. We spent the rest of the day ferrying the people and their scant possessions to Messumba. As the school was on holiday, there were plenty of classrooms in which to store the furniture, and we found room in the dormitories and hospital for the women and children, and those few men who had not fled to the mountains. The burning of Chiwanga was typical of the many senseless acts that the Portuguese troops committed. To be sure, two of their lorries had hit landmines near by a few days previously. But it was obvious that the villagers had had nothing to do with the planting of them, or they would have run away when they saw the troops coming. The result of such burnings was simply to alienate the villagers still more from the Portuguese; to drive more people into joining the guerrillas; and to leave more room for Frelimo to roam at will.

A few days later, as planned, Borges de Brito picked us up at Mónduè in the Roman Catholic Mission's boat, and we sailed to Cóbuè. The lakeshore was a very different place from my first sight of it. It was now a silent, uninhabited, ruined landscape. We passed the deserted villages of Chia, Ngoo, Mala and many others, without seeing any sign of life at all. On reaching Cóbuè, we were met by some Portuguese army and naval personnel who, surprisingly, were very friendly. They took us up to what had been the Mission, which they had now taken over completely. Padre Menegon and I slept on camp beds in the sacristy of the church and Borges de Brito in Morais' house. The latter was clearly embarrassed by the presence of Padre Menegon and myself and hardly spoke. Apart from about a dozen who were employed by the military authorities, the only Africans we saw were some twenty pathetic people living a primitive existence in a long shed. They had apparently been found by the troops when making various sorties into the mountains. Next morning Padre Menegon said Mass in the church with myself for congregation, and then the two of us sailed for Likoma. There I spent the next five or six days, while Padre Menegon returned to Cóbuè most evenings.

Likoma Island, over-populated at the best of times, was now seething with people. Fr John Parslow, the priest-in-charge, had an enormous problem on his hands with so many refugees. The Portuguese had sent maize flour from Beira to Likoma in order to help with the feeding, but the flour was not of the texture to which the Nyasas were accustomed, and some said that the Portuguese had put poison into it. I met many of our Christians and was even able to pay some of our employees their overdue wages. I was happy to find Fr Odala, from Manda-Mbuzi; Fr Polela from Cóbuè; Fr Chizuzu from Ngoo; and about a dozen other Mission employees. And there were hundreds of villagers from across the water. In the whole Cóbuè area, the only place still inhabited was a small group of villages between Cóbuè and Wikihi. Our priest and his catechist from there came to Likoma to see me briefly, but it was not long before they, too, fled from Mozambique to Likoma.

When I told the Mozambicans why I had come with Borges de Brito to Cóbuè, they said that he might be fair, but what about Morais and the armed forces? How could they be expected to return after the terrible things the Portuguese had done? Now, they heard that all our teachers at Messumba had been arrested, and that Chiwanga had been burnt within the last week. How could anyone trust the Portuguese? There was no answer to their questions. I returned briefly most days to report to Borges de Brito. He suggested that he might meet some representatives of the refugees on a boat on the Lake to discuss the situation, but no one wanted to talk with any Portuguese official. Portuguese planes were constantly (and quite illegally) buzzing the Island, and this hardly helped our embassage, as most of the refugees had already been bombed or machine-gunned out of their villages across the water. When I told Borges de Brito about this, he was very annoyed, and, in my presence, radioed Vila Cabral to ask that the pilots should stop this immediately. So perhaps we did accomplish something for the refugees.

The Chief of the Island held a meeting, to which Padre Menegon and I were invited, and we were politely asked to stop suggesting that people return to Mozambique. The refugees were guests on the Island; and if they were to be asked to return to Mozambique, Dr Banda would send the appropriate instruction. We were always welcome at Likoma, but only as visitors. Padre Menegon argued a little, but I was very content to accept this ruling. Just after the meeting, Canon Mwenda (he originally came from Cóbuè, though he worked on Likoma) came to see me, and advised me to leave before some people got the wrong impression about where my sympathies lay.

After some five or six days of shuttling back and forth between Cóbuè and Likoma Island, it was clear that we were making no headway whatever, so Padre Menegon and I left, though Borges de Brito stayed on at Cóbuè for another six months. I think that his only achievement was a cordial, though inconclusive, meeting with a representative group of refugees on a boat midway between Likoma and Cóbuè.

One thing, however, was quite clear, and that was that Likoma Island could not possibly absorb all these refugees. Even in normal times the Likomans relied heavily on the Mozambican lakeshore for supplies of food, firewood, building materials and countless other necessities. Eventually many of the refugees left to live in other parts of Malawi.

On my return to Messumba, I was not altogether surprised to find that many people had fled from their villages around the Mission. Apparently Frelimo had become more active in the area, and each time people heard the naval launches with the dreaded *fusileiros* passing by, they panicked, not unnaturally, and ran away. There were still quite a lot of people about, however. And, of course, we had all those Chiwanga refugees living on the Mission. One of my problems was to feed and clothe them. Fortunately there had been a good harvest that year; so from time to time we drove to Chiwanga, and elsewhere, to collect the maize that had been stored in small granaries near people's burnt-out houses, though the troops had burnt a great many of these, too. Also, just before my abortive attempt to go to Manda-Mbuzi a few months earlier, I had bought a large quantity of maize from Mpochi and Mt Chisindo, which I was now able to grind into flour with a small maize mill that I had recently bought in Blantyre. I foresaw, however, that if the number of refugees on the Mission was to increase, as seemed probable, we would not be able to continue feeding the people with our own meagre resources. The scorched-earth policy of the Portuguese reduced drastically the amount of land which the people could bring under cultivation. I wrote, therefore, to the World Council of Churches, explaining the position and asking for money to help us buy food and blankets in Vila Cabral. This was readily and speedily forthcoming. The Portuguese said that they would help, too; but I doubt if we received more than about twenty-five sacks of flour and beans from them during the whole time I was there.

11   Isolation

It must have been about 12 August 1965 that a village youth came to me with a note: 'We have mined the roads to Metangula and Maniamba. Please do not use them.' It was signed by the *Chefe do Base*. This was the first communication of any kind that I had ever had from Frelimo, and I was rather alarmed, but there was nothing I could do, and the messenger said that he had to hurry off. At dusk hundreds of villagers fled into the hills. I shall never forget the absolute terror that gripped the people, nor the frantic speed of their flight, women with babies on their backs, and small children struggling to keep up. Some people, before they went, came to my house and left their more treasured possessions on my verandah – bicycles, suitcases of clothes, camp beds and almost anything that one could imagine. Charles Wright made it his job to list everything, and to stow it away in the classrooms, with all the belongings of the Chiwanga refugees that we were already looking after.

It was clear that everyone had been warned of possible reprisals against the population for the mining of the road. At about nine o'clock that evening, three Frelimo soldiers arrived at my house. I did not recognize any of them. They were very polite, saluted me and said '*Seja louvado o Nosso Senhor, Jesus Cristo*' which is a greeting sometimes used by peasants in Portugal. They asked me if I had received the note about the mines, and told me that they had sent a similar one to Padre Mondine at the Roman Catholic Mission a few miles along the road towards Nova Coimbra. They went on: 'We want to tell you that we have nothing against missionaries and civilians: we only wish to liberate our country from the Salazarists who have been exploiting it for so long. We hope that you have not got a gun, and that you will always receive our comrades well. We know that the Portuguese will, as is their custom, retaliate mercilessly against the local population and therefore we would ask your cooperation in sending to our base those who have not already gone there.' I told them that the only gun I possessed was a twelve-bore shot-gun, which I used for killing monkeys that were robbing people's crops, and that I would always be prepared to receive anyone on the Mission. I asked them not to station troops on the Mission, however, as I did not want a pitched battle between them and the Portuguese. And as for sending people to the base, I could not possibly regard this as part of my job; though if people wished to go, they would be free, of course, to do so. Meanwhile I would keep our work at Messumba going for as long as I could. Before leaving, they particularly stressed that I should not attempt to drive on the road. They left my house courteously, and I had the impression that they were dedicated and efficient men. After they had gone, I realized that on the wall of my office were the framed photographs I had been given of the Portuguese President, Salazar, and Costa Almeida, and I removed them rather hastily.

During the next six or seven weeks we lived a strange and totally isolated life. The villages around Messumba were deserted, apart from two obstinate old men who had refused to budge. Most people had fled to the hills, but on the Mission some 250 had found sanctuary, sleeping wherever there was room. Messumba Mission had become a refugee centre. Reggie slept in the garage, but during the day would usually go to his village, unless he heard the dreaded naval launches approaching. His pattern of living was typical of most people's.

I had not before realized that there were so many of the mentally disturbed in the area. Those people who had gone into hiding in the mountains had left the poor things behind lest they inadvertently betray the whereabouts of the rest to the Portuguese. Now it was up to us to look after them. They were all fairly harmless, I discovered. From time to time goats and cows would wander through the Mission, and dogs and hens would appear; all had been left behind by the fleeing villagers. One man who owned many cattle asked if he could build a stockade for them on Mission land, and this was most useful to us as we were never thereafter short of milk or cheese.

We were very much on our own now. Apart from a supply aeroplane that flew over every day on its way from Metangula to Nova Coimbra, there was at first no evidence that we were in Portuguese territory at all. I took one piece of precautionary advice that Borges de Brito had recently given me and every day hoisted the Portuguese flag. I am sure that this stopped our being attacked. Only once did any Portuguese soldiers appear, and then they came just to drink some water as they passed through the Mission. The supply plane was also used as a spotter plane, and frequently disappeared into the mountains looking for signs of Frelimo. Three ancient Harvard bombers flew past the Mission fairly frequently, and it was rather alarming to say Mass while they circled over the church. As Charles and I came out of church late one afternoon, one of the bombers dived straight at us, very obvious targets in our white cassocks. There was nothing to do but to stand stock still, and I am sure that if we had run for cover they would have opened fire. As it pulled out of the dive, the second bomber came in, and then the third, and this exercise was repeated for about twenty minutes. I do not know what their object was: maybe the church was good for target practice, or maybe the pilots were just trying to scare us. That evening, when our refugees returned from their villages to sleep on the Mission, many expected to find us dead. Later, I complained to the civil and military authorities about this performance, but they all professed complete ignorance of it.

The planes were based at Vila Cabral, but there were landing strips at Nova Coimbra and at Metangula, both of which were by now sizeable military bases. As the road was mined, there was little movement between the two – at least not after the first convoy had hit a couple of mines. One morning Charles and I, from the hill on which the Mission stood, saw a convoy going towards Metangula, and we could see that it was preceded, on foot, by half a dozen Africans. We realized that we were witnessing one of the army's more macabre practices – the use of human mine detectors. Looking closely through binoculars, we recognized one or two of our employees who had been taken on Black

Saturday. (Lord Kilbracken, who visited Messumba a few weeks later, wrote in the London *Evening Standard* of 27 September: 'I asked at Maniamba how they located mines . . .; a young soldier told me . . . it was not too difficult. They simply drove . . . "the blacks" along the roads believed to have been mined. And he mimicked the "knees-up" stamping march they were made to adopt . . .')

Messumba and the villages immediately surrounding it were not molested at all by the Portuguese at this time, even though the inhabitants had either fled to the mountains or were living on the Mission itself. Not a single house was destroyed nor a bomb dropped. However, all the houses on the roadside and all the grain stores were burnt down. We often saw planes bombing and machine-gunning the villages and hide-outs in the mountains; but with little success, I think, as we seldom heard of any casualties.

On the other hand, we were constantly visited by Frelimo soldiers and their 'hangers-on'. During this time, Frelimo people came to see me as often as five nights out of seven. They often brought a note asking for cigarettes, soap, sugar, salt, tea, paper, envelopes, cloth, and so on – and sometimes brought money. Only twice was I ever asked for 'military' supplies: petrol, which I knew would be used for burning the wooden bridges on the road, and which I refused to give them, though there would not have been much I could have done if they had insisted; and oil for their weapons. I allowed them to take what they wanted from the small drum of used sump oil we always kept in the garage for anyone who wanted it. I am not sure how good it was for their weapons, though. They often asked for medicines, and these, of course, we gave them, especially as most were to be used for the children who had fled to their bases. Of all the Frelimo people who came to visit us, only one group was slightly unfriendly, though they could hardly be said to be hostile.

Every evening we would see the scores of villagers who had fled to the mountains being escorted by a few Frelimo soldiers through the Mission to collect food from their villages or to visit their families still at Messumba. Some of our employees who were in hiding would come to collect their previous month's wages from me, and many soldiers and civilians would visit friends and relations in hospital. It was all far removed from our normal lives, and I was surprised to find myself rather at a loss on the nights when nobody came. The Frelimo soldiers were usually armed with Thompson sub-machine guns and Mausers, but they also carried an odd assortment of weapons, including a sort of chimney brush which, I was told, was for knocking out sentries. They had cut all the telephone wires to Vila Cabral; and by the time that I finally left in 1970, these had still not been repaired. Occasionally we could see the flashes of a battle going on somewhere, usually at Nova Coimbra or at Maniamba, and often the three bombers would fly in the direction of Chia, from where we would hear the sounds of a bombardment. But at Messumba itself all was peaceful.

I came to learn quite a lot about the local Frelimo bases, one of which, Matenje, I was to visit at the end of September. It was the one to which most of the Messumba villagers had fled. The Frelimo Commander-in-Chief of the area was a man called Mabote; and though I received notes from him occasionally, I do not think I ever met him. The Frelimo Commander that I did meet fairly often was Henrique Calumbaine, who called himself Catarina, and was in charge of a near-by base. He had been a schoolboy at Messumba but was now about twenty-four years old. He was always very friendly. One rather dangerous habit of Frelimo was to write their requests for things in a duplicate order book, and I was always worried that these books would be found by the Portuguese; but there was little I could do about this, as our Africans were notorious for keeping diaries, letters, and records of everything. Sometimes I would receive a note from a catechist requesting me to send his back pay to him by the messenger.

One morning Padre Mondine came to see me, having walked along bush paths from his Mission. He asked me if I was intending to close down Messumba. I told him that the thought had never occurred to me. We still had about 250 people living on the Mission; while people came from their hide-outs in the hills to have their babies baptized, and several even came to Mass on Sundays. We were still able to provide medical care and attention, not to mention food. He said we were lucky, since at his Mission there were only fourteen people left. The Portuguese garrison at Nova Coimbra, although visiting his Mission to draw water, was hostile to him, as they suspected him of harbouring the Frelimo soldiers who sometimes attacked them. In fact, the Captain had gone so far as to tell him: 'My soldiers distrust you so much that I cannot be responsible if they attack you personally when you come here to say Mass.' Once again, I was thankful that Messumba was not situated anywhere near a Portuguese military base, and that the danger of mines on the roads kept Portuguese detachments from visiting us.

A few days after Padre Mondine's visit, I went to visit him, and saw Portuguese soldiers coming to collect water. We were all in what was virtually Frelimo-held territory, and here was the Portuguese army, heavily armed, collecting water, with soldiers jumping off their trucks and surrounding the little water pump. Padre Mondine and I bought things from one another. We might be short of soap, and he of salt, and so on. In the face of the Portuguese army, our two denominations were drawn closer.

One night a couple of Frelimo soldiers came to see me and asked if they could go into church to say the rosary. I readily agreed, but asked them to leave their arms outside the sacristy. They were not very happy about this, but I promised to look after their weapons; so they agreed and went into church. They knelt down reverently, took out their rosaries and said their prayers. Afterwards they asked me if I could sell them some rosaries, as there were many people at their base who wanted them. A few days later I was able to buy some for them from Padre Mondine.

On another occasion, a Frelimo soldier said he brought greetings from the Bishop of South-West Tanganyika, whom I had met a few years previously in England!

Some Frelimo people, like the British in 1939, were suffering from exaggerated optimism – 'it will all be over by Christmas'. One evening when a group of them were visiting us, I was asked: 'We hear that you are intending to re-open the school in September, but what books will you use?' I told them that I could only use the books I had in the book-store. 'That is all right for now,' they said, 'but you will receive our books that are being printed in Tanzania in time for the term that starts in January.' We never did receive them, of course. Most of the Frelimo people who came to the Mission to see me were ordinary villagers with a gun, though there were some who had been to Algeria and elsewhere for training.

Charles Wright was far too intrepid for our comfort, and when one day he said he would cycle to Metangula to see if there were any letters for us, Irene and I begged him not to go, but he insisted. On the way, near Chiwanga, he came across the dead body of the wife of Salathiel Chizuzu (who had by now fled to Malawi). Although, like everyone else, she must have known that the road was mined, the poor woman had taken the risk and trodden on a mine. More distressing was the half-dead baby tied to her back. Charles put the pathetic little wounded body into the mailbag and returned to Messumba, but the baby died that evening. Charles then went back to the mother and buried her body by the roadside.

He was deeply disturbed by this episode, and resolved to do something to prevent any recurrence. He wrote out several posters '*Mina aqui*', stuck them on split bamboos, and set off on his bicycle to put them wherever he thought there might be a mine. He said he could easily tell where these had been laid. Again Irene and I asked him to stop doing this as he might get killed himself. Everyone knew that the road was mined, and if they chose to walk on it they did so at their own risk. It was not worth risking his life. He only gave in when Irene said: 'Charles, if you are killed by a mine, that's one thing, but if you are wounded then I will have to nurse you, and I do not want such a responsibility, especially as we have no contact with any doctor.'

That night I was awakened by an urgent knocking outside my house and a voice calling: 'Senhor Padre, Senhor Padre.' I got up and opened the door, though as always it was not locked, and in came some angry Frelimo soldiers. 'We told you that the road is mined, why do you allow Fr Charles to destroy our work by putting notices on the road?' I told them that I had spoken to him about this and that he had agreed to stop. 'Well, if he does it again, we shall come to his house as we have come to yours, and when he opens the door we shall kill him. You are head of this Mission, Fr Charles is your subordinate, so it is up to you.' With that they left. I went over to Charles' house to tell him what had happened, and he was most apologetic that he had caused such trouble. He assured me that he would stop his campaign, but his docile mood vanished the next morning when he found that his bicycle had disappeared: 'That's just the sort of dirty trick they would do!' In actual fact, it was one of our mental cases who had taken the bicycle, which was later found near Nova Coimbra.

One morning, a few days after this, as I was sitting in my office, I suddenly saw a strange European, accompanied by an African. I knew the latter by sight as he came from Metangula, but who the former was, I had no idea, except that he was obviously not a Portuguese. It was Lord Kilbracken – and never have I been more astonished to see anyone than I was to see this member of the House of Lords, in my house, in the middle of Africa, in time of war. He told me that he was in Mozambique on a fact-finding tour, and that ever since he had arrived, he had been seeking a way to visit the Anglican Mission at Messumba. It had been very difficult to get here, but thanks to Zilhão, the Naval Commander at Metangula, he had got a lift on a gunboat. He had been dropped off at the beach with only an hour to see us. No official was with him, and he had come at his own risk. After all he had heard of the war in the area, he was surprised that we were living fairly calmly and that, although the surrounding villages were deserted, there was obviously still a settled community on the Mission itself. He had seen Bishop Pickard in Lourenço Marques, who had spoken of withdrawing the Anglican work at Messumba. I told him that I had no intention whatever of leaving: our presence was necessary to the refugees, and if ever we should fulfil our long-held role as the guardians of the Nyasa people, it was in difficult times like these. He saw over the hospital, and then I drove him over rough tracks to the beach where the boat was waiting for him. The crew were obviously frightened and rather annoyed that Kilbracken had been away for so long. I also got the impression that they expected me to be accompanied by a large band of Frelimo soldiers.

Mozambique: Memoirs of a Revolution

Lord Kilbracken returned to England, and on 27 September 1965, some two or three weeks after his visit, the front page of the London *Evening Standard* carried the headline: 'I find the Unknown War'. Every day that week, the newspaper printed articles by Lord Kilbracken about his trip to Mozambique. Charles was angry, as he thought Kilbracken had made all too good a story of Charles-and-his-bicycle. The Portuguese, too, were very angry about the articles; though Zilhão told me privately that he thought they were fair. (He was soon replaced.) However, the world now knew, almost for the first time, that a very serious contest was going on in Mozambique, which the Portuguese had done everything in their power to hide. Portugal had made a great mistake in inviting Lord Kilbracken, for he reported a true picture of what he had seen.

His article in the *Evening Standard* of 30 September was entirely about his visit to Messumba:

Of more than 2,000 inhabitants, almost half were still in the mountains ... but to Messumba, where there is Christian charity, they are returning ... the sick come from many miles around. They have nowhere else to go – except the Italian Catholic mission a dozen miles away ... When I was speaking to the Brigadier in Vila Cabral, a monocled nonentity who reminded me of a Prussian colonel from the First World War, he implied – in a most offensive way – that Father Paul and his mission were on the side of the Frelimo. This was rubbish. He isn't on the Frelimo side – nor on the Portuguese side, either. The Brigadier, I believe, had drawn his conclusions from the fact that some Frelimo leaders are graduates of the school. It never seemed to occur to him that most leaders are educated – at least to the point of being able to read and write. The very few scattered mission schools, most of them Italian, provide the ONLY educational facilities in all this troubled country. The Anglican school at Messumba is the biggest and best of them. How could it be otherwise than that some Frelimo leaders should be counted among its alumni? ... Father Paul's policy is to remain as neutral as possible and hope he may continue his ministry in peace. There was such a feeling at Messumba of security in the midst of danger, and so much vital humanitarian work in progress, that I found it difficult – indeed almost ridiculous – to pass on the Bishop's message ... that ... he should consider withdrawing the mission.

At least I was able to send some mail by Kilbracken, including a letter to Bishop Pickard in which, among other things, I explained that we were safe but completely isolated. I also said that, in the circumstances, and as the school now had barely eighty pupils (instead of ten times that number, as was usual), Joan should not return to Messumba. The Bishop agreed, and Joan was transferred to Inhambane. A year later we regretted this, as her experience and dedication were needed at Messumba; but by then she was firmly settled into her new job in the south.

When the people first fled to the mountains, we were left with only about two hundred round the Mission; but little by little, the people drifted back to Messumba, where they felt safer from the Portuguese and where medical and educational facilities were available. Our main trouble was shortage of supplies (at one time we were down to a solitary half-bar of soap on the whole Mission), and it appeared that we might be forced to close down. Help came rather surprisingly when some Frelimo soldiers visited me one evening, asking for cigarettes. I had to explain that we did not have a single one on the Mission, and that as the road to Metangula was mined by them, we could not buy any more, nor anything else. If they wanted things from us, they would have to make it possible for us to get to Metangula. And this they promised to do.

A few days later, a Frelimo soldier walked confidently into my office and handed me a note. Although he was not in uniform, we all knew who he was, and his apparent brazenness in coming in broad daylight caused some consternation. The note read: 'We have removed most of the mines from the road; this comrade will accompany you; don't forget my cigarettes.' We set off immediately; Reggie following in the lorry, while I drove the land-rover with the Frelimo soldier at my side. He warned me not to drive too fast, and then after a couple of miles, told me to stop. We got out and he showed me exactly where there was a mine. He then wished me a safe journey, assured me that there were no other mines on the road, and warned me to be very careful to follow in the same tracks on my return. He disappeared into the bush, and we drove along a deserted road. When we arrived at Metangula, the few people there stared at us in absolute amazement, as if we were visitants from another world. At the shop we loaded up the cars with all the supplies we could get from a delighted shopkeeper, for whom business was now practically at a standstill. Only a handful of Africans remained in Metangula now, the rest having fled to the mountains, and the army and navy canteens supplied their people with most of the things they required.

I went to see the Chefe do Posto, Soares de Cruz, and as I did so met about a hundred of the people seized on Black Saturday, who had just been brought from Vila Cabral via Meponda on a naval launch. Their thin, tattered, and, worst of all, thoroughly cowed, appearance told its own tale. But it was a joy to see them and talk with them, as they came up and shook hands with me. Soares de Cruz came out and told them that he would, that afternoon, get all their papers in order, and then take them back to Messumba in a launch the following morning.

He then invited me into his house for lunch; so I gave Reggie some money and told him to get something to eat. Soares de Cruz asked me if we had many people at Messumba, and was surprised when I replied that by now there must be about five hundred. At Metangula, he said, everyone had fled, and even now there were less than fifty. He had almost no staff, so would I please excuse a rather poor lunch. Just as I was leaving to go home, one of the released prisoners came up and in an agitated manner told me that Reggie had just been surrounded by some *fusileiros* and taken into the naval base. I instantly told Soares de Cruz who became angry and, before I could say anything, jumped into his jeep and went off. He went straight to the naval base, then to the army headquarters, then back to the base, and finally returned to me. We went to his house again. I was myself both furious and fearful, and told him that Reggie could not conceivably be involved in 'subversive activities'; he had already suffered unjustly at the hands of the police in Vila Cabral prison, and would not have risked another similar experience. Soares de Cruz said that he agreed with this and had therefore ignored repeated requests from P.I.D.E. to arrest him. He could only assume that this was why the armed forces had been asked to do so.

I was shown various telegrams and other communications that he had received. Apparently, P.I.D.E. had been told that Reggie was in radio contact with Frelimo. I said this was ludicrous. First, although he possessed an ordinary wireless, he had had no training in telecommunications; secondly, he had been sleeping in the garage, and I knew exactly what was there; and thirdly, he went to his village infrequently, just to tend his fields, as his possessions were all stored on the Mission. In addition he was an elderly man by African standards and would probably not be particularly interested in what Frelimo was doing. Soares de Cruz made it clear that he agreed with all this; and when he told Costa Matos what I had said, the Governor also agreed. A couple of days later I went to the naval base and asked to see Reggie, but was told that he was being held 'incomunicado' (I knew the sinister implications of that word now), in the room at the top of the 'lighthouse', until they were able to send him up to Vila Cabral. In that room I knew the *fusileiros* were at liberty to work out their frustrations with the guerrillas on anyone unfortunate enough to be sent there. I never saw Reggie again, as he did not return to Messumba until August 1972 – seven years later, and long after I had left Mozambique.

Bitterly angry, anxious and frustrated as I was feeling over Reggie, I had another, immediate problem: how to get the second lorry, which Reggie had driven, back to Messumba? This was solved with the arrival by plane from Vila Cabral of Padre Jorge, who was hoping to get a lift to the Roman Catholic Mission near Nova Coimbra. I was glad to let him take the land-rover, but told him that the road would only be safe as far as Messumba, where he could spend the night with us, and go on to Nova Coimbra by footpath in the morning. I also warned him about the one remaining mine on the road.

Padre Jorge was a strange character, but I think he cultivated this role. He came from an aristocratic Portuguese family, and was some sort of ward of his Bishop, Dom Eurico Nogueira. He had a rather sentimental, yet casual, attitude to life, but later on showed other, more solid, qualities. When we got to Messumba, he walked round the Mission, commiserating with everyone, and then came to the *mezane* for supper. During the meal

I was called outside to speak to some Frelimo soldiers, come to ask me if I had been able to bring cigarettes from Metangula. Padre Jorge came out to chat and smoke with them. He asked them what the movement was trying to do; rather a naïve question, I thought. They told him quite simply that they wanted to liberate their country.

Next morning I walked with him part of the way to the Roman Catholic Mission; and as we went we saw those three bombers, flying overhead and dropping bombs in the hills where we knew there were many people in hiding. The bombardment went on for about twenty minutes, and then the bombers returned to Vila Cabral, and Padre Jorge walked on to Nova Coimbra. All that day people poured into Messumba – men, women and children, who had been bombed out of their make-shift camps. There did not appear to have been any casualties. Our population quadrupled overnight.

The following morning I received a message from Padre Jorge: after the bombers had attacked the camps, the troops from Nova Coimbra had moved in. On their return, they had passed through the Mission, telling Padre Jorge that they had only fired into the air to scare the people back to the Missions. However, later on, a wounded teacher had been brought in who told him that people had been killed at Matenje. Padre Jorge had gone there at once and found seven bodies. Two, his companions told him, came from the Roman Catholic Mission, and these he took back to the Mission for burial. The other five were Messumba people; but he could not remove them as he had insufficient helpers, and Messumba was that much farther away.

Irene (who came in case we should find any injured) and I set off for the area with some porters; but others chose to come with us, and in the end it was quite a procession that wound its way into the hills. It took us about two hours to find the place near Matenje as I had never been there before. And after that day, I did not intend to go there ever again. The make-shift camp was in a thick bamboo forest in a valley. The bombs had all, mercifully, fallen short of it; and so we could see the collection of small grass shelters that the people had constructed. There was an enclosure which, we gathered, had been a church, for we found there a number of religious books. There was even a tiny stockade which we later learned had been used as a 'prison' for those who had been suspected of collaborating with the Portuguese. Life had obviously been extremely primitive and the conditions appalling: no fresh water, no land for crops, few possessions. It showed how great was the fear of the Portuguese that had forced several hundreds of people to exist in such conditions. About twenty-five Frelimo soldiers had guarded the camp, but often other Frelimo militants would pass through on their way to or from other bases, and sometimes there would be political meetings during which some leader would explain to the people the aims of the struggle for liberation. Sometimes a Frelimo medical team would come and vaccinate people against smallpox and other diseases. (We had given quite a number of medicines to our Frelimo visitors.)

I was grateful to Padre Jorge for having carried the five remaining corpses to a central place, where each one was covered with a blanket. They had been dead for two days, and the sickly-sweet smell of human flesh rotting in the African sun was all-pervading. I shall never forget the look on Henrique Zindo's face when he pulled the blanket off one face and saw that it was his father. None of the people who had been killed was a Frelimo soldier: they were just ordinary villagers who had gone into hiding in their fear of the Portuguese. We took it in turns to dig a mass grave and, between shifts, searched the ruins of the place for anything that had been left behind. Eventually the grave was ready, and into it, with great reverence, we placed the five bodies. When all was ready, I said the burial office, and the sad procession returned to Messumba.

12 Zona Neutra

The day following my visit to Metangula was the day that the Portuguese bombed the people out of their refuge at Matenje. It was also the day that Soares de Cruz brought home, by launch, some of the Black Saturday prisoners. I went in the lorry to Mónduè to meet them and drive some of them up to the Mission. What a pathetic sight they were as they huddled together, hardly able to believe that they were free. And many of the prisoners had not returned; so that there were heart-rending scenes as women searched for husbands, sons or brothers among those released, and failed to find them.

Soares de Cruz held a *banja* in the centre of the Mission. On one side were the released prisoners; on the other three sides were those who had been living for the past two months as refugees on the Mission, most of whom had at least one relation amongst the ex-prisoners. Soares de Cruz said that he was sorry not everyone had returned, but that within a month more would be released. The events of Black Saturday had been like a net cast into the sea, and both the guilty and the innocent had been caught. Only in this way could the Government separate the guilty from the innocent, and the latter were now home. But he was sad to see that some had obviously been ill-treated while in prison. He told them all that they could now return to their village homes and live in peace. He had agreed with the military and naval authorities that they would not be molested, and that Messumba would in future be classed as a 'Neutral Zone'.

People asked him how the troops would know that Messumba was a neutral zone. He said that he would, with my help, put up notices saying 'Zona Neutra', on various paths leading into the area. He was also asked what would happen if the Portuguese troops were to find Frelimo forces in the area, and he replied that he hoped Frelimo would respect the Zona Neutra as the Portuguese intended to do. The people said that they had no power to prevent Frelimo from coming into the area. What would happen if Portuguese troops found Frelimo footsteps outside a house? He answered that the best thing then, would be for them to get up early every day and, if there were any Frelimo footprints outside their houses, to obliterate them.

The people went off to their villages; those who had been bombed out of the mountains also returned; and by the evening the villages around Messumba were once more inhabited. It looked as if we might even be resuming our normal life.

At first it was difficult to extract much information from the ex-prisoners, because they were still in a state of shock. But during the course of the next few months, I was able to obtain a fairly accurate picture of what had happened to them. And the stories that they told were corroborated over and over again.

They had been taken in open lorries from Metangula to Vila Cabral. When they reached the prison, they were herded through the narrow entrance like cattle, as Portuguese soldiers, police and bystanders struck and beat them. Jaime Cumpenda (our senior carpenter, aged about fifty-five) had nearly all his teeth knocked out by a blow on the side of his face. João Rashide (a senior hospital orderly, aged about thirty-seven) received such a cut on his arm from what seemed like a piece of steel wire that four years later he could not bear to be touched where the blow had fallen. There was nothing systematic about this : anyone might be hit as he went through the gate, and a few even managed to push through untouched. They were all put into a single room, where the sanitation consisted of two or three buckets, emptied once a day. There was no furniture of any sort except the buckets, and no blankets. They were fed from time to time, but the food was quite insufficient, and requests for more were answered with a blow. The stench in the room was foul from the excreta and unwashed bodies. For Nyasas, who normally bathe in the Lake twice a day, this represented an additional ordeal. Conditions deteriorated as more people were pushed into the room, until it became impossible for them all to lie down and sleep at the same time.

By the time that these men had reached Vila Cabral prison, most of our teachers and others who had been called into Met-angula during the previous weeks had already been taken from there to Nampula or Lourenço Marques. Buanacaia and a few others of the Black Saturday haul were also moved from Vila Cabral within a few days of their arrival, but my informants did not know where. The released prisoners told me that while they were in prison, most of them were not interrogated at all beyond having to inform their captors of their identity, but almost every day, a few of the prisoners would be taken into another, smaller room, where they were beaten and tortured. If a man fainted, a bucket of water was thrown over him and the torture resumed, as had happened to Reggie the year before. They were shouted at and abused until they were forced to confess something no matter what, true or not. Many people named under torture were, of course, then arrested. Some of the tortured men were not seen again. One who died was Guilherme Mishindo, a young villager about twenty-five years old. All that was known was that one day about six of his fellow-prisoners had been called out to dig a grave, and were then given Guilherme's body, on which they saw the marks of the cruel beatings he had received.

Of course, I only heard the stories of a small percentage of the prisoners, but the pattern was the same. They never knew what was going to happen next. Suddenly a man was summoned; sometimes he returned, sometimes he did not. Often people were taken out to accompany troops as 'guides', 'mine detectors', or porters. Jaime Chipungu (30) and Jaime Cumpenda (22) – a nephew of the senior carpenter – were among those used as mine detectors. They had to walk in front of a troop convoy the seventy miles from Vila Cabral to Nova Coimbra. Jaime Cumpenda told me he had been among those whom Charles and I had seen, walking in front of a convoy between Nova Coimbra and Metangula just after my return from Likoma Island. Jaime Chipungu was kept with the garrison at Nova Coimbra and accompanied the soldiers as a porter on their sorties into the mountains. He told me that, on one occasion, they came under fire from a lone Frelimo soldier who was eventually wounded and captured. The soldiers wanted to kill him, but their officer was a decent chap and ordered Jaime and the other porters to carry the wounded man. Despite the repeated demands of the soldiers for his death, the man was still alive when the party reached a rendezvous with the navy on the lakeshore. They were all taken to Metangula, and the wounded Frelimo soldier sent to Vila Cabral hospital, where I later visited him. His home had been near Chicale, though I did not remember having met him before. He was ultimately returned to Messumba, but was permanently crippled by the long delay that there had been before he received medical attention.

I made repeated requests for Jaime Chipungu and Jaime Cumpenda to be released from Nova Coimbra, and eventually they were both allowed to return to Messumba, a few days after the arrival of the first batch of released prisoners.

Among those who had been returned to Messumba was a seventeen-year-old, André Chucua, who had been taken on Black Saturday while doing some labouring job at the Mission. He had never been a very intelligent lad, but he was now a complete simpleton, neither moving nor even eating unless made to do so by someone else. Apparently, while they had all still been at Metangula, he had asked permission to go outside the wire fence one evening, since no sanitation was provided inside. As he returned, he was set upon by the soldiers and hit so brutally with rifle butts that he had literally been knocked out of his senses. When he reached Vila Cabral, he was not subjected to further physical punishment, and some kind fellow-prisoner took care of him. A few days after his return to Messumba, Padre Jorge revisited us, and when he saw what his fellow-Portuguese had done to André, he wept bitterly. Some three years passed before the lad regained his sanity.

While they were still at Metangula, some of the men had seen Charles pleading with the P.I.D.E. agents to be allowed in; and they had heard that when I passed through Vila Cabral on my return from Malawi, I had tried to get into the prison. They knew that I would never be allowed to see them in the condition they were in, and apparently some of the guards had made very caustic comments about my audacity in asking to see a bunch of terrorists. None of these prisoners had been a Frelimo militant, and I doubt if more than half a dozen of them had even bought Frelimo membership cards: they were just ordinary villagers.

One of the prisoners was Carlos Messosa, who had been the catechist at Chicale during my first years at Messumba and was now about fifty years old. Every day he led the people in prayer; Christians, Muslims, and heathens together. And then the day came that it was his turn to be summoned. He and several other prisoners were taken on an army truck somewhere to the south of Vila Cabral and there they had to accompany the soldiers in a hunt among the mountains for Frelimo hide-outs. On their return, the trucks drove over the rough roads with great speed towards Vila Cabral and home, and Carlos was thrown out of his truck by the jolting. As all the prisoners were roped together, he was dragged along the road behind. The driver would not stop despite the pleas of the other prisoners, and so Carlos was dragged to his death. Before they reached the town, the truck stopped and the soldiers untied his body, throwing it into the bush for the hyenas.

Of the 300 prisoners collected on Black Saturday, about 50 had been returned from Metangula before the rest were taken to Vila Cabral. Now, two months later, 120 had returned, and after three weeks another 80 were released. Of the remaining 50 some had already met their deaths in one way or another. The two months between Black Saturday and the return of the 120 coincided very nearly with the time that we had been completely cut off at Messumba, so that apart from my vain attempt to visit the prison on my return from Malawi, I had been unable to get to Vila Cabral at all. It was fortunate that our students at the Escola Técnica were on holiday during this time; otherwise they would no doubt have been arrested as well. For P.I.D.E. swooped on the population in and around Vila Cabral, arresting the Nyasas, including Fr Litumbi and the intelligent and charming Carlos Juma (eldest son of Fr Juma) who, after his return from studying in Lourenço Marques, had left the Mission and gone to work first in Salvado's office and then as a senior clerk in the local secretariat. These two were among those who spent only a very short time in Vila Cabral prison before being sent on elsewhere. After P.I.D.E. had seized most of the Nyasas working in Vila Cabral, they then took the Yaos, and those who returned to Messumba told me that the Yaos had been consistently treated in a far more brutal manner than the Nyasas.

The Yaos, as already stated, were about ninety-eight per cent Muslim, and Portugal displayed an almost pathological hatred of Islam. (Portuguese history books are full of stories of how the Portuguese Christian people drove the Moorish hordes from their country. Every Portuguese has heard the stories of what the Moors did to the Christian Portuguese in the name of Islam, and for centuries Portugal was torn between Christians and Muslims.) The Yaos had remained staunchly Muslim, and neither the Roman Catholics nor ourselves had had much success in converting them to Christianity. To call a person a Muslim had even become something of an insult. Not only did the Yaos, therefore, have a severe handicap because of their religion, but they also suffered because they inhabited what were considered to be Portuguese 'settler' areas, and so were additionally suspect. Finally, they did not enjoy the protection of white missionaries, as did the Christians; and so P.I.D.E. did not run the risk, as they did with the Nyasas, that missionaries would tell tales. I have almost no first-hand information as to how they were treated, but it was said, not infrequently, that some had been thrown out of aeroplanes.

Until the end of 1965, P.I.D.E. did not have a permanent office in Vila Cabral, but controlled operations from Nampula, where Campos was the Inspector. Rosa, at Vila Cabral, was his subordinate; and the brutal treatment meted out to the prisoners there had been his direct responsibility. The prison at Vila Cabral was run by the P.S.P. (Polícia de Segurança Pública) and had been built for common-law prisoners. However, P.I.D.E. was all-powerful and, when necessary, took over a wing of the prison and even employed the P.S.P. to do their dirty work for them. P.I.D.E. was, I repeat, all-powerful. Originally it had been the private army of Salazar; now it was the political arm of the Portuguese state. Everyone feared P.I.D.E., even the Governor-

General, and there were no lengths to which P.I.D.E. would not go to root out all opposition to the régime. The majority of their agents were sadistic thugs, for whom the only way to treat an 'enemy of Portugal' was to eliminate him. Worst of all, they were responsible to no one.

When I had learned all the terrifying truth from the released prisoners, I went to see the Roman Catholic Bishop of Vila Cabral, Dom Eurico Nogueira, to ask if he could do anything to stop the brutality. He was a Portuguese and had the same official standing as the Governor, Costa Matos. The Bishop already knew much of what I had to tell him, because what had taken place at Messumba seemed to have been general policy. But in spite of his many protests, there had been no change whatever. Indeed, he himself had not been allowed to visit the prisoners, and Padre Piquito, who had, at least, been allowed to say Mass on one occasion, had only been allowed to do so for the common-law (not the political) prisoners. The Bishop suspected that all his mail passed through the hands of P.I.D.E. before it reached him, and he was obviously very unpopular with the authorities because of the complaints that he had made.

Dom Eurico also told me that he had brought up the subject of P.I.D.E.'s brutality at the latest Episcopal Conference, but that most of the other bishops were unsympathetic to his point of view: 'Their dioceses are in areas which are not yet affected by this sort of thing, and they simply have no idea of the anguish we feel here.' The Bishop was clearly very concerned about the official Church reaction in Mozambique to what was going on in Niassa, and continued himself to be outspoken; so it was no surprise to me to learn, a few years later, of his transfer to the See of Sá da Bandeira in Angola. For the Portuguese, the last straw must have been a pastoral letter in which he wrote:

I have been given information, almost always too late, of excesses which attain the dimensions of atrocities ... to affirm that terrorism can only be defeated by terrorism is politically monstrous and un-mitigatingly criminal.

Meanwhile at Messumba we had the comfortable thought of our Zona Neutra; and I went ahead with the painting of a dozen or more signs, which I hoped would serve until the signs that Soares de Cruz had promised to have made at Vila Cabral were ready. We then agreed where each of these signs should be placed, and I nailed them to a tree or a pole. The signs gave the villagers a feeling of great security and they felt able to move about as they pleased within the area. Hundreds of people returned every week from the mountains near Chia, Chicale, Mpochi and even Ngoo, to seek the comparative peace of the Zona Neutra. By Christmas 1965, the population of Messumba must have been at least 7,000, and we had almost 1,000 children at school. It had been agreed that no one should leave the Zona Neutra without a pass; so every day Charles and I issued hundreds of passes to people who wished to tend their fields outside the area, or visit Metangula or Nova Coimbra. If they happened to meet any Portuguese troops, they just produced their passes. Anyone found without a pass outside the Zona Neutra might be in trouble. On one occasion when I was in Metangula, I saw about five people I knew by sight from Messumba outside the army headquarters (by that time there was a battalion stationed at Metangula). I was told that they had been caught fishing outside the Zona Neutra and were, therefore, suspect. I assured the authorities that they lived at Messumba and then persuaded the people to own up to the army that they had followed a shoal of fish which had taken them outside the authorized zone. This they did, and were allowed to return with me to Messumba.

I was always fearful lest one side or the other would abuse the Zona Neutra, but on the whole there was little trouble. Once, the *fusileiros* burnt two or three houses within the area in an excess of enthusiasm after burning down what few houses still remained at Chia. When I complained to Soares de Cruz, the owners were given a minute monetary compensation, and I was told that it had been a mistake. On another occasion, when I went to see if one of the distant signs was still up, I came across some twenty-five Frelimo soldiers, all armed, but they remained just outside the Zona Neutra and told me that they were awaiting the return of three of their comrades (including Mário Chaomba, who had been beaten up with Reggie the previous year), who had just gone, in civilian clothes, to visit their families.

For six months after the return of the prisoners from Vila Cabral, everything was very peaceful, if hardly normal, at Messumba itself, though this was far from the case elsewhere. There were always plenty of Frelimo and Portuguese soldiers about, but they never clashed within the Zona Neutra. Every night I drove our cook to his home at Mónduè and I often met Frelimo soldiers walking freely along the road. On one occasion, a section was all lined up to greet me as I turned the land-rover round to return to the Mission. The man in charge brought them all to attention and they presented arms. One morning I found a Frelimo soldier, who had recently been at the Escola Técnica, sitting on the church steps. I asked him to clear off, as I did not want the Portuguese to find him and start a battle outside the church. He answered with a smile: 'Whose bloody country is this?', and, still smiling, sauntered off in the direction of the Lake.

Messumba was a haven of peace in a very troubled area, and while one never knew quite what would happen next, our main troubles were concerned with issuing countless passes, and giving out food to some six hundred people every day. This was bought largely with money which we had received from the World Council of Churches. We had to evolve a strict rationing system and could give the people only the minimum of food. But this at least kept them alive. Irene at that time had as many as three hundred out-patients a day at the hospital, which was very short-handed as so many of her trained staff had been taken prisoner by P.I.D.E. Often the troops came from Nova Coimbra to collect water from our taps rather than go down to the Lake. I shall never forget one afternoon when they went to Charles to ask if they might take some water: 'Clear off,' he said. 'Here are a couple of buckets. You are quite young enough to go down to Mónduè and fill up your water-tank there.'

It was clear that the Portuguese troops were not at all pleased by the Zona Neutra. They even went so far as to bring up a long-range field-gun to within a mile of the Mission, and every fifteen minutes or so fired a shell low over the Mission and into the hills beyond. This noisy and alarming bombardment went on for about two hours, and we expected the Mission to be hit at any moment. I complained to Soares de Cruz; but, of course, he said that he knew nothing about it.

The Zona Neutra covered a very large area and included not only the villages immediately around the Mission, but also that part of Chiwanga that had not been burnt; and Soares de Cruz felt that it would be better for everyone if the population moved out of it as little as possible. At his suggestion I opened a small shop, where we sold a few basic things like salt, sugar, and cloth. This was an excellent idea, but it produced new problems for us. We had to keep the shop stocked when transport was particularly difficult, and it was impossible for us to prevent soldiers of both sides from using it.

The Roman Catholics had similar problems: for, although their Zona Neutra was very much smaller, and they had less than a thousand people living there, they were nearer to both the Portuguese and the Frelimo bases. At Metangula, the situation was quite different. Although Frelimo frequently sent people to buy supplies from the shops there, the responsibility for keeping Frelimo out rested with the Portuguese army and navy, who were stationed at the place in considerable numbers. Padre Mondine and I were under constant suspicion, but we were powerless to do anything about that.

Towards the end of 1965, Chief Manhica of Ngoo came to see me. He told me that ever since Carlos Catatula's murder, his people had been living in the hills near by (though not at a Frelimo base). He had heard about the Zona Neutra at Messumba and wondered whether it would be possible to establish one at Ngoo. I told him that even if it were possible, it would be extremely difficult to guarantee the area any real degree of safety, as there would be no missionary there to protect the inhabitants from either the Portuguese or Frelimo. I suggested that they should all come to the Messumba Zona Neutra, but he reminded me of the traditional rivalry between the two communities. There was also the important matter of his people's fields which were, of course, at Ngoo. I finally agreed to take three representatives to Metangula to see the Chefe do Posto – now called the Administrador do Posto.

Soares de Cruz was very pleased by the Chief's request to

establish a Zona Neutra at Ngoo and readily agreed, although I told him that I was extremely doubtful about the wisdom of the plan. Within a few days, it was agreed with the naval and military authorities that the people could return to Ngoo, and they did so with joyful alacrity.

Only a couple of days later, however, word reached me that the whole population had again fled to the mountains, after a gunboat had opened fire on some fishermen, killing one of them. I immediately went to Metangula and told Soares de Cruz what had happened. He was clearly distressed by the incident, but felt that it had only happened because the gunboat had not been aware of the establishment of a Zona Neutra at Ngoo. He would go to Ngoo, and, declining to cycle there with me, made arrangements for another gunboat to take him, along with an official called Cláudio.

Cláudio was a fat, pompous man employed by the *psico-sociológica* organization which was, in fact, a department of P.I.D.E. He had recently arrived at Metangula and lived with his wife in a caravan behind Soares de Cruz's house. He was nicknamed by the Africans 'Ka-pipe' because he always had a pipe in his mouth, and I think he rather relished his nickname. He was a jovial person, but I could see that he did not care to have me go with them on their mission of explanation to the people of Ngoo. Soares de Cruz explained to him, however, that their mission would be fruitless unless I went, too, and I agreed to accompany them.

On 1 January 1966, Soares de Cruz, Ka-pipe, and I went in the gunboat up the Lake to Ngoo. We saw no one as we ran the boat on to the sand. My companions obviously were on edge; so I said that I would put on my white cassock and walk along the beach and into the reeds. After fifteen minutes, I came across a youth with some cattle. I told him that I wanted to see Chief Manhica; and that I had some Portuguese with me who wanted to see him, too. The youth led me to the Chief, and I explained that the death of the fisherman had been a mistake, and that the Portuguese wished to apologize. I repeated my fears that the establishment of a Zona Neutra at Ngoo was very risky, but he still insisted that his lands should be properly inhabited again.

'The land' is of deep spiritual importance to Africans, and they are accordingly concerned to keep continuous possession of it.

I returned to the gunboat and told the waiting officials that I would take them to meet the Chief, provided that they came unarmed and attended by only one *cipai*. Chief Manhica and his villagers were very much in command of the situation; and as soon as Soares de Cruz and Ka-pipe realized that there were no Frelimo people about, they relaxed. Everything was discussed and explained, and the Chief and his people were assured that everyone could return to Ngoo without any further risks. I remained doubtful, but the Ngoo people were determined to come to an agreement with the Portuguese. Soares de Cruz, Ka-pipe, and I returned to the gunboat, and we were soon back at Metangula. Later, I regretted that I had had anything to do with the whole affair : but such was the determination of the people at Ngoo to return to their homes, that at the time I felt it impossible to withhold my help.

After all the troubles and tragedies at Ngoo during the previous year, it was quite out of the question to expect any of our employees to accept a posting there again, so I visited Ngoo very frequently myself. My first visit took place within a week, and I stayed for a couple of nights in the house that we had built for Susan Andrew. This was no Zona Neutra such as we had at Messumba, for down on the lakeshore there was a detachment of troops. They had instructions to keep themselves strictly to themselves, but I was told of a number of misdemeanours, especially concerning women. The villagers at Ngoo had had no experience of Europeans apart from missionaries and the occasional Government official. The presence of the Portuguese troops increased my unhappiness about the situation, but the people doggedly refused to join us in Messumba.

I set off on the return journey with Rafael, a Mission employee I had brought with me from Messumba; and as we rounded a corner in the path near Chia, we cycled straight into a group of five Frelimo soldiers. I do not know which of us was the more surprised. Luckily the leader came from Chiwanga and knew me; so it was a cheerful encounter. They told me that they had been to the rice fields to harvest the abandoned crop. We continued on our way, and just after we had crossed the River Fúbuè, those three Harvard bombers appeared and circled overhead. Rafael was very frightened; but I assured him that as I was in a white cassock, they would hardly think that I was a Frelimo soldier. And I tried, similarly, to reassure myself.

On another occasion, I went to Ngoo by naval gunboat, which then went on to Cóbuè before returning to pick me up. It was very late, and the sailors were only interested in returning to Metangula. We boarded the boat in great haste and set out in a storm. The Lake was very rough, and I became seasick. The Commanding Officer kindly lent me his cabin and for company a small book: *The Thoughts of Mao*, in Portuguese, which they had got hold of somewhere. It seemed rather odd to be reading *The Thoughts of Mao* on a Portuguese gunboat in the middle of Lago Niassa, but I found it very interesting. On deck, things were just as interesting, but rather more lively. The sailors had not secured any of our belongings properly; and, among other things, the large tin trunk in which I kept most of the church plate and vestments went overboard. I was very angry; but as a hitch-hiker, and a very seasick one at that, there was little I could do. On most of my subsequent visits to Ngoo, I kept to dry land and my bicycle.

13 Convoys

Although Frelimo did not mine the seven miles of road between Messumba and Metangula after September 1965, it became generally accepted that, elsewhere, roads were always dangerous. The weekly bus service between Vila Cabral and Metangula was discontinued after the bus had been 'warned off' with machine-gun fire earlier in the year. (There had been no casualties.) Army convoys now were the only vehicles on the road, and I nearly always attached myself to one when I wished to drive to Vila Cabral, or beyond. If I had gone independently, and had hit a mine, no help would have been forthcoming, as no one might pass along the deserted road until weeks later. Only when there was no convoy available, and not likely to be one for weeks, did I take a chance and drive to Vila Cabral by myself. As I passed through the 'forts' on the way, the soldiers would stop and stare at me in great surprise and suspicion. Along the road were places ideal for an ambush; and when I came to them, I stopped the car, and walked up the road for a mile or so in my white cassock, to show anyone who might be watching that I was on my own.

Convoys were quite unpredictable. I might be told that one would leave Nova Coimbra at 5 a.m. next morning, and I would be there in good time, only to wait around until it left at mid-day – if it left at all. On one occasion, I was told that a convoy was leaving Metangula at 7 a.m.; but when I got there at 6 a.m., I found that it had left two hours before. I followed at my own risk, the Battalion Commander told me. When I arrived at Vila Cabral, everyone was surprised to see me, and asked me all about the ambush near Maniamba. Apparently there really had been an ambush and in spite of my explanation about the early departure of the convoy, some suspected that I had been warned by Frelimo not to accompany the convoy. But there never was any collusion between Frelimo and myself about using the road, except for the two occasions I have already mentioned (August and September 1965). It was suggested once, unofficially, by Frelimo that we paint our own vehicles white; but as this would have been blatant collusion, I refused. With Reggie in prison, Charles and I were the only drivers, and he sometimes went to Vila Cabral instead of me. On one occasion I was told by Frelimo soldiers that the presence of Charles and the lorry in the convoy had prevented an ambush between Maniamba and Nova Coimbra. So the Portuguese even had some reason to be grateful to us for making use of their convoys.

On other occasions, they – and I – were not so lucky. While we were never ambushed between Messumba and Vila Cabral, a vehicle sometimes hit a mine. The soldiers reacted very violently, even if there were no casualties. They seemed incapable of realizing that this was routine guerrilla warfare. The Portuguese themselves placed 'booby-traps' for Frelimo, especially underneath bridges. Other hazards were the scores of trees that had been felled across the road, and sometimes it took as long as three days for the convoy to reach Vila Cabral from Metangula, so that we would spend the night in our vehicles. The soldiers burnt the villages on both sides of the road, whether or not these were inhabited, and anything they found, such as livestock and furniture, they appropriated. Once, we came across a group of women near Maniamba, who were immediately arrested. They all had passes from the Administrador to go to their fields, but if Padre Menegon and I had not been there, I am sure they would have been shot.

Portugal was continually proclaiming that the situation was well under control. But, in fact, this was far from the case. The Portuguese troops were stationed in 'forts', but outside of these, Frelimo really controlled the whole area. The need to travel in convoy became greater and greater as Frelimo spread farther and farther south, and by 1969 it was accepted that anyone who travelled alone as far as Nova Freixo (250 miles from Messumba) did so at his peril. Many lorries were blown up by landmines.

Travelling in a troop convoy was very frustrating. There were interminable delays when vehicles broke down or had punctures or got stuck in the mud. Sometimes our own vehicles were to blame, and this incensed the already suspicious soldiers. More than once I have been told by a subaltern that if our lorry broke down or got stuck in the mud again, I would be left to fend for myself. Delays at every 'fort' where we had to stop were always long, while the soldiers greeted one another and delivered supplies.

By mid 1965, there was no sign of any African village between Nova Coimbra and Vila Cabral, as they had all been burnt to the ground. At places like Maniamba, were living some villagers who had, for the most part, been 'found' in the mountains and re-settled where they were under the strict control of the Portu-guese authorities. The troops fortified some of the settlers' shops on the road, which they simply took over. At one place, where a Senhor Dias had spent years cultivating coffee, the officer ploughed up all the bushes and planted potatoes instead, since these gave him a quick return with a minimum of effort. Within a few months, the army had undone even the little that the civilians had tried to do during the previous thirty years or more, and this caused very bad feeling between them.

Most of the shopkeepers along the road left when Frelimo became active in the area. But near Unango Mission there were a few potato farmers, who had apparently come to an under-standing with Frelimo that the road between them and Vila Cabral would not be mined, in return for which concession they dropped off a sack or two of potatoes at specified places on each journey that they made to Vila Cabral. Knowing of this, I found it a little galling to reflect on how ill-deserved was our own collaborationist reputation. I never met any Frelimo soldiers anywhere except at Messumba itself, and then we never talked about what day it would be safe to go to Vila Cabral. But often, when Portuguese soldiers saw that Padre Mondine or I was in the convoy, they would say: 'No mines today, chaps, we have missionaries with us!'

The idea of there being any collusion between the Missions and Frelimo persisted even after I hit a mine in the land-rover. At about 8 p.m. on the day after my visit to Ngoo with Soares de

Cruz and Ka-pipe, as I was working in my office, I heard an explosion not far away. We were so used to such noises that I did not think very much about it, until a small group of people came running to tell me that they thought a man had been injured by the explosion. I set off in the land-rover in the darkness and pouring rain, and on the main road between Messumba and Nova Coimbra found an elderly Muslim who lived at the Roman Catholic Mission. He had obviously trodden on a mine and was very badly hurt and in need of immediate surgical treatment; so I put him into the land-rover and drove to the army base at Nova Coimbra, where there was a chance that I might find a doctor. Unfortunately the doctor had left, but the troops gave me a flask of saline and some other drugs, and I drove back to Messumba. As we passed the place where the man had been hurt, the land-rover hit another mine. Luckily it, too, was an anti-personnel mine, but the land-rover was seriously damaged. I was stunned by the explosion for a moment but, very fortunately, not hurt at all. My passenger was still just alive. I jumped out of the land-rover and ran on to Messumba, where I collected Charles and some others to help carry the man to the hospital. But by the time we got back to him, he was dead. We made a rough stretcher and the men carried the corpse to the Roman Catholic Mission. The land-rover was completely out of action, and we had to leave it where it was.

Next morning there was another explosion, and I took Irene with me to see what had happened, in case immediate medical attention was needed. This time an army truck from Nova Coimbra was the victim. About five soldiers had been slightly wounded and all were very frightened. Irene did what she could for them, and then we took the more serious cases in the lorry to battalion headquarters at Metangula. When we came back, we went to have a look at the land-rover, to see if there was any way that we could get it back to Messumba. Beside it we saw the Company Commander of Nova Coimbra shouting at an elderly African to walk all over the area, in order, presumably, to detonate any other landmines. When I protested, he coolly informed me that this man had laid the three mines. The poor old man was just an ordinary villager, and it was quite ludicrous for the Captain to expect me to believe that he had been laying the mines. When I pointed this out, he became embarrassed and tried to ignore me, in spite of the fact that I had just taken his wounded soldiers to Metangula, after having hit a mine myself the previous night. A few days later, some Frelimo soldiers came to see me and told me how sorry they were that the land-rover had been blown up. They had hardly expected anyone to be going along that bit of road during the night.

A few weeks later, I went to Blantyre, intending to fly on from there to Beira and Lourenço Marques; and on the way between Messumba and Maniamba, the lorry got stuck in the mud. In spite of everything that we could do, it only became more firmly embedded. There was nothing for it but to walk to Mani- amba, about ten miles away. On the journey we saw no cars or people, but abundant evidence of war – the usual burnt bridges and, rather surprisingly, hundreds of expended cartridge cases. When my African companion, Rafael, and I walked into the military camp at Maniamba, the troops were staggered to see us and full of eager questions. It was then I learnt that a battle had taken place between them and Frelimo on the previous night. I told them about our lorry and asked if they could come and help pull it out. This they were obviously, and understandably, unwilling to do, as most of them had been up all night, and they were in no mood or condition for another pitched battle with Frelimo. Finally, however, they came and pulled the lorry out of the mud, and Rafael and I continued our journey to Vila Cabral unescorted – which, of course, only added to the troops' suspicion of Messumba.

On arrival at Vila Cabral, Salvado told me that P.I.D.E. had now opened a permanent office there. He advised me to go and pay my respects to Inspector Maia and tell him where I was going, for although I had a passport, Rafael did not. The P.I.D.E. headquarters was housed in what had, until a few years previ- ously, been the town's primary school, and from the outside it looked the same as ever, apart from a brass plate inscribed 'P.I.D.E. – Passports'. And inside it was like any other office. Maia knew who I was (his file on me was, I have no doubt, fairly thick), and when I told him that I wanted permission to take

Rafael with me to Malawi, he said that he would need a passport or, at least, a proper authorization. Either would take a week or two, as photographs, finger-prints and various personal details needed to be produced. I replied that I was not able to spend so long in Vila Cabral and, indeed, was surprised that there should be any difficulty. There had never been any in the past, when I had taken an African employee. 'That's O.K., Padre Paul,' he said. 'If you don't want to cooperate with me, I shall not co-operate with you.' And with a shrug of the shoulders, he walked away. Outside I met a friend who asked what on earth I was doing, talking with 'that brute'. When I explained, he told me that the only authorization that was needed for any African labourer to accompany anyone into Malawi was that of the immigration people at the border-post at Mandimba, who were, in any case, P.I.D.E. agents. I asked various other friends just to make sure, and they all agreed that no authorization was needed from Maia. When I explained all this to Rafael, he said that he was prepared to take the risk. My Vila Cabral friends told me that there was a convoy leaving for Massangulo the following morning, and that it would be most unwise not to join it, as there had been quite a number of ambushes; though the road beyond Massangulo ought to be safe.

The next morning we joined the convoy. The country between Vila Cabral and Massangulo was very fertile and used to be fairly thickly populated. Now, apart from one 'fort', there was no sign of life. All the people's houses had been burnt to the ground, as had a tiny church, one of our outstations. The people responsible for all this devastation were some Portuguese commandos, who had an even worse reputation than the *fusileiros*, and rejoiced in the nickname of 'the Shelltox' (an insecticide which claimed to be the most thoroughly effective killer on the market). Everyone knew of their infamous reputation, but, like most Portuguese soldiers, they were charming to meet off-duty in the Vila Cabral cinema, bars, and cafés.

The stories that people told me in Vila Cabral about 'the Shelltox' were corroborated over and over again by Frelimo soldiers who came from there, some of whom had been to school at Messumba. The commandos would suddenly arrive at a village and start burning the houses and granaries and shooting at any living thing in sight: cows, chickens, goats – and people. Some of their human victims were first captured and then eliminated. But, in any event, by the time that the troops had finished with a village, the only survivors were those who had fled to the hills. Written in charcoal on anything that could be written upon, were obscenities and phrases like 'The Shelltox don't play games.' At Massangulo, the priests told me of a group of some twenty women who had been found on the road by 'the Shelltox'. All except one had been assaulted and then killed. The sole survivor had found refuge on the Mission.

The road beyond Massangulo was considered then to be fairly safe; and, while no military vehicle would risk it alone, some civilians did. In places the road forms the international frontier with Malawi, and all along here were stuck propaganda posters portraying Frelimo leaders 'living it up' in luxury hotels at the expense of those who were supporting the movement. There were other posters depicting the misery suffered by those who followed Frelimo, and the bliss enjoyed by those who remained faithful to Portuguese rule in Mozambique. I had often seen propaganda posters before, since we were frequently given them at Messumba, and sometimes an aeroplane would drop them over the fields, while all administrative secretariats were plastered with them; but never had I seen such a forest of them.

At Mandimba, Rafael found no difficulty whatever in getting permission to cross the Malawi border with me, and my only fear was that he might take this opportunity of running away, which would mean trouble for us all at Messumba when I returned without him. But happily my fears were unfounded. We came across several people in Malawi who had recently fled from Mozambique. All were eager for news, and all had heard that Messumba was the only place of any size in the north where life was still fairly stable. A number of our Yao Christians who had lived near the Malawi border told me that they had managed to escape just before 'the Shelltox' reached their village.

I then flew to Beira, where I stayed a night with a friend who told me that, while things were fairly peaceful there, many of the Nyasas working in the town had been rounded up by

P.I.D.E. and sent he knew not where. He himself had been questioned by the Beira P.I.D.E. For some extraordinary reason, Inspector Lontrão thought that Frelimo and I were using this friend's post-office box as an accommodation address! Lontrão was all too soon to be transferred to Vila Cabral to replace Maia. The P.I.D.E. building in Beira was an innocent-looking, large, detached house in a smart residential quarter of the town; but I later learnt that its outward appearance, as with all P.I.D.E. buildings, belied what went on at the back, and in the cells below ground.

This was my first visit to Beira since Rhodesia's Unilateral Declaration of Independence (U.D.I.) of November 1965, and Britain's blockade of Beira. For us at Messumba, U.D.I. was a matter of only passing interest. We were too busy with our own grave and immediate problems. U.D.I. had no effect whatever on our life at the Mission, except that we found great difficulty in exchanging the Rhodesian money and postal orders that our people working there sent home. The Portuguese press gave it some coverage, but not very much. For there was a clandestine U.D.I. movement among certain whites in Mozambique which was passionately opposed by Lisbon, as hostile to the fundamental concept that Portugal was a pluri-continental nation.

Most Portuguese people I met were in sympathy with the Rhodesian U.D.I., but I think that this was mainly because they disliked the Labour Government in Britain so much. (Generally speaking, the Portuguese disliked white South Africans and Rhodesians, who they felt despised them.)

In Lourenço Marques, where there were plenty of Rhodesian tourists to be seen, I heard more about the Rhodesian situation. I heard from people working in shipping agencies how much they were losing because of sanctions, and certainly the British blockade of the port of Beira was extremely unpopular. In my contacts with members of the diplomatic corps in Mozambique, I heard that the staff at the British Consulate were unpopular, and they declined to attend official parties if Rhodesian representatives were also to be present. There was a story, too, of an over-zealous member of the British Consular staff who was asked to leave Mozambique by the Portuguese authorities for having spied on the trains taking petrol through Mozambique to Rhodesia. Although Beira had been blockaded, Lourenço Marques was not. There was also a loop line from South Africa through Mozambique to Rhodesia which bypassed Lourenço Marques at Moamba.

At Lourenço Marques, I stayed as usual with Bishop Pickard, who told me that Fr Paulo Litumbi was in the Miguel Bombarda Hospital with both legs broken, and I lost no time in going to see him. The Miguel Bombarda occupied a large area, with many vast pavilions, and was considered to be an excellent hospital. I found Fr Litumbi, eventually, in a rather overcrowded and smelly ward, but he assured me that he was being well cared for. This was the story he had to tell:

'I was arrested at our Mission in Vila Cabral a week or two after Black Saturday. I did not know why, as I had had nothing to do with Frelimo since Administrador Simões Carneiro held that *banja* at Messumba in January 1964. I was taken almost immediately to the P.I.D.E. headquarters in Nampula where I found many other prisoners, including most of our teachers. In Nampula we were beaten most terribly with whips, *palmatórios* and even iron bars – I cannot tell you how awful it was. The food was disgusting and we were treated like animals. Most of the people who beat us were Europeans, but there was also a Nyasa, Pedro, from Cóbuè, and he, I think, was the worst. How we didn't die under the beatings, I shall never know. It must have been the Grace of God. I tried to pray for our torturers, as I knew that not all Portuguese people were as evil as they were.

'After a few months, during which we never had any exercise, we were taken to Lumbo on the coast. There we were put aboard a ship. It was night and the police cuffed us as we went up the gang-plank, saying 'Faster! faster!" We didn't know that we were to be thrown straight into the hold of the ship like sacks of flour. I fell and broke both my legs, and without the kind help of my fellow prisoners I would surely have died, but they shared their meagre rations with me during our ten-day journey to Lourenço Marques. A few people died during the voyage, and others, too, broke an arm or a leg as they were pushed into the hold. It was a terrible journey, and when we reached Lourenço

Marques, everyone was taken from the hold. I was unable to move, but luckily my life was spared, and I was brought here where people have been kind to me. I have had an operation, and I hope I may be able to walk again one day, though I suppose I shall have to go to prison when I leave here. Really I've done nothing "subversive", and I thought that my brief connection with Frelimo in 1963 had been forgiven as the Administrador told us so long ago.'

As far as I could make out, few of his fellow prisoners had had even as much to do with Frelimo as he had, and simply had no idea why they had been arrested.

Although I was appalled by his story, I was deeply moved that he was so forgiving. He was clearly a well-liked person in the ward. No one bore him any malice, and the nurses were obviously sympathetic towards such a dedicated Christian.

He told me that he had heard that Reggie, Buanacaia, and Carlos Juma had been flown from Vila Cabral to Lourenço Marques. But he did not know where they were, nor where his fellow passengers from the ship had gone.

I was in a quandary: I knew Inspector Vaz was the head of P.I.D.E. in Mozambique, but Fr Litumbi begged me not to interfere, as, during their brutal interrogations, they had often been asked about me. He felt that if I was to make a fuss with P.I.D.E., those who were still prisoners would suffer even more than they had done already. I was very angry about all this, not least because we had done all we could to come to some sort of *modus vivendi* with the Portuguese. But it appeared that anyone, especially missionaries, who was working with or for Africans, was now in exactly the same position as myself.

During my few remaining days in Lourenço Marques, I visited him every day. He had several visits from Anglicans working in Lourenço Marques, but not unnaturally they were a little apprehensive about seeing him, in case they themselves should fall under the suspicion of P.I.D.E.

When I reached Blantyre on my return to Messumba, I was thankful to find that Rafael had not disappeared. He told me that Henrique Calumbaine (the Frelimo Commander 'Catarina' of Chia) was in Blantyre Hospital, so I went to visit him. He had been totally blinded in some bombing raid that the Portuguese had made near his base, but otherwise had escaped injury. He told me that the only other casualties had been civilians. He had somehow escaped to Malawi, where he still is today.

I crossed back into Mozambique at Mandimba as usual, and spent the night at Massangulo Mission, since I heard there was a convoy leaving for Vila Cabral on the following day. The missionaries told me that life was being made increasingly difficult for them by the presence of Frelimo near by, and by a company of Portuguese troops stationed uncomfortably near the Mission. Many villagers had fled to the Mission for protection; though not in such numbers as at Messumba, since Malawi was so near, and many had fled across the frontier when 'the Shell-tox' began their campaign of terror.

The following morning, I experienced my first and only ambush. The convoy was about fifteen miles north of Massangulo when we were fired upon from a hill. We jumped out of our vehicles and lay in the ditch – much to the detriment of my white cassock. I think Frelimo only fired a couple of shots to scare the troops; but the troops fired mortars and rifles for about half an hour, before the convoy continued on its way to Vila Cabral. Several soldiers maintained that the only reason Frelimo had stopped was because they could see that one of their missionary friends was in the convoy.

Near Maniamba, the trucks detonated two or three mines which considerably damaged the vehicles concerned, but happily no one was injured. However, as emergency repairs had to be carried out, we spent the night there. Rafael and I went for a walk; but as we found numerous Frelimo footprints, we returned to the land-rover rather quickly. Next morning, as we left, one of the Africans who had 'hitched' a lift on a lorry asked the driver to stop because he had left his jacket behind, hanging on the branch of a tree. As he ran to retrieve it, he stepped on a mine. His foot was practically blown off and dangled by a piece of skin from his ankle. He was unconscious, but a medical orderly gave him a shot of morphia and tied a tourniquet on his leg. Then a young officer came up and, with a penknife, severed the foot. He put the man into a jeep and took him the ten miles or so to Maniamba, from where he was flown to Vila Cabral hospital. He recovered, and I met him later on several occasions.

At Maniamba, I met Padre Menegon, who told me that Padre Mondine had been transferred from Nova Coimbra to Unango, and that within a week of his arrival the Mission lorry had been ambushed. Padre Mondine had been blinded in one eye and would shortly be returning to Italy. Unango Mission had never been popular with anyone, and it was accordingly no surprise to me to hear that a lorry from there had been ambushed. But Frelimo obviously could have had no idea that Padre Mondine, who had only just arrived there, was in it.

Padre Menegon, with another priest, was waiting at Maniamba to catch a convoy for Metangula; but because of the mines between Vila Cabral and Maniamba, and the time it had taken, the officer-in-command said that they would return to Vila Cabral the next day, and not go on to Metangula, after all. I suggested to the priests (the second was Padre Mário Tellusi, newly come to Nova Coimbra) that we take a chance and go from Maniamba on our own. I was already much later than I had intended to be and did not want further delay. Padre Menegon said that he would follow half an hour behind me, and the Administrador, on hearing our plan, said that he would follow an hour or so after Padre Menegon; as, if there were any mines on the road, the chances were that one or other of us would have detonated them first. My journey home was quite uneventful, but the troops at Nova Coimbra were deeply suspicious of me as I called in with their mail and a note from the convoy commander explaining why he was not proceeding farther than Maniamba.

Padre Menegon and Padre Mário left Maniamba as planned, and halfway down the escarpment were machine-gunned. Padre Menegon was wounded in the foot. Padre Mário jumped out in his white cassock and shouted: 'What in the hell do you think you are doing ambushing a Mission car? Where's your boss?' After a few moments, two or three extremely penitent Frelimo soldiers appeared: 'We are terribly sorry, Senhor Padre, but we thought it was the Administrador. Please forgive us, but we are new to this area.' Padre Mário got back into the land-rover (which was, unfortunately, identical to that of the Administrador), and drove with all haste to Metangula, where Padre Menegon was flown back to Vila Cabral. After a week or two in hospital, he recovered.

I watched the casualty list grow during the first few months of 1966 with some concern: I had hit a mine very near to Messumba; Padre Mondine had been blinded as the result of an ambush, and now Padre Menegon had been injured in this latest ambush. Of course, I realized that we were taking risks because of the landmines, but I was alarmed that three of these should have been placed so very near Messumba, and that two Mission vehicles had been ambushed. Did Frelimo really wish us, too, to leave Mozambique? I decided that my best course was to talk about the subject in church, since what I said there would be bound, somehow, to reach Frelimo ears. So, from the pulpit the next Sunday, I explained that if the people did not want the Missions to close down, then Frelimo must exercise more discretion. My words bore fruit, for we were not ambushed or mined again during the rest of my time at Messumba, and my Frelimo visitors made it plain that they did not want us to withdraw.

14 The Army Takes Over

Rivalry between the armed services of any country is common, and so are contrary opinions between the civil and military authorities. In Mozambique, the situation was aggravated by the total lack of consistent policy from one official (whether civil or military) to his successor.

Five or six months after the setting up of the Zona Neutra at Messumba, Lieutenant-Colonel Damião was appointed Battalion Commander at Metangula. The battalion had companies stationed at Nova Coimbra, Maniamba, and at Lunho (near Mpochi). Damião was a militarist and viewed the whole of his area as a battleground. He had little use for civilians and regarded all missionaries as enemies. On one occasion, Damião remarked to Padre Scotini, a Brazilian priest who had just arrived at Nova Coimbra, how strange it was that Mission vehicles never hit landmines. Padre Scotini replied: 'Padre Paul has hit a landmine, and I hope that, if ever I hit one, you will be with me and that it will be on your side of the car.' Only a Portuguese or a Brazilian could have got away with such a remark.

Damião told me frankly that he considered Messumba clearly sympathetic to Frelimo, as he knew we entertained Frelimo soldiers from time to time. I told him that we had no option; and if he wished to stop Frelimo from coming into the Zona Neutra, he had better post guards outside the area. He said that he had never heard of anything so preposterous as a Zona Neutra, and asked how I dared declare part of Portugal to be neutral in this patriotic war. I told him that the whole idea was Soares de Cruz's. Within a few weeks, Damião had pulled down all the 'Zona Neutra' signs, much to the consternation of the villagers who had found refuge within the area. When I protested to Soares de Cruz, he preferred to know nothing about the whole subject, and very soon afterwards he was transferred else-where.

One day not long after this, when I was in Vila Cabral, Damião told me complacently that on my return to Messumba, I would find a platoon of soldiers billeted on the Mission, who would ensure that all collusion ceased between Frelimo and ourselves. (The Roman Catholic Mission near Nova Coimbra had also had some soldiers thrust upon them.) When I returned to the Mission that night, I discovered that the soldiers had taken over Joan Antcliff's house right in the middle of the Mission. This seemed to me to be quite the wrong place: if Damião wished to stop Frelimo from coming into the area, he should have placed the troops outside the Mission. Most of Joan's belongings were still in her house, as she had taken little with her; so Irene and I salvaged what we could. But by then a lot of damage had been done, and many of her things had been turned out by the soldiers. This was hardly an auspicious beginning to our association with the subaltern and fifteen soldiers billeted on the Mission, and I could see that it would not be long before there was serious trouble.

The young subaltern commanding our 'protectors' was quite a pleasant person and did all he could to see that his soldiers disturbed the work of the Mission as little as possible. After the first few days, they stopped walking around the place with their guns and became more relaxed, and we were glad that they kept themselves to themselves. At night they occasionally went on patrol, but most of the time hung around Joan's old house. Their officer told me that his soldiers had been amazed to find so many people apparently living quite peacefully. They were even a little shy because some of them were illiterate, and here, on a foreign Mission, nearly everyone could read and write. When we had our annual school sports, with much singing of African songs, the soldiers were delighted with it all and said that if I took a group of the children to Portugal to perform, they would get a full house wherever they went.

The troops seldom left the Mission; but early on in their stay, other units of the army staged two ambushes in the area. The first was near Matenje, when some troops from Nova Coimbra shot and killed a Frelimo soldier; the second near Mónduè, where the *fusileiros* told me that they had killed two soldiers from a group of three. When I went down there next morning to look for the dead, I found only one corpse, that of a middle-aged villager.

Messumba was shortly afterwards honoured by a visit from the Commander-in-Chief of Mozambique, General Carasco. He had told me sometime earlier that he would come when he was next at Nova Coimbra, but no definite arrangements had been made for a particular day. The General arrived about midday with an enormous convoy of army lorries. They pulled up outside my house; and all the soldiers, fully armed, jumped off and took up positions round the centre of the Mission, as the General and his two aides-de-camp came to greet me and tell me they had come to lunch. This was one of those times when Irene's housekeeping talent rose so nobly to the occasion. The General sent all the soldiers, except his two aides, back to Nova Coimbra, telling them that he knew he would be quite safe 'in the company of Padre Paul'! The Company Commander, looking like a bullfrog in enormous goggles, was clearly sceptical and begged his General not to dismiss his guard in such hostile country; but the General replied by simply ordering him off the Mission.

Lunch was a ceremonious meal – and an interminable one, as the General chose to make a speech for nearly two hours, all about the glories of Portugal and the advantages which her rule had brought to Mozambique and which wicked bandits were now trying to destroy. The General's aides became slightly overcome by the whisky that they had drunk before the meal and very wisely, I thought, on a number of counts, went off for a walk. Charles dozed uncomfortably in his chair, and Irene hardly understood a word; many times, to my envy, she was called down to the hospital, and so managed to miss a good bit of it. Eventually a pause occurred, at which I hastily suggested to the General that he might like to see where the troops were billeted on the Mission. He agreed, and we went off to Joan's house; passing on the way his two aides, who had nodded off as they sat on the bench outside my office. The troops sprang to attention as we approached, and at the same time the convoy and Captain 'Frog' reappeared to collect their General. The latter once more became quite cross, repeating that he was with friends, and sent them to Nova Coimbra again! It was another hour before he would let the troops on the Mission escort him back to Nova Coimbra.

When Irene went on her furlough soon after this, she was replaced by another English nurse, Pearl Maskelyne. Pearl and Irene were different in so many ways, but both were excellent and dedicated nurses. Indeed, very soon after her arrival, Pearl had a grim opportunity to prove her worth.

Shortly after 8 p.m. on an evening in May 1966, we heard the noise of rifle fire and explosions very close. Since the troops had come to the Mission, we had grown quite used to the occasional firing of shots from their quarters, but this was something quite different. I went over to the *mezane* to get Charles, but he did not think that anything serious was happening, and the noise soon stopped. I was on the point of returning to my house when the officer in charge of the troops came hurrying up to us, very worried: 'Senhor Padre, we've just had to storm one of your classroom blocks, as we heard there were some Frelimo soldiers there. I don't know if we got any, but there are some dead, and my soldiers are bringing along the wounded to the hospital.' (The block of classrooms he spoke of was being used by refugees from Chiwanga and elsewhere, of whom I had a complete list in my house.)

As we went quickly towards the hospital, we saw a group of people carrying the casualties. Pearl was just tidying up for the day. When she saw the casualties, she ordered everyone but her two remaining assistants out of the building, and immediately set about treating the alleged Frelimo soldiers: Bonomali, a thirteen-year-old schoolboy and the son of one of our builders; António Mtambo, a seventeen-year-old trainee nursing orderly; Jaime Chipungu, who had been taken on Black Saturday and employed as a 'mine-detector' and porter before being released from Nova Coimbra. There were also two or three village people with minor injuries. A Portuguese soldier had a graze on his hand which Pearl covered with a piece of plaster. The Africans who had helped bring the injured men and boys along were in a state of great shock and fear, so I sent them along to my house to wait for me there, while Charles and I went down to the classroom where the attack had taken place.

A scene of unbelievable chaos met us, with broken doors and windows and furniture, and four bodies. By the faint light of the moon, it was a nightmarish picture. We covered the corpses with blankets and returned to my house. We did not go to tell the relatives of the dead then, as they would have been far too frightened to come from their villages.

I told the shocked and terrified survivors that they could sleep in my house for the night. There were no beds for the twenty or so people, all men that I knew well, so that they had to sleep on the floors of the various rooms. I asked them what had happened and they told me they had been chatting peacefully in their temporary home before going to bed when they heard soldiers shouting at them to come out. They were too terrified to move, and the soldiers opened fire and hurled grenades into the building. The men assured me that there had been no Frelimo people there at all.

When I had got them settled down, I went outside and found the officer waiting on my verandah. I asked him why he and his men had done this horrible thing. He had the decency to be very apologetic and said that he had acted on false information. If there was anything he could do to help me, he would be glad to do so. He asked me why the people had not come out of the classroom with their hands up, as he and his men had shouted at them to do. I told him that, quite apart from the fact that they did not know enough Portuguese to understand what was being shouted at them, all troops had a terrible reputation among Africans, whose immediate reaction to the shouting would have been to panic. He could not seem to grasp that village Africans are not brought up on 'cowboys and indians', and so have no idea that on such an occasion you are expected to file out quietly with your hands up.

Next morning I had to break the news to the relatives of the four dead: Dunstan, a simple soul, partly crippled, who did odd labouring jobs for the Mission; Benedito Cantinte, who had just left school and was filling in time working in the *mezane* kitchen (in fact it was he who had prepared our meal on the evening he was killed); Jaime Chatupa, who, like António Mtambo, was a trainee nursing orderly; and a cripple, who spent most of his days hobbling round the villages on a crab foot.

Amid the wailing of the bereaved, the graves were dug, and we prepared to bury the dead before nightfall. The soldiers kept very quiet, staying in their house all day, and none went near them.

During the morning I received a note from Barnabé Mbuna, who slept in the same classroom block and who worked in my office. He had not turned up that morning and his letter apologized for this, saying that he had managed to escape during the confusion, and was far too frightened to leave the house where he was now hiding.

I went to the house and found Barnabé still trembling with fear and shock. He asked how many dead and wounded there were. Like everyone else, he had panicked when he heard the Portuguese shouting outside. He had managed to escape out of a window through which a grenade had just been hurled. I tried to quieten him down and told him I thought it would be best for him to come to the hospital where he could receive treatment. Very reluctantly, because his instinct was to remain hidden, he came with me and was admitted into the ward where the wounded men were being treated.

Late that same afternoon, as I was leaving the cemetery after the burials, I saw about eight Portuguese men coming towards me and was horrified to recognize two of them as P.I.D.E. agents. I knew we were in for trouble. They asked me if I knew the dead personally, so I gave them their names. They then told me that Frelimo had definitely been in the classroom block the previous night and that it was just unfortunate that they had all escaped while others had been killed and wounded. I told them that Frelimo had never been in the classroom block; since not only had all the men who had been there told me so, but the officer and his soldiers had admitted, in so many words, that they had made a mistake. The men from P.I.D.E. then insisted that they had ample evidence that the soldiers had been fired upon from the building. This was the first I had heard of this, and I told them it was nonsense. 'Why then do you think that one of the soldiers has been wounded in the hand?' they asked. One of the soldiers had sustained a very superficial injury, but I naturally assumed this to have been caused by a piece of broken glass or something. The P.I.D.E. agents then showed me a rifle that had a hole in the stock, which *might* have been a bullet hole. 'If you don't believe Frelimo were there, how do you account for that?' they asked triumphantly. It is always useless to argue with P.I.D.E., and sometimes one needs the mind of a Lewis Carroll to follow the workings of theirs.

The P.I.D.E. agents wanted to see the wounded, which I took to mean they were seeking further evidence that Frelimo had been around the previous night. They showed little interest in the wounded, but spent some time by poor Barnabé's bed. A doctor in the party agreed with Pearl that two of the men who were seriously wounded should be taken to the hospital in Metangula. P.I.D.E. told the doctor that they thought Barnabé should be taken there as well. At this suggestion, Pearl protested vigorously, maintaining that he would be far better left at Messumba to get over his shock. But they were insistent, and once again I felt myself to be a traitor: if I had not persuaded Barnabé to leave the house where he had been safely hiding, this would never have happened. Short of physical violence, there was nothing that I could do now. I was conscious of my utter helplessness in the face of the Portuguese machine.

The following day, I went to Metangula to try to rescue Barnabé, but he had already been taken to Vila Cabral; and in spite of my repeated requests to be allowed to visit him, I did not see him again until he returned to Messumba several months later. Apparently he had been roughed up by the P.I.D.E. officials until he was forced to say that Frelimo soldiers had been with them that evening. He was kept in one of the cells behind the P.I.D.E. building in Vila Cabral, where, like the other prisoners, he was treated as an animal. He knew that his arrest was none of my doing, and never bore me any ill-will.

In June of that year, Charles left Messumba and returned to

England a few weeks later. We were all sorry to see him go. I was particularly sad, as his experience and courage had been a great support during his time at Messumba.

15 Rivalries

At about the same time as Damião became Battalion Commander at Metangula, António Brasão de Silva was appointed Administrador at Maniamba. And very soon after his arrival, there were many administrative changes, one of which was that Metangula became the administrative headquarters, instead of Maniamba, so that Brasão de Silva moved there.

There were also many changes of nomenclature. Chefes do Posto had become Administradores do Posto; the 'circunscrição de Maniamba' became the 'circunscrição do Lago'; cipais were called milícias; Metangula was now called Augusto Cardoso*; and, coincidentally, the slang for Frelimo came to be 'turras'.

On my first visit to Brasão de Silva, he spoke to me in good English, and showed me, with considerable pride, a photograph of his father with some member of the British royal family. He also said that he was not in the least bit frightened of Frelimo. 'Why, then,' I asked him, 'do you have an automatic pistol on your desk?' He replied: 'Well, you don't think I'm a fool do you?' He was clearly disposed to be very friendly, and we talked as equals.

He seemed to be trying to present the appearance of a cultured person, and the woman who lived with him had been an art teacher in Portugal. For an Administrador to live in an official house with a woman who was not his wife was, of course, very irregular, but when I asked my friends why a blind eye was turned to this particular case, I was told: 'It's extremely difficult to get anyone to take the job at Metangula because of all the complications with the army and navy, so the Government has to take anyone who was willing to come.'

Brasão de Silva had frequent disagreements with the military

* See note on p. 18.

authorities, partly because he was something of a 'frustrated soldier' himself. A short time after his arrival, the troops at Messumba were replaced by *milicias*, who were not just *cipais* but a sort of para-military force under his command. He did not want the army occupying what were civilian areas, and this became general policy. It was, in theory, a sensible change, as the Administrador, and not the military commander, was in charge of civilian affairs.

Joan's house was now occupied by about fifteen African *milicias*, some of whom were nothing more than toughs. Others had been Frelimo associates who were tired of waiting for Frelimo to win the war, and had come to Metangula, where they were drafted into this para-military force. We had not only Nyasas among them, but also Yaos and Macuas. Many could not read or write, but they were paid the same salary as our middle-ranking teachers. They were told that if they did not behave, I would report them to the Administrador – and they were certainly troublesome.

On the first Sunday after their arrival, in accordance with the Administrador's orders, they paraded for the customary hoisting of the national flag. As usual, we were all grouped round the flag-pole, and up 'marched' the *milicias*, resembling nothing so much as the local 'Dad's Army'. Most of them had no idea about drill, and few knew their left from their right. They scuffled into position to the sniggers of the schoolchildren, and when the ceremony was over they all turned in different directions as they were dismissed. Everyone roared with laughter, and I do not remember them ever again taking part in the ceremony – except as observers.

On Saturdays and Sundays, there was usually beer to be had in the villages. The *milicias*, with so much more money in their pockets than most people, took advantage of the ready sale of drink, and many returned to the Mission completely drunk. Some became aggressive in their cups and asked people for their *cartões de identidade*. The frightened villagers would hand these over, and be dismayed to see them torn in half. The unhappy possessors, tied by the hands, would then be brought back to the Mission. Many I had to rescue as they were led by a rope to the *milícias'* house. Once I was able to retrieve a torn-up *cartão*, and on the following day took the *cartão* and its owner to Metangula. Brasão de Silva now had absolute proof of the things that I had complained about. The offending *milícia* was duly punished, but there was little improvement in the behaviour of our guards.

One Saturday, some people came running to complain that two *milícias* were drunk in their village and were being extremely offensive. I went to the village and reprimanded the offenders, one of whom was a Nyasa, and the other a Macua. The Nyasa agreed to return with me to the Mission, but the Macua refused. At this point, Brasão de Silva turned up unexpectedly and asked me what all the noise was about in the village below. When I explained what had happened, he promptly went off and arrested the drunk Macua and brought him up to the Mission. Then he called the drunk Nyasa and, shouting at him, asked why he had obeyed me and returned to the Mission, while the Macua had not. The Nyasa explained that all Nyasas knew 'Padre Paul' and did what he said, but Macuas were strangers in the place. Brasão de Silva ordered the Nyasa to slap the Macua on the face repeatedly, crying 'Harder! harder!' I nearly broke down myself before this brutality, which I had no power to prevent, and walked off. I think the man must have been slapped in the face about fifty times. Eventually Brasão de Silva left with the battered Macua as a prisoner. The Nyasa begged to be taken too, as he feared the consequences to himself from his fellows, but the Administrador refused.

Next morning, I asked the *milícia*-in-charge, himself a Macua, to come and see me, together with another Macua and the Nyasa who had been involved in the incident. The Macua in charge was very upset by the whole incident but extremely understanding both of my position and the whole attitude of the authorities. He said that what had happened had been typical of the Portuguese, who always sought to set one tribe against the other. Indeed, I found most of the *milícias* reasonable.

Soon after this, dissension was aggravated, when Damião sent three of his soldiers to live in the same house as the *milícias*. This move, predictably, produced total confusion. Caught be-

tween the army and the civil adminstration, no one ever knew
who was in charge at Messumba.

Bishop Pickard came to see us shortly after this, and, on his
return to Vila Cabral, Brasão de Silva invited him to spend a
night at his house, as he would then be on the spot to take the
plane early the next morning. I drove the Bishop to Metangula,
where I also dined with the Administrador. He had previously
given orders that a *milícia* accompany us to Metangula, but the
man never turned up, so that Bishop Pickard and I arrived unescorted. Brasão de Silva was very angry and said that on my
return I must take Erasto, an African I knew well, who would
bring the *milícias* to order. After dinner, therefore, I left Metangula with Erasto keenly on the alert beside me, pointing his
sub-machine gun out of the land-rover. When we had gone a few
hundred yards, I told him not to be such an ass, and we stopped
for a swim in the lake. Erasto suddenly said: 'Senhor Padre,
look, there are some headlights of a car.' We got hastily back into
the land-rover and drove to Messumba, just ahead of the other
vehicle. This contained, we found, Brasão de Silva's *aspirante*,
who had been sent to withdraw all the *milícias* from Messumba
and bring them back to Metangula as a punishment for not
having sent one of their number to accompany the Bishop. It
was midnight by this time, but all the *milícias* had to pack their
belongings and leave. The three Portuguese soldiers who were
left were so frightened at being alone that I let them spend the
night in my house.

There must have been a tremendous row between the Administrador and the army in Metangula as a result of all this, for the
milícias never returned, and in their stead a platoon under the
command of a sergeant was posted to the Mission. This remained
the position for the rest of my stay in Mozambique.

These sergeants were in fact *furieis* – that is, conscript sergeants, and most were very pleasant people. As conscripts, like
their subordinates, they were divided in their attitude to the
war: one section thought all this soldiering in Africa was an attempt to defend an unrealistic and therefore pointless situation;
the other section held the official view, that Mozambique was
Portugal and would remain so even if it meant killing all the

Africans there. Consequently, although I may, in instancing the shocking things that happened, have given the impression that all Portuguese soldiers behaved like brutes, this was by no means the case. Many had been caught up in the system most unwillingly, but had accepted the situation in fear of the ever-present P.I.D.E. informers.

A *furiel* usually had two corporals and ten soldiers under him, and the detachment often had a couple of African 'prisoners' (sometimes ex-Frelimo soldiers) with it. The soldiers attracted a number of schoolchildren to them, since these could earn a few escudos by doing odd jobs. This had its disadvantages, especially if the *furiel* for the month was uncooperative with the Mission. Children would absent themselves from lessons, fail to return home at night, and insult their teachers (whom the soldiers often referred to as a bunch of *turras* in front of the children). They also picked up a mass of Portuguese slang and pornography, and sometimes I heard of homosexual practices which were anathema to the ordinary village Nyasa. But, most dangerous of all, the children would often accompany the troops on their journeys to Nova Coimbra and Metangula, where there was always the danger of an ambush. The soldiers, however, regarded the children as a form of insurance against such attacks. The Portuguese peasant, who formed the great mass of the army, usually came from a large extended family, and so was delighted to have children around him. The fact that they were black and yet could speak Portuguese appealed to him, and I am sure that Portuguese military intelligence benefited greatly from the children's difficulty in keeping secrets. I felt that the juxtaposition of the soldiers and the children was unhealthy in every way.

The time-consuming and potentially dangerous troop convoys to Vila Cabral became less and less frequent, because other ways were found of obtaining their requirements. Meponda (Porto Arroio), only thirty miles from Vila Cabral, was now firmly established as a port, and it was both easier and safer to send supplies there and then take them by landing craft to Metangula. Meponda also came to have another significance which the Portuguese did their best to conceal. Across the Lake is the Malawi port of Chipoka, and the railway line from there goes directly south to Beira. This Meponda–Chipoka crossing was in constant use, especially for transporting fuel to the naval and military establishments in Metangula. In this way, there was no risk of tankers and lorries laden with drums of fuel hitting landmines. Without the cooperation of the Malawi Government, the military situation at Metangula might have been very different.

A large boat, painted green, would leave Metangula for Meponda, where the crew would change into civilian clothes before making the comparatively short trip across the Lake to Chipoka. They would return by the same route with fuel which had been brought by rail from Beira. The sailors who went on these trips would also buy things like fishing nets and clothing which were cheaper and of better quality than any available in Metangula, and then sell them to the local Africans at grossly inflated prices.

We at Messumba, however, were not able to use this new means of transport – in fact, we were not supposed to know anything about it. As troop convoys became infrequent, I sometimes spent as much as three weeks in Vila Cabral waiting to return to the Mission. This was not only boring and time-wasting, but frustrating, as there was so much to do at home. Sometimes I stayed with friends, sometimes at the hotel, and every evening would go to the barracks to ask if there was a convoy leaving next day. At that time the only aeroplanes that flew to Metangula were military ones, and naturally they did not welcome civilian hitch-hikers. There was also the problem of getting the Mission lorry back to Messumba, if I flew. On occasions I was able to come to an agreement with someone to drive the lorry back in the next convoy while I went by plane, but this was rarely satisfactory. Once I found a driver who agreed to do this for what was, to us, a great deal of money. When the convoy stopped for the night at a 'fort', he became very drunk and turned on the headlights. Whereupon the soldiers dragged him from the lorry and beat him up, calling him and his assistants *turras*. When he finally arrived at the Mission, he was badly bruised, and many of the things on the lorry had been stolen by the troops who had said that a Messumba lorry must be a Frelimo lorry. There was nothing I could do, apart from complaining to Brasão de Silva, as the 'fort' was forty miles away, and I only had the word of a man who had been drunk at the time.

Vila Cabral bore little resemblance to the quiet, dusty, slow-moving place that it had previously been. It was now a garrison town, bustling with activity. Our outstation was only a few miles away, and whenever I was in Vila Cabral I tried to help out with services, as the priest-in-charge there was both elderly and often away visiting other villages. When I was staying with friends in the town during one of my long waits for a convoy, it was agreed that I would say Mass for him the following morning at 6 o'clock. At about 4.30 a.m., I was awakened by gunfire which was more sustained than usual. Having, at Messumba, become quite used to this sort of thing, however, I set out for the church, rather to the alarm of my friends. As I drove out of town, I realized that the shots were being fired uncomfortably close, so I reluctantly turned the land-rover round, and returned to my anxious friends. By the time that the gunfire ceased, it was too late to hold a service, since the people would be off to work.

At about 8 o'clock, two men turned up at the house to tell me that Inspector Lontrão, who had just been transferred to Vila Cabral from Beira, wanted to see me. When I asked if 10 o'clock would be convenient, they said that I must accompany them right away. I put on a jacket and went off in the police land-rover, sandwiched between the two men, to the P.I.D.E. headquarters. I hung around for about half an hour until Lontrão arrived and then went into his office, where we were alone. At first, he pretended he did not know who I was, asking me to what Mission I belonged, and obviously not realizing that my Beira friend had already reported P.I.D.E. conversations about me. He asked me what I was doing out early that morning when there was gunfire, and I told him. He asked me if I had anyone, apart from Africans, who could back up my statement that I had intended to go to the outstation. I told him that not only my hosts, but also Padre Piquito had known of my intention. This seemed to satisfy him, though he did not seem to be certain who Padre Piquito was.

Lontrão then asked me what I meant by referring to European policemen in derogatory terms: did I not realize that he was one? When I said that I did not know what he was talking about, to my horror he produced a file of all the letters I had written to Brasão de Silva, including some complaining about the behaviour of some policemen who had been stationed by him at Mónduè. I told him that Brasão de Silva had asked me to be frank with him, so I had been – very frank! I felt a fool for having been so naïve as not to realize that he would pass my letters on to P.I.D.E.

His next question: 'What is all this money for, that you have received from Geneva?' – indicated that he had been investigating our bank account, or my letters to the World Council of Churches, or both. I told him that it was to buy food and blankets for the many refugees living on the Mission.

Lontrão went on: 'Padre Paul, we know you have been at Messumba several years, that the Nyasas trust you and that you know them well. Will you please tell me who are the Frelimo informers on your Mission?' I told him quite honestly that I had no idea who they might be. Anyway I would consider it no part of my business to tell him, even if I did happen to know that there were any, or who they were. He then said: 'So *you* don't know, you who know your people so well! It's funny, isn't it, that we know who the Frelimo informers are at your Mission.' I replied: 'Well, if you know, why do you ask me?' Changing the subject, he asked me where Chizoma was, and I told him that he was on the Mission. He then hinted something about the senior nursing orderly, but I could not make out what he meant.

I was back with my hosts within a couple of hours, thanks to my white skin and that invaluable British passport. It would, I knew, have been quite a different story if I had been an African. My friends said that they had been very worried. If I had not returned by noon, they would have brought my lunch along to me; and, such was the fearful reputation of P.I.D.E., would have contacted the British Consul-General.

In the months to come I often saw Lontrão at the hotel, and he would always take me on one side, asking questions to which I usually gave no answer, unless it was 'I don't know', which might even have been true. He did not look like anyone's idea of a secret-police interrogator, but his looks belied the terrible things he did, directly and indirectly. The people who died under torture would be taken from the building in the very early hours of the morning and dumped some five miles outside the town. Padre Menegon told me that a tractor-driver had come across some of the corpses one day when ploughing.

One day I met in Vila Cabral an ex-college student who had been a Frelimo soldier. Coming up to me quite openly, he said that he had been captured and handed over to Lontrão, who had received him very well. This was typical of P.I.D.E.'s attitude to Frelimo militants who were taken prisoner or surrendered: they were usually treated fairly well, and then became either P.I.D.E. informers or *milícias*. The people who were tortured or killed were in general ordinary villagers who could not be made use of. This particular lad spent the whole afternoon with me, helping me to load the lorry and so on, but he was very frank with me, and asked no questions. (Several months later an aeroplane dropped hundreds of anti-Frelimo leaflets over Messumba, bearing his picture and a signed letter from him, and our Escola Técnica students told me that they were always very wary of him.) About a year after our encounter he was killed. He had been taken by some soldiers as a guide to seek out Frelimo bases; and after walking for days and finding nothing, the soldiers shot him, telling P.I.D.E. when they returned to Vila Cabral that they had run into a powerful Frelimo unit and had had to retire, their guide 'unfortunately' being killed in the skirmish. I learned this later through one of the soldiers who had been on the exercise and was outraged at this blatant murder by his comrades.

Although there were now troops stationed on the Mission itself, and there were *milícias* at Mónduè, this did not stop Frelimo soldiers from coming to Messumba, though they usually came in civilian clothes, and their visits were far less frequent. On 31 December 1966, on my return from Mónduè one evening, a man called Kishindo, whom I knew to have been a Frelimo soldier or associate, stopped me and said that he wished to leave Frelimo and live at Messumba. I told him that, as a newcomer, he would have to present himself to the authorities and be registered as a resident. He was very frightened at the thought of encountering 'authority', but I promised to take him to Metangula myself the following morning. I told him I was sure the Administrador would be delighted to receive a Frelimo deserter. Brasão de Silva was not in his office the next morning, New Year's Day, and I eventually found him in a huge crowd assembled outside the battalion headquarters, where the new Governor (Costa Matos' successor) was handing out gifts of clothing to the assembled villagers. I whispered to Brasão de Silva that I had a Frelimo soldier in the car, whereupon he left the crowd, almost ran to the land-rover and embraced Kishindo. As I had foreseen, he was very pleased with Kishindo, who soon found himself working as a junior clerk in the secretariat.

Unfortunately, the new Governor had not been so busy with his handing out of gifts that he missed seeing me, and on my next visit to Metangula, the Administrador told me that the Governor had considered himself insulted because I had not gone up to pay my respects to him. I excused myself as best I could, pointing out that my mind was occupied with Kishindo's problem and that the Governor was obviously engaged in his New Year's Day presentations. And anyway I was not suitably dressed for a ceremonious occasion (a very important consideration with the formal Portuguese). However, on Brasão de Silva's urgent advice, and realizing the prudence of it, I wrote a letter of apology to the Governor. This, in fact, turned out to have been wise, as relations between the new Governor and myself were thereafter always friendly. Although he was a Lieutenant-Colonel in the army, he was far less of a militarist than Costa Matos had been, and more of an administrator.

What I feared would happen occurred early in 1967: Frelimo attacked the troops at the Mission in the middle of the night. The troops were stationed less than a hundred yards from my house, with only the church between us, so that I was soon roused by the firing of mortars just outside my bedroom window. At dawn, I went to the troops, and was relieved to find that there had been no casualties. The house had received some damage, and, though four of the windows of the church had been blown out, it had suffered no further hurt. The *furiel* told me that he thought there were probably some dead or wounded *turras*, but that his troops had been too frightened to investigate

Mozambique: Memoirs of a Revolution

during the night. They were still frightened on account of booby-traps, so I went by myself to the place from which the attack had been made. I found no sign of anyone, but I did find some light arms and ammunition which I brought up to the soldiers. During the course of the morning, Fr João Sululu handed me a note which, he said, he had been told to hand me the night before, but he had been too frightened to do so. It warned me that Frelimo would attack the troops that night and instructed me not to leave my house during the attack as they did not wish to shoot me by mistake.

The situation at Ngoo, as I had expected, deteriorated rapidly. Ngoo was administratively in the Cóbuè area, and shortly after the people's return to their village at the beginning of 1966, a new Chefe (now Administrador) do Posto was appointed to Cóbuè. He was a black man from the Cape Verde Islands, and had obviously been placed at Cóbuè because of the colour of his skin and the need to demonstrate the theory that in Mozambique there was no colour-bar.

After Portuguese colonial oppression had been so obviously brought to the world's attention by the events of 1961, Portugal had started re-settling Cape Verdeans in Mozambique, and the Cape Verdeans were very ready to leave their poverty- and drought-stricken islands. The blood of many races ran in their veins, but their language was Portuguese. At home, they had been terribly oppressed, and now in Mozambique they were given the chance to be masters. Some, of course, were very pleasant people; but unfortunately many took advantage of their newly acquired power. Visiting M.P.s and journalists were allowed to think that these blacks were Mozambicans. But, in fact, until the late 1960s, there were very few Mozambique Africans in any position of authority at all.

To the casual visitor, this new man at Cóbuè was a perfect example of Portuguese non-racial attitudes: he looked like an African, and his wife was almost white. His mother-tongue and his children's was Portuguese. In Cóbuè he behaved fairly well, as he had the army and navy to keep him in order; and as he was just across the water from Likoma Island, his special object was to present to the people there a picture of a benign, non-racial Administrador do Posto.

When he went to Ngoo, however, he became quite a different person. Here he was all-powerful, for the only Europeans were a few soldiers under the command of a corporal, who had noth-thing to do with civilians. The *milicias* came directly under his command. While he was very friendly towards me when I visited Cóbuè, his attitude was very different when I visited Ngoo.

The Portuguese were now starting to move the people of Niassa into *aldeamentos* (fortified villages), after the example of the British in Malaya during the 1950s. The authorities maintained that this was the only way to prevent the *turras* from infiltrating the villages; but, in effect, it meant that the population was under constant surveillance. Frelimo did all that they could to dissuade the people from going into the *aldeamentos*, and I myself was openly against the practice for several reasons:

1. The system had not proved successful in Malaya (where the inhabitants merely threw food over the wire to the *turras*);
2. It represented a traumatic break with the Nyasas' traditional way of living;
3. As the fields of the villagers would necessarily be outside the *aldeamento*, the crops would be at the mercy of the monkeys, whose depredations had previously been kept down because the village houses were close by the fields;
4. Every movement, however innocent, of every person would be watched, and unscrupulous police and soldiers would undoubtedly abuse their position.

It was also clear to me that the very innovation was tantamount to an admission of defeat by the Portuguese, because it effectively allowed Frelimo to roam at will everywhere else.

As a result of many protests and arguments, *aldeamentos* were never established at Messumba and Chiwanga while I was there. At Ngoo, the situation was quite different. The *aldeamento* was sited in a marshy area near the lakeshore where there had been no houses previously, and it excluded the church on which the people's lives (especially at Ngoo) were centred. One of the first buildings to be erected by forced labour was a reed house on the lakeshore for the Administrador do Posto. The villagers were then forced to build new houses for themselves, within the area of the *aldeamento*, and according to measurements which specified not only the area of the house, but also the distance between houses and the width of the 'roads' between each row. No sanitation whatever was provided, but at least at Ngoo the *aldeamento* was on the lakeshore. This 'urbanization' of the village was in complete contrast to the people's traditional way of living. Their fields were all outside the perimeter of the high fence that surrounded the *aldeamento*, and when they went to them, or to church, they passed through the official exits, where they had to clear themselves with the *milícia* who was stationed there. Their former houses were burnt, and no compensation of any sort was paid to them. During the construction of the *aldeamento*, including the Administrador's house, a landing-jetty, and the barbed-wire fence, they were hardly ever allowed to go to their fields, which, in addition to remaining untended, were despoiled by monkeys. When I visited the *aldeamento* for the first time with a nursing orderly, I was deeply disturbed to find acute malnutrition among the people. Many times, in the future, even in cases of serious illness and childbirth, permission was not granted for patients to be brought into Messumba, because, it was alleged, the villagers were being 'lazy' about constructing the *aldeamento*.

The Cape Verdean did not like the Ngoo people, and told me many times that they were all *turras*. I argued with him constantly, and he hated my visits there. More often than not, he left his wife and children at Cóbuè and chose whichever woman he wished to enjoy during his stay at Ngoo, while any husband or father who complained was mercilessly beaten with the *palmatório*. There was nothing that anyone could do: people were far too frightened to make any formal complaint to Brasão de Silva (the Cape Verdean's immediate superior); and, anyway, they were virtual prisoners, since they could not leave Ngoo without an official pass. The stories I heard were innumerable, but there was nothing that I could do either: I had no proof with which to back up the charges; and, besides, it appeared that no one had any effective control over what the man did, though other officials were quite prepared to admit that he was a rascal, and worse. This lack of control over a junior administrative official typified the whole pattern of Portuguese rule in Mozambique; though whether this was intentional or incidental, I never discovered.

Chief Manhica of Ngoo was elderly and not very intelligent, but as the Chief, it was he who bore the brunt of the Administrador's cynical inhumanity. He was told that his people were undisciplined; that they were hand-in-glove with Frelimo; and that it was he who was to blame. The Chief owned several head of cattle which grazed outside the *aldeamento* and were brought in only at night. The Administrador of Cóbuè coveted these cattle very much and from time to time, however much the Chief might protest, would appropriate one to himself, for sale to the army or navy at Cóbuè. The military authorities were very isolated and asked no questions, since they were only too pleased to be able to buy fresh meat. Inevitably, the day came when the Administrador accused Chief Manhica of supplying meat to Frelimo, and arrested him. The Chief was sent to P.I.D.E. in Vila Cabral to be interrogated under Lontrão's supervision. In due course his clothes were sent back to his relatives.

16 Fluctuating Hopes

By May 1967, I was some years overdue for furlough, but because of the situation in and around Messumba, it had been impossible for me to get away earlier. Now, however, I felt that I could safely leave the Mission, if only for a few weeks. I spent a couple of days in Beira on my way to London, and while there, I was asked to call at the Malawi Consulate to see Jorge Jardim.

After the coup in April 1974, the name of Jorge Jardim figured prominently in the news. I write of him as I knew him in the years up to 1970.

He was an extremely wealthy businessman, with a multiplicity of financial interests both in Portugal itself and in Mozambique. He owned an executive jet aeroplane and a newspaper. He was also Malawi's Consul in Mozambique. Most important of all, he was known to be Salazar's 'man in Mozambique', and there can have been few political manoeuvres in which he was not involved. From time to time we met by chance at Metangula, and he was always extremely friendly, inviting me to his private suite at the naval base. He used to ride up and down the dusty road at Metangula on a moped, and always said that he was coming to see us at Messumba but, as far as I remember, never came. My Portuguese friends used to tell me that in Jardim I had a powerful friend and that, so long as I kept on the right side of him, P.I.D.E. would not dare touch me. He appreciated the importance of the Anglican Mission at Messumba to the Nyasa people, and recognized that the authorities had far more to lose than to gain by interfering with our work.

At our meeting in May 1967, he was, as usual, most affable, but rebuked me mildly for being so outspoken about P.I.D.E. and the troops. When I protested that I could hardly ignore the terrible things they did, he agreed, but said I should be more temperate in what I said, as the way I had been behaving was not helping the extremely tense situation. I told him that I seemed to be the only person who *would* speak for those who were being ill-treated and had given up hope of getting anywhere by protesting for themselves. He seemed to accept this, and we parted quite amicably.

On the plane leaving Beira, I found myself sitting beside a Belgian White Father, Padre Pollit, who told me that he was being expelled from Mozambique. He had been at Lundo Mission not far from Inhaminga; and, although Frelimo had not yet begun military activity in the area, he and his Africans had been subjected to constant harassment by the Portuguese. As a result of this, some of his staff had fled to Dar-es-Salaam; and that was where he was intending to go, too. Several of his people had been arrested by P.I.D.E. and tortured. One of the tortures had been to make the victim drink a *garafão* (5 litres) of water and then for the interrogator to beat, and jump on, his abdomen. Padre Pollit had complained bitterly about this to his diocesan superiors, but had received no help from them. We spent most of the flight talking about the iniquities of Portuguese rule in Mozambique; though, as I was intending to return, he suggested that we speak very quietly, for there were doubtless P.I.D.E. informers on the plane.

I stopped off in Lisbon for a few days to see various friends, who were astonished when I told them about my experiences in Mozambique. Owing to strict press censorship, they had no idea that there was much more than the occasional skirmish with Frelimo on the frontier with Tanzania, and, while they knew that Portuguese troops had been dispatched to Mozambique in some strength, they had no understanding of the extent to which there was now, virtually, a war in progress. They were incredulous when I told them of the widespread and indiscriminate brutality of P.I.D.E. and the troops. Not unnaturally they were shocked to learn that their 'gallant' soldiers could behave in such a way. In Portugal, as in Mozambique, there was seldom any news in the papers about the fighting, and what there was, was usually confined to a brief military bulletin published about twice a month on an inside page, listing the number of enemy soldiers killed, the number of enemy bases destroyed and the number of weapons captured. There was then usually some heartening statement, such as: 'Our armed forces continue to repulse the enemy. During this period, our armed forces suffered five casualties, three of which were caused accidentally.'

In England, Lord Kilbracken's reports in the *Evening Standard* had been forgotten, and I found a similar disbelief when I said that the situation in Mozambique had deteriorated considerably. Portugal had learnt her lesson after his lordship's visit, and had become more careful in her choice of those journalists whom she allowed into the 'war zone'. Thanks to the very competent public relations firm which Portugal employed in London, one heard and read only about the enlightened racial policy pursued by Portugal in Africa. I despaired of ever convincing even my friends of the true situation.

In July I left England to return, a trifle apprehensively, to Messumba. This time I went overland to Lisbon, accompanied by an old Ely friend, Jim McGowan. In Paris I collected a new Peugeot truck in which we drove to Lisbon, and which was then shipped out to Mozambique.

Earlier in my furlough, I had paid a brief visit to Oporto to meet a new and important recruit to the Diocese of Lebombo. This was Dom Daniel de Pina Cabral of the tiny Lusitanian Church (which is in full communion with the Anglican Church). Dom Daniel had recently been consecrated a bishop and would shortly be leaving to become Bishop Pickard's assistant in Mozambique. Bishop Pickard had now been in office for almost nine years and wished to retire soon. He realized, as did the missionaries in his diocese, that the continuation of the Anglican work in Mozambique depended upon our getting a bishop of Portuguese nationality.

Daniel de Pina Cabral was made for the job. In his mid forties, and married with four children, he was a highly qualified lawyer and extremely 'well-connected', socially as well as politically. He disliked Salazar and had even spent some months in Penamacor prison for failing to sign, during his military service, some document affirming his loyalty to the régime. This 'crime' was noted in his passport; so that whenever he went abroad, P.I.D.E., who were responsible for immigration formalities, would know there was an anti-Salazarist leaving or entering the country. He spoke good English and was sympathetic to the high-church tradition of the Diocese of Lebombo.

His consecration as a Bishop of the Diocese took place in Lisbon and was widely publicized on radio, press, and television. The Roman Catholics and the Portuguese Government were officially represented; among the distinguished guests were Marcello Caetano, who had been professor of administrative law when Pina Cabral had been a student at Lisbon University, and also the Minister for the Overseas Territories. It appeared that Portugal was at last giving official recognition to the presence of the Anglican Church in Mozambique.

I was relieved to find that during my absence from Messumba, the only notable incident had been another attack by Frelimo on the troops billeted on the Mission. One unknown Frelimo soldier, thought to be a Maconde, was shot dead, and Fr Juma had buried him the following day in our cemetery.

Within a few days of my own return, Bishop Daniel came to visit us at Messumba. The Bishop of Vila Cabral came out to greet him at the airport, as did the Governor and the military commander of the area. Everyone of any importance seemed to have heard of the Pina Cabral family, and, although it was a mystery to them how such an eminent Portuguese could be a Protestant, a 'bishop' of a foreign mission, and yet receive such evident support from the establishment, they were enthusiastically cooperative with him.

The Africans were naturally somewhat alarmed, as their experience of the Portuguese had not been a very happy one, but the Bishop soon dispelled their apprehension by his charm, courtesy, and sincerity. When the local Chiefs came to pay their respects, he explained to them (through me as interpreter, since few of them could understand Portuguese) that he knew of the sufferings of their people, particularly during the last few years, and he intended to do all he could to alleviate their lot. He hoped that they would trust him. Even though he was Portuguese and could not speak Chinyanja, he made a great impression on them.

Like all our visitors, the Bishop was impressed by the long traditions of Messumba, the dedication of our missionary nurses and the high standard of the services in the church. The music struck him, as it had me, as very discordant, and he asked me why I had not taught the people to sing properly. I explained that this was their traditional style, and Messumba missionaries had not felt that they should impose an alien, Western one instead.

I had no difficulty in arranging for a naval launch to take us to Ngoo and Cóbuè, any more than I had had in arranging for an aeroplane to bring him at once from Vila Cabral to Metangula. Never had such help and support come from everyone, and I suspected, with some justification, that the Roman Catholic missions were a little jealous.

His reception at Ngoo was almost hysterical. He was shocked to find that the church and original Mission buildings had been excluded from the *aldeamento*, and reacted similarly to all that I told him about the Cape Verdean Administrador. At Cóbuè, there were now about a hundred people, most of whom had been found in the mountains. They were nearly all Anglicans. The Cóbuè *aldeamento* was far less sordid than the one at Ngoo, and there was a much happier atmosphere there. The Bishop and I were received with honour at the officers' mess, and the Administrador came in to pay his respects and then waited outside, as he had become *persona non grata* in the mess for some reason or other. As we walked down to the launch on our return, the Bishop took the Administrador aside and spoke to him fairly severely about not abusing his authority.

I accompanied the Bishop on his return from Metangula to Vila Cabral, where he stayed with Dom Eurico Nogueira, and together we went to see the Governor. The Bishop impressed upon me that, on these occasions, it was very important to maintain one's position, as Government officials were very conscious of their dignity. One should address them as an equal: which, as a priest, one had a right to do. The conversation between the Governor and the Bishop was very formal, but there was no doubt that it was Bishop Daniel who was in command of the situation. Next morning the Governor and the Bishop of Vila

Cabral went to the airport to say good-bye to Bishop Daniel: a courtesy that came to be standard practice, but which had never been accorded to any previous Anglican bishop.

Bishop Daniel was very critical of the Portuguese administration and of corruption in high places, and while he was, of course, prepared to pay his respects to the civil administration, he had no use for P.I.D.E. whatsoever. Like Jardim, though, he was also critical of my attitude to the armed forces and kept on saying: 'You always blame the troops; they have their work to do, as you and I have ours.' He seemed to think that my stories of brutality by the troops issued not from my own knowledge but from my susceptibility to pro-Frelimo propaganda. While he was prepared to admit that a rare reprehensible act might have been committed by a small group of soldiers, this was only inevitable in such warfare. As a Portuguese, he believed that pluri-continental Portugal was an ideal worth fighting for, while Portuguese citizenship was a privilege that had been accorded by Portugal to all the peoples of her African 'provinces'. I protested that, for the people in the villages of Mozambique, as well as at Messumba, Portugal was another world. But he would infer that, if this *was* the case, we obviously had to do more to convince them how lucky they were to be part of the Portuguese nation; even though it was, for the moment, ruled by Salazar. He could not bring himself to believe me when I told him of mass forced labour and arbitrary arrests being so frequent. 'All are citizens of Portugal,' he would say. 'Of course, with Salazar, there are many injustices in Lisbon, but it cannot be quite so terrible here as you make out.'

One day, when I was on my way to the *mezane* with the Bishop, a *milícia* came up to me and asked me, in Chinyanja, if I could possibly help him to buy any chickens. He had been sent by the Administrador to Messumba for this purpose, but had failed to persuade anyone to sell to him. The Bishop asked me what the *milícia* wanted and I told him. The Bishop then advised me to tell the *milícia* to go and inform the Administrador that he had been unable to get any. When I gave him the Bishop's reply, the *milícia* looked frightened and perplexed, and said: 'If I return to Metangula without any chickens, I shall be beaten.'

The Bishop refused to believe that this could happen, while I knew only too well that it would. I found it almost impossible to convince Bishop Daniel that his own countrymen were so brutal to the Africans. (One recalls how blind the Germans were to the brutality practised by their countrymen; and after the overthrow of the Caetano régime, how shocked were so many Portuguese to learn about the widespread use of torture by their own D.G.S. – Direção Geral de Segurança.)

I liked Bishop Daniel and came to have great respect for him, but in the months that lay ahead, I found that he was isolated, as were most Portuguese people, from what was really going on in Mozambique. In subsequent visits to Messumba, though he never neglected his pastoral duties, he would always make a point of spending at least half a day at the naval and/or military headquarters at Metangula, even if he was only at the Mission for three days. To the Messumba people, these were their enemies; these were the people who had killed Carlos Catatula, who had beaten up Reggie, who had burnt scores of villages and raped their women. They would remark significantly: '*Apita kucheza ni wantu wao*' (He has gone to chat with his people). I sympathized with the people; but what they did not realize was that, as a consequence of his friendly visits to Metangula, we received considerable help, without which I doubt if we could have carried on at all. One simply had to mention that Bishop Daniel was coming, and officials almost jumped to attention. The Bishop naturally saw the whole situation from a Portuguese standpoint, and had little insight into that of the Nyasas. Since he had never worked among them, and had lived always in a country with strict press censorship, this was hardly surprising.

As he was esteemed by Caetano and other influential people, there was nothing that the Portuguese civil and military authorities would not do in order to please him, and on his arrival anywhere the local Portuguese would dress up in their best uniforms to greet him. Such was his influence that he was accorded almost the same privileges as a Roman Catholic bishop, including free transport by land, sea, or air – an unprecedented concession to an Anglican bishop. As the diocese was so vast and scattered, free air transport was an enormous help financially, though we continued to receive no direct financial aid for our work.

I became a little apprehensive of where this treatment would lead us. Now that our Church was being accorded (albeit unofficially) many privileges previously only accorded to the Roman Catholic Church, I feared that before long, instead of fulfilling our traditional role, we, like the Roman Catholic hierarchy in Mozambique, would be seen by the very people we had come to serve as little more than an instrument for their deliberate Portugalization.

Bishop Daniel certainly seemed to find difficulty in altogether understanding my own position. He told me that before he had left Lisbon, he had gone to pay his respects to the Minister for Overseas Territories, and had been told that I was a law unto myself, since I had declared Messumba to be a neutral zone, but that I had been brought to heel. I was amazed that the story had reached Lisbon, and explained that it had not been my idea, but Soares de Cruz's. The Bishop was clearly sceptical that any Portuguese official could have behaved in this way, and I do not think that he believed my explanation.

The Bishop also asked me why some of our employees, including Fr Paulo Litumbi, were in prison; and I told him that I really did not know, since the Frelimo cell had been disbanded almost eighteen months before they were arrested. He considered it monstrous that P.I.D.E. should have done this to the Mission, and he promised to do what he could to get them released as soon as possible.

At least I now knew where most of them were, as they were allowed to write letters. Fr Litumbi and most of the teachers were in Mabalane prison camp, some 130 miles from Maciene; and Buanacaia, Reggie, and Carlos Juma were in Machava prison, just outside Lourenço Marques. They wrote to their families about once a month, and each letter carried the censor's stamp. They were only allowed to write in very general terms, and any reference to themselves, except to say they were well, was scored out with an ink scribble, though one could nearly always make out what was underneath. They were not even allowed to write: 'It is raining heavily today.' They had to give the impression that they were all happy, healthy, and spent the days in perfect weather and conditions. Obviously this could not be true, and I knew what their conditions had been at Vila Cabral, Nampula, and on that boat. When I saw in a newspaper a picture of Reggie and some other Nyasas, in clean white shirts, doing a Nyasa dance in the Lourenço Marques Stadium, I knew only too well that this had been especially organized to give a good impression to the outside world. The particular dance that they were doing, the *ng'anda*, is usually performed by unmarried men, and never by anyone as old as Reggie. Furthermore, that dance is only performed in times of peace, and since the beginning of the war, it had not been performed at Messumba. The picture might delude foreigners and most Portuguese, but not the Nyasas, or anyone who knew anything about their customs.

Not long after my return to Messumba in 1967, Bernardo Chitupila turned up like a gift from heaven itself. He belonged to a near-by village and had been a rather boisterous adolescent, but in 1961 had volunteered, at Borges de Brito's suggestion, for the army. He had been a driver in the army and had spent most of his service near Lourenço Marques and Beira. Now, after six years away, he had come home, a most presentable man of twenty-seven. For two years I had to do practically all the driving myself, which had taken up a great deal of time that I should have spent on administration, accounts, etc. – the bane of a missionary's life. Now here was someone who was not only asking to be employed as a full-time driver, but also prepared to accept the small wage I could offer him – along with the hazards of troop convoys – because he wanted to get married and settle down at home with his family and friends. My only fear (and his, too) was that Frelimo might try to recruit him into their ranks. He was a trained soldier who knew quite a lot about the Portuguese army, so that he could be extremely useful to them; but fortunately the local Frelimo commanders were mostly Nyasas and realized that Bernardo was needed at Messumba if we were to carry on at all. He had friends and relations in Frelimo, and presumably they respected his wish to settle down in his home village after so many years of absence. As far as I know, he never met any Frelimo militants until after he had been with us a year – and that meeting was both incidental and arranged by myself. As neither of us wished to run the risk of his being abducted by anyone, I arranged for him to sleep on the Mission itself.

The boisterous youth had given place to a retiring adult, and his six years' experience of the army had taught him a lot about the Portuguese. He knew exactly how to deal with them in any given situation and he was in every way a notable acquisition for Messumba where we all came to like him very much. Certainly life became fractionally easier for me, though the arrears of office work, on top of the active day-to-day administration of the understaffed Mission, still remained a daunting task.

If Bernardo thought that he was returning to Messumba for a quiet life and a little gentle driving, he was soon to be disillusioned, for within his first six months he was to revisit, as a civilian, several places where he had served as a soldier.

His first task was to accompany me to Nacala, a rapidly growing port on the Indian Ocean and beyond Nampula, to collect the Peugeot truck which I had had shipped out from Lisbon. For various reasons we had to spend several days in Nampula, both on the way to and from Nacala. Borges de Brito had recently been appointed the Mayor of the town.* Lontrão had succeeded Campos, who had been transferred to P.I.D.E. headquarters in Beira. Nampula was now one of the most important towns in Mozambique, as it was the headquarters for all military operations against Frelimo and also one of the main army training centres. One often saw African recruits trotting along the street and heard them reciting mind-numbing chants: 'To the north, we'll go; we'll kill every enemy of Portugal; we are true Portuguese. To the north!'

Borges de Brito had somehow managed to get some Nyasas released from the terrible P.I.D.E. prison on condition that they worked for him and did not return to Messumba. These now formed a nucleus of Anglicans who together with some of the soldiers in the barracks made up a small congregation. The newly appointed Bishop of Nampula, Dom Manuel Vieira Pinto,

* In Mozambique, as in Portugal, this was a Government appointment.

was most helpful in allowing me to use one of his private chapels for services.*

Lontrão was not pleased when he heard that I was staying in Nampula and informed Borges de Brito of his displeasure, but the latter told Lontrão that we had been good friends for many years and that I was always welcome at his home.

Bernardo's second task was to take him away from Messumba for almost two months. The diocese had just bought us a five-ton lorry, and this was awaiting collection in Lourenço Marques. We were able to fly to Lourenço Marques without any problem; but once there, we had to obtain the documents necessary for him to travel through other countries, since in 1968 there was still no all-weather road within Mozambique from Lourenço Marques to Messumba.

The first people to see about the necessary permits were P.I.D.E. Bishop Daniel was able to give me a letter of introduction to Santos Correia, the sub-inspector of P.I.D.E., whom I visited at the new P.I.D.E. headquarters in Avenida Pinheiro Chagas. He told me that provided I could produce various documents about Bernardo, there would be no difficulty as far as he was concerned, but that I would also need a visa from the Rhodesian authorities. He said that there was little point in my seeing the South African authorities, as it was extremely improbable that they would give permission for an African to travel through the Republic.

I eventually managed to obtain all the necessary documents; but as Bernardo was unable to travel through South Africa, it meant that we had to take the very poor dirt road to Malvérnia and the Rhodesian border. The road ran parallel to the railway line for some three hundred miles, and it was both interesting and instructive to see that nearly all the traffic consisted of petrol tankers : sanctions-busting with a vengeance. Then, having spent almost two days passing countless petrol trains, we arrived at the Rhodesian frontier just beyond Malvérnia to find that there was strict petrol rationing there. I had to inform the authorities of the mileage that I expected to do in Rhodesia before leaving the

*Dom Manuel was expelled from Mozambique just before the *coup* which overthrew Caetano, but was able to return immediately afterwards.

country, and the coupons I was given were barely sufficient, though I was told that I could buy some more in Salisbury. However, the real shock came when I was told that I was now in a restricted area and was not permitted to stop for another 150 miles. This, I later discovered, was the Gonakudzingwa detention area, where the Smith régime had been keeping some of the African leaders of that country for several years.

We spent a few days in Rhodesia before crossing the Tete 'pan-handle' and so into Malawi. In Blantyre I met, quite by chance, Amós Sumane, whom I had not seen for five years. He told me that he had left Frelimo; joined Coremo (a small rival organization); and then helped to form U.N.A.R. (União Nacional Africana da Rombézia), which was based in Blantyre, and had the tacit support of the Malawi Government. He explained that U.N.A.R. was a movement which wished to gain independence for northern Mozambique (and hence Rombézia, that part of the country which lay between the Rovuma and Zambezi rivers) by political and not military means. Such a partitioning of Mozambique was not a new idea. Some Portuguese I had spoken with had said: 'We might as well give the north to the blacks for what it's worth and keep the rest ourselves.' Portuguese official propaganda was also directed to a policy of splitting up the nationalists where possible, so weakening Frelimo. The leaders of Frelimo mostly came from the south, and the Portuguese, with some small degree of success, had told the northerners that they were just being used as fighting fodder. Frelimo official policy was entirely opposed to the partitioning of Mozambique in such a way, and so was Portuguese official policy.

I was not altogether surprised that U.N.A.R. was tolerated in Malawi, and that its literature later found its way through the post to Messumba. For the Salazarists, U.N.A.R. was useful as a splinter-group; and for 'liberal' Portuguese, who saw that some concessions must be made to the nationalists, the establishment of a docile Malawi-type state to the north, while the Portuguese presence continued in the south, was a possibility worth consideration. U.N.A.R., while attracting many Nyasas, eventually petered out as more and more Africans realized that colonialism in Africa was doomed.

Bernardo and I eventually reached Vila Cabral where, to my considerable annoyance, I found that I could go no farther, because of mines and ambushes. It was almost Easter, and I had to get back to Messumba. Regretfully I left Bernardo and the new lorry and flew to Metangula. Bernardo and the lorry arrived a month later, having gone with a troop convoy to Meponda, and from there to Metangula by launch.

17 The Last Chapter

In 1968, Marcello Caetano was appointed Prime Minister of Portugal. Bishop Daniel, like many others, was full of hope that this would mean a real liberalization of the régime. A civilian Governor-General, Baltazar Rebelo de Sousa, was appointed to Mozambique. The Minister for the Overseas Territories remained Silva Cunha, whom the Bishop knew well.*

Bishop Daniel brought pressure to bear on P.I.D.E. to release more prisoners. Buanacaia, Jaime Farahane, Fr Litumbi, and several others were set free; but after hearing their stories, I was even more concerned for those who remained: Reggie, Carlos Juma, Alexandre Ncalamba, and many others.

Those who had been released clearly wished to forget the years that they had spent in prison; and I was unwilling to ask too many questions, not only because I did not wish to place them in a compromising position, but also because I knew that they did not wish to be reminded of their terrible experiences. It taxed my emotional resources to hear of the horrors suffered by people to whom I had come close. However, I gathered some information during the course of the next eighteen months before I left Messumba, which tallied with the experience of those released before:

1. Very few of them had been involved, even trivially, in 'subversive' activities. I had had far more to do with Frelimo than any of them.

2. They were beaten and tortured terribly during their time of interrogation, until they were forced to say something, anything, whether true or false.

---

* Silva Cunha, after the *coup* of April 1974, was sent into exile with the President and Caetano, but was later brought back to Lisbon and detained.

3. Their cells were grossly overcrowded, so that the men slept like sardines, with the head of one man resting against the feet of another.

4. Disease, especially diarrhoea, was rampant, and there was seldom any medical attention.

5. They were given nothing to lie upon; and if blankets were supplied, which was seldom, they were soon full of lice.

6. Food was quite inadequate and, what there was, extremely bad.

7. Anyone who dared to complain about anything was ruthlessly punished.

8. There was no prison pay; though money that was sent to them usually reached them, and they could then get sympathetic guards to buy things for them.

9. Mabalane was better than Machava, since there at least they worked outside instead of being kept indoors like caged animals.

10. The few who saw Red Cross representatives were those who bore no tell-tale scars. All international teams had to speak through an interpreter, so that the prisoners could not tell the whole truth without fear of reprisals afterwards.

Most of the released prisoners returned with an official piece of paper declaring that they had been in prison because they had indulged in 'subversive' activities. One reason given might be that they had not reported the presence of Frelimo in their areas. (This was fatuous, as we all knew that Frelimo was everywhere, and if we had all gone to tell the authorities, the Administrador would have been confronted with about a thousand people outside the secretariat every day.) Another might be that they had, at some time, been members of Frelimo; or even that they had failed, before their arrest, to show themselves sufficiently anti-Frelimo.

I was particularly angry about Buanacaia. I am quite sure that he was kept a prisoner for so long only because of his connection with me. I knew that he had had nothing to do with Frelimo at any time, and none of his close relations had joined Frelimo. He had been subjected to brutal interrogation about me.

The hope of liberalization under Caetano proved to be an empty dream. P.I.D.E. came in time to be called D.G.S. (Direção Geral de Segurança) but otherwise was the same organization in every way. The new title dispelled some of the stigma that the dreaded P.I.D.E. had attached to itself, but soon acquired its own evil reputation. Government policy changed from killing all enemies, to trying to win the hearts and minds of the people; but, curiously, by the same means.

People had to be shown somehow how wicked Frelimo was, and that it was the Portuguese who really had the interests of the Africans at heart. They would go to almost any lengths to 'prove' the futility of Frelimo. A propaganda film was made in Vila Cabral with the approval of Major Custódio Augusto Nunes and Captain Caetano (no relation of the Prime Minister, I think). Some youths who worked in the barracks were taken out into the hills in tattered clothes where they were given captured Frelimo weapons to act the part of '*turras*'. Then they were surrounded by Portuguese troops and taken prisoner. The film was shown in the Vila Cabral cinema to the applause of the whites in the audience, and to the amazement and barely concealed amusement of the blacks who, of course, recognized the 'Frelimo soldiers' as people who normally worked in the army barracks.

Another piece of propaganda was staged at Messumba, and could be entitled: 'The kidnapping of people by Frelimo'. Several times I was told that Frelimo had come the previous night and taken people off. I realized that Frelimo might have had some justification for collecting recruits in this way. But the people apparently captured were, for the most part, hardly suitable as recruits, and nearly always managed to escape. One day there was great excitement, since not only had some villagers been taken, but a grenade had been left behind. I went to the spot, Bernardo picked up the grenade, and we took it to the troops stationed on the Mission who did not seem in the least bit disturbed. I could not dismiss these stories entirely as it was possible that Frelimo might take someone they wanted, or someone they suspected of being an informer.

Certainly the immediate effect of the kidnapping upon the Messumba people was to make them very frightened of Frelimo. They felt that Frelimo was annoyed with them for remaining settled at Messumba under Portuguese influence. As the kidnapping seemed to serve the interests of the Portuguese much more than Frelimo's, it more than once crossed my mind that the kidnappers were, in fact, *milicias* and others dressed up in Frelimo clothes, who had been sent specially into the villages in order to discredit the *turras*. Those who escaped usually said that they had not had much difficulty in doing so; and, as far as I now recall, they had not recognized any of their captors. The civil and military authorities took the kidnappings calmly, but also stressed how necessary it was for the people to be resettled in *aldeamentos* like Ngoo, and how necessary it was for the population to be guarded against *turra* incursions.

One afternoon, a middle-aged woman came to tell me that the soldiers on the Mission had just shot her son dead in the village below. Fr Juma, who was distantly related to the woman, happened to be in my house at the time. He said that he would go down to the scene of the incident and suggested that I remain in my house. An hour later he returned, saying that he had been given short shrift by the *furiel*. The dead man, it appeared, had recently returned to Messumba from Rhodesia and was a little simple-minded.

I went at once to the troops' house, where I found the *furiel* in rather an anxious state. He told me that as he and some of his soldiers had been walking down to the River Lunho, the man concerned had shouted offensively at them, though they had not understood what he was saying. Since he had continued to be offensive, and would not shut up even when they threatened to shoot him, the *furiel* had shot him at point-blank range as a *turra*. I was appalled, and told the *furiel* that the man had been nothing of the kind. The *furiel* protested that when they had searched his belongings, they had found Frelimo-type boots in his suitcase. I asked to see these, as I was sure that they were simply boots which he had brought back with him from Rhodesia. The *furiel* refused, and would not let me go near the body until he received permission from his superiors at Nova Coimbra for the man to be buried. I told the *furiel* that even if they had thought him a *turra*, he and his soldiers could have arrested him and then made the necessary investigations. To shoot first and ask questions afterwards was murder, especially as the man concerned was not even armed. The *furiel* by this time realized his mistake. When permission was granted for me to bury the body, I found that the soldiers had themselves dug the grave, and some half-dozen even attended the service at the graveside. I assume that the *furiel* had been reprimanded by his captain, and told to make some sort of conciliatory gesture.

One of the most terrible things that ever happened at Messumba took place on a Sunday morning, while I was conducting the main service of the day. P.I.D.E. agents had gone to visit the soldiers on the Mission, bringing with them some 'stranger' they had arrested on the way. In the house beside the church, twenty yards from where I was celebrating Mass, they suspended him from a beam in the roof and tortured him. I only heard the story, from some deeply shocked soldiers, later on that morning, after the P.I.D.E. agents had left with their prisoner. There was nothing I could do; always there was nothing I could do; I could not even persuade my own Bishop that in reporting such horrors I spoke the truth.

The troops billeted on the Mission seldom left their house after dark, and posted guards and set booby-traps around it every evening. These consisted of a piece of string, one end of which was tied to a fixed grenade and the other to a stick in the ground, thus forming a 'trip-wire'. I protested vigorously against this dangerous practice which, with so many people about, was a real risk to life. Some of the *furieis* were very slack about dismantling most of their traps at a sufficiently early hour, and those on one side of their house were permanent fixtures. The grenades were constantly being set off by stray animals and birds, and at every explosion there was a burst of fire from the soldiers. Occasionally someone would trip over the wire and set off the trap, but luckily no one was seriously injured by them. If I ever returned from a journey after about 5.30 p.m., I would either have to ask the soldiers, in advance, not to put down the trip-wire on the road until I had passed, or I would have to stop the vehicle before I came to the trip-wire, blow the horn and wait until a soldier came and removed it. There seemed absolutely no point in having soldiers on the Mission: they neither 'defended' the Mission, nor prevented Frelimo from coming to it (though now they nearly always came in civilian clothes). The soldiers

Mozambique: Memoirs of a Revolution

seemed to regard their stay at Messumba as a respite from their headquarters at Nova Coimbra. They went about quite freely, chatting to people, and there was always some woman who was prepared to sell herself to a soldier.

Jorge Jardim's visits to Metangula became ever more frequent, and whenever he saw me he would make a point of coming up to me and telling me about the wonderful success that Portugal was having in winning over the hearts and minds of the Mozambicans; how fruitful were his contacts with Malawi; and how impressed the Government there had been by the happy race relations that existed in Mozambique. Malawi sea cadets were now being trained by the Portuguese navy at Metangula, so that Malawi might have her own navy on the Lake, as the Portuguese did.

Relations between Malawi and Portugal were rather ambivalent; for while Portugal trained a navy for Malawi, and Metangula received its fuel from Malawi via Chipoka and Meponda, the Portuguese troops did not hesitate to violate Malawi territory when chasing *turras*, and villages near the border had been bombed by Portuguese planes. On at least one occasion, the *Ilala* had been boarded by *fusileiros* who arrested some African passengers. None of this was ever reported in the press.

In December 1968, Bishop Daniel came to visit us, bringing with him my Ely friend, Jim McGowan, who was teaching at a school in Swaziland. Jim expressed his surprise that the Mission could carry on at all, now that we were so clearly in a war zone. We visited Ngoo and Cóbuè, and the Bishop was later able to start negotiations for the church at Ngoo to be included within the *aldeamento* and for us to resume some form of educational and medical work there.*

During the Bishop's visit, Fr Juma asked him if he had seen his son, Carlos, when he had visited Machava prison to say Mass. The Bishop replied that he had not seen him on the last occasion he had been there, but thought that he was quite well. Afterwards the Bishop told me that apparently Carlos had been in some sort

---

*Negotiations concerning the church were not successful during my time.

of trouble, the nature of which he could not discover, and that he was rather worried about him. (Carlos died at the prison in 1970, almost exactly a year later.) I spoke again to the Bishop about Reggie, and how grossly unfair it was that he, of all people, should still be in prison. Since he had worked so faithfully for Messumba for so many years, could the Bishop use his undoubted influence to get him released? He asked me to write out Reggie's life-story, and armed with that he would do what he could. But another three and a half years were to pass before he was successful, and Reggie returned home.

The Bishop left after a few days. Jim stayed to spend Christmas and the New Year with us, and during his stay persuaded me to return with him to Swaziland for local leave, which by then I was badly needing.

Jim had flown to Vila Cabral from Tete, where he had left his car; so we flew to Tete and then drove to Salisbury, Rhodesia, where we stayed with the Bishop who was a friend of Jim's. During my stay there I met Susan Woodhouse who within a year was to become my wife. She was the Bishop's secretary and I had often heard about her. Strangely enough, I had met her father twelve years previously on Salisbury station, when I was on my way to Messumba for the first time.

I spent only a few days in Salisbury, and, as Jim had other engagements, I went to Beira for the wedding of one of Jorge Jardim's daughters. He had taken over a vast hotel in the centre of the city for the occasion, which turned out to be not only a glittering social event, but also a diplomatic jamboree and a masterpiece of propaganda.

The Nuptial Mass was celebrated in the hotel by no less than three Bishops, and among the seven hundred guests were the Governor-General of Mozambique, some Brigadier representing the Rhodesian régime, and a representative of the South African Government. Aleke Banda was there as the personal representative of Dr Hastings Banda, President of Malawi. Also present were many of the foreign diplomats stationed in Mozambique, and a sprinkling of Mozambique Chiefs from the far north, who looked unhappy and out of place on this very formal Portuguese occasion. Jardim made a special point of introducing me to the

Governor-General, Aleke Banda and the African Chiefs. Cristina's son, who was working for Jardim, came up and whispered to me: 'There are at least four of "them" mingling with the guests,' and I knew he was referring to P.I.D.E. agents, as I had already spotted Campos and taken care to keep well clear of him.

I was fascinated by the whole performance. Jardim had clearly made excellent use of his daughter's wedding to proclaim to the world the thoroughly relaxed and contented situation that was supposed to exist in Mozambique. He had set out to demonstrate how powerful and confident was the Portuguese presence in Mozambique, and he made me feel how feeble and doomed to failure were my lonely efforts to fight the system on behalf of the people in Niassa. My attempts to get official evildoers brought to justice, or to obtain redress or even trial for those arrested and detained for no crime, could not succeed against the machine here so intimidatingly portrayed.

I returned to Rhodesia almost immediately after this wedding, and, together with Jim McGowan and Susan Woodhouse, drove to Johannesburg, stopping for a couple of days with Garfield and Grace Todd, for whom Susan had worked for eight years before becoming secretary to the Bishop in Salisbury.

Jim and I went to Swaziland where I left him and went on to Mozambique for Bishop Daniel's enthronement as Bishop of Lebombo. Like the wedding, though rather less so, this was a strange experience for me. Bishop Daniel, without any difficulty, obtained permission from P.I.D.E. for us to meet the Archbishop of Cape Town, Robert Selby Taylor, who was coming for the occasion, when he got off the plane at Lourenço Marques. As we drove to Maciene, the conversation inevitably turned to the situation in northern Mozambique, as the Archbishop was very interested in Messumba, which he had visited many years previously. Bishop Daniel tended to make light of it, saying that although he could sympathize with Frelimo in many ways, because under Salazar things had been so bad (after all, he had been in prison himself), now, with Caetano, considerable improvements were being gradually introduced. Caetano could not possibly undo, in an instant, all the evil that Salazar had done in the preceding thirty years. The great thing was that, unlike

South Africa, every African in Mozambique had the same legal rights as any white Portuguese. He foresaw that Mozambique would eventually be incorporated as a semi-autonomous country within a Lusitanian Commonwealth. What the Bishop had against the independence movement was that if Mozambique became a militant black African state, South Africa would soon step in, bringing with her the atrocious apartheid policies to which she was committed. Such policies were in direct conflict with what Portugal was trying to do, and also in direct conflict with the teaching of the Gospel as he saw it.

That evening, the Archbishop told me that he did not entirely agree with all that the Bishop had said in the car, and asked me for my opinion. I told him that nearly all Portuguese seemed to believe that they held a unique position in the field of race relations. In fact, what they said and what they did were two very different things. I could not, of course, speak with authority about Africans in southern Mozambique, but my suspicion was that Bishop Daniel, though a very intelligent person, had little idea what the Africans really thought about the situation. I emphasized, however, my belief that we were lucky to have him. I was convinced that, so long as Portugal ruled, we had, in him, the saviour of Anglican work in the country.

Bishop Daniel's enthronement was a very grand occasion, attended by the Governor-General whom I had to meet and conduct to his seat in the Cathedral. I am sure that he had never been inside a non-Roman Catholic church in his life. There were also the British Consul-General, the local Governor, the Minister of Education, a representative of the Archbishop of Lourenço Marques and several other Portuguese people (among whom, no doubt, were a few P.I.D.E. agents). We were rapidly becoming part of the Portuguese establishment, to my disquiet.

Back in Lourenço Marques, the Bishop took me to task for failing to produce the Messumba accounts for so long. I knew all about the overdue accounts and letters; they had been hanging over my head for longer than I cared to remember. But I tried to explain to the Bishop how impossible it was for one missionary to do all that had to be done on such a large mission even in peace time – let alone during a war, with all the added difficulties of transport, soldiers, arrests, the displacement of whole villages, the feeding and housing of so many refugees. Originally, Messumba had had a European staff of five or six; we were now reduced to three, two of them nurses. I had to run the school, which was larger than it had ever been, and that in itself was recognized to be a full-time job. If the diocese required accounts, it had better do something about sending someone to do them, as I simply could not continue to run the place as it should be run. While I became angry with the Bishop, he became exasperated with me and the whole situation – though we parted good friends.

On my return to Messumba, I went down with a severe attack of shingles and was in bed for almost two months. I had all too much time in which to realize the impossibility of carrying on in so intolerably frustrating a situation, and I tried to warn those closest to me, Buanacaia, Bernardo, and Fr Juma, that I felt it time to leave Messumba. I feared that unless the Bishop could somehow increase the missionary staff, the place might even have to close. They were very worried, since to them, even more than to me, Messumba meant so much.

In April, Bishop Daniel visited Messumba again. I had recovered sufficiently to meet him in Vila Cabral and accompany him on the various journeys that he made during his short visit, but again I was deeply disturbed by the amount of time that he spent with the Portuguese authorities, at the expense of being with his people. At Macalogue, a remote, but extensive, Portuguese garrison, which we visited on 9 April 1969, we spent almost the entire time in the officers' mess; and, apart from saying Mass, he cannot have spent more than half an hour with the members of his African congregation. These Africans had been 'found' by the troops hiding in the surrounding hills and were now kept in an *aldeamento*. This was the first time that they had seen their Bishop for many years, as most of them originally came from our most distant outstations, which were rarely visited, even by me. This was the great day in their lives, and I was deeply shocked that Bishop Daniel, in whom I had placed so much hope, should neglect his flock to dine with their captors.

Within a week or two of the Bishop's departure, I became ill again, but Jim came for another visit and was a great source of strength to me.

At the beginning of May, we always had our annual school *festa*, and I was well enough to attend. But I was not pleased when I saw the recently whitewashed walls of the school buildings plastered with Portuguese propaganda posters. While I was still confined to my house, I had been told that the troops had done this, without asking anyone's permission, but I was not expecting to see quite so many. There was hardly a single square foot of wall to be seen. Some of the posters were untidily peeling off because of the wind. It is possible that some of the smaller children had been mauling them, but the teachers told me they had been very firm in telling everyone to leave them alone.

A few days later, our teachers and Irene told me that three soldiers were going through the classrooms and wards sticking up more posters. They asked me to intervene, as the lessons were being interrupted and the patients disturbed. They also told me that the soldiers were behaving in an arrogant and threatening manner. I went to see for myself, and there was hardly a single building that was not covered with posters on the outside, as well as having a fair sprinkling within. Then I saw that they had not spared the church. When I went inside and found a few pasted up even there, I tore them down, and was sorely tempted to do the same with all the others on the Mission, but decided that it would be wiser to leave them alone and see the Company Commander next time he visited his troops on the Mission.

During the customary *sesta* after lunch, I was awakened by a single shot fired fairly near. I rushed in the direction from which I assumed the shot had come and found everyone in a state of alarm. Apparently, the three soldiers had accused a man, Mateus Wemba, of having removed some of the posters they had put up. He had denied this, and one of the soldiers had fired a shot a few inches above his head. They had then taken him prisoner. (I found the bullet buried in a wall.)

I went to the house in which the soldiers were billeted, and found Mateus being guarded by a soldier whom, of course, I knew well. I told him that if any posters had been removed, other than by the wind, I was to blame, and requested him to exchange

Mateus for me. The poor soldier was very frightened. He said that he could not possibly do this, and the person I should see was a subaltern who had arrived that morning from Nova Coimbra with two soldiers for the purpose of sticking up the posters.

It did not take me long to find the young officer and his subordinates, and I told him that they had arrested the wrong man. It was I who had removed the posters from the church; while any others missing had probably been blown off by the wind, since the teachers and children and everyone else would have been far too frightened to do so.

The subaltern asked me if I still had the posters I had ripped off, and I said that I would fetch them. As I returned with the posters, he shouted: 'Don't you dare put them on the ground: I'm warning you!' His gun was in his hand, with his finger on the trigger, and I knew that he would not hesitate to shoot if I dropped them; so I told him that I would put them on the table in the house reserved for the Bishop. Shortly afterwards Mateus was released and spent the rest of the day, and that night, in my house, as he was too frightened to go to his village.

But Aidão Lilinga (the headmaster), and two other teachers, all of whom had fairly recently been released from Mabalane, were seized and taken to Nova Coimbra that evening. On their return next morning, Aidão told me what had happened: 'We were taken to the garrison and put into a room. After dark, the Captain and some others came to see us and shouted that you were an enemy of Portugal, and that you had encouraged us to rip off the posters that had been stuck up. We said this was not true. I was told to take off my shirt and I was whipped on my back. We were given neither food nor a blanket. It was like being at Mabalane again.'

I asked Jim to come in, and in his presence I took two photographs of Aidão's scarred back.

Two days later, Bishop Daniel arrived unexpectedly. 'What have you been doing about posters, or something? Yesterday I was called to the Governor-General's office, as he had received information that you were indulging in anti-Portuguese activities.' I told the Bishop the whole story. He was furious with the Captain at Nova Coimbra: for ordering the posters to be stuck up at all without first seeing me; then, for the shot fired over Mateus' head; and lastly for the whipping given to the headmaster of the school. I told the Bishop about the photographs I had taken of Aidão's scarred back, with Jim as my witness. The Bishop said: 'I think you had better destroy the film in case P.I.D.E. find out about it; and also I think you should destroy all those notes you have received from Frelimo for the same reason.' Stupidly I did destroy the letters, but I kept the pictures. When he had returned to Lourenço Marques, Bishop Daniel sent me a telegram saying that he had explained the story of the posters to the Governor-General, and that I was now entirely free from any blame. Knowing his fellow-Portuguese, he probably thought that sending a telegram was the best way to broadcast the fact.

The Bishop now agreed that I was badly in need of a long holiday from Messumba and suggested that I return with him to Lourenço Marques. But he took Jim's advice that I should get right out of Mozambique, and so very shortly I found myself in Salisbury staying with the Woodhouses. The doctors recommended five months' sick leave, which the Bishop agreed to allow. But during my convalescence I realized that it would be unwise for me ever to work again at Messumba, at least while the Portuguese were there; and I was also a little doubtful about the wisdom of my working again in Mozambique. When Susan and I decided to marry, I wrote to Bishop Daniel, telling him that we would be prepared to return to his diocese, but not to stay at Messumba for more than a year. I was hardly surprised, but rather shaken, when he replied that he felt I needed a complete break for at least two years.

It seemed to me, however, that it was no good half-shutting the door on such a large part of my life and that this must be the final break.

Susan and I were married at the end of 1969, and a few weeks later we went back to Messumba to pack up my belongings and say good-bye. This last journey was very different from my first just thirteen years previously, when I had spent days in trains and boats.

We flew to Metangula, where we were met by Bernardo and

Irene. The Lunho was in spate, so we left the lorry at Chiwanga and walked to the river's mouth which we crossed by dug-out canoe. From where we started our walk, it is a distance of about three miles up to Messumba, but it took us nearly two hours since, for the people, this was our wedding. They crowded round us singing wedding songs, each one wanting to shake hands with us. As we approached the Mission along the familiar paths, inches deep in mud after heavy rains, I found myself leading a procession hundreds strong, with Susan somewhere in the middle of it. By the time we reached my former house, we were the dirtiest bride and groom imaginable.

Throughout our visit, during which I tried to restore the electricity and water supplies which had failed, people kept coming to the house and bringing us gifts. Each encounter was a most moving experience, as the people who gave so gracefully had so little from which to give. But the costliest gift of all came from Bernardo's widowed mother: she brought a little scraggy chicken to us with a murmured apology for its meagreness, but it was, she said, the last one in her village.

After Mass on the Sunday, there was a formal ceremony of gifts and speeches and singing. We sat on a verandah with a table before us, on which were placed two trays; and, after the custom of the Nyasas, people came forward and put one coin into Susan's tray and another into mine. One of the younger priests gave a formal address on behalf of all the people and then handed it to me. They were not only pleased that I had come to say good-bye in person, but also that I had brought Susan with me so that they could celebrate our marriage.

We spent barely ten days at Messumba, but in Beira, where we spent a few days, the Nyasa Anglicans working there held a similar reception for us.

One of the last things I did before I left Africa was to send Reggie a registered envelope containing the few Mozambican bank-notes that I still possessed. I well knew the address at Machava, C.P. 1951, Lourenço Marques. But a year was to pass before he finally received it, since he, like Carlos Juma, had been subjected to disciplinary treatment; though, unlike Carlos, Reggie survived to return to Messumba.

Two years after I had left Messumba, Bishop Daniel asked if I had any idea of returning to Mozambique. I told him I had none – but Messumba will never be far from my thoughts.

FAREWELL ADDRESS TO ARCHDEACON
JOHN DOUGLAS PAUL AND HIS WIFE*

In the Name of Messumba District: Chiefs, Clergy, Teachers, Nurses, Elders and All Christians:

WE GREET YOU

All of us are very happy to see you today, but we are sad at heart because you and your wife have come to say good-bye to us. Are you really leaving? Who will live with us now? We find it difficult in your presence to recount your acts of kindness to us, as we do not wish to give the impression that we are only thinking about ourselves.

However, we shall recount a little, though much more remains in our hearts. You have lived with us for eleven years, from 1958 to 1969. We have not time to speak about your early years, but we would like to say something about your kindness to us during these present troubles.

Like a shepherd you have really given yourself to your Christians. You have cared for everyone here at Messumba, at Cóbuè, at Ngoo, at Manda-Mbuzi, at Lucambo, those in the hinterland and those at Metangula. You arranged places to sleep, a water supply, food, clothes, and blankets. You agreed to store the belongings of those who asked you, and afterwards when they collected them, they found them as they had left them. You welcomed, without question, all who came to you, and helped people who found themselves in unexpected distress at any time – even at night.

Because of your *nous* and your love for all your Christians, you came to an agreement with the civil authorities that people might live together peacefully in areas such as Messumba, Chiwanga, Nova Coimbra, Metangula, Ngoo and Cóbuè.

* Translated from the original Chinyanja.

Thus we know that God chose you as the means of saving us your children, and you, by the Grace of God, obeyed His Will by sacrificing yourself in this way.

We were very sorry that you were ill and had to go to a proper hospital for treatment, but we are happy you were well cared for and have recovered.

We are sad that you are leaving us alone and will no longer work among us, but we are pleased that on 30 December 1969 you were married. Now, because of your good heart which we know so well, you have come here so that we can see your wife. We are happy to see your wife in our midst, and count today as your wedding day for us at Messumba. Please forgive our poverty of which you yourself are only too well aware.

Receive this little present from your Christians, which is for both of you.

Also, the Mothers' Union wish to present your wife with a little gift.

We are very sad that you are leaving us, but because it is God's Will that the rest of your life should be spent elsewhere, we can only say THANK YOU.

Have a good journey. May God be with you wherever your next job may take you, and we pray you may work there as well as you have worked here.

We shall not forget you in our prayers, and please may you remember us.

GOOD-BYE

We, your beloved children, the Christians at Messumba.
8 February 1970

Epilogue

Developments in Mozambique since August 1974 have, for the most part, been encouraging. Undercurrents of dismay among some small sections of the population at the turn of events may have led to outbreaks of violence, but the moderation shown by the new rulers augurs well for the future.

The ill grace with which President Spínola was reported to have recognized the independence of Guinea-Bissau on 10 September 1974 served to strengthen my own conviction that he was not the man to lead Portugal in her negotiations for a truly independent Mozambique. Costa Gomes, his successor, has shown himself far more aware of political realities by his acceptance of the fact that there can be no halfway-house between colonialism and independence for the peoples of Mozambique and Angola. I make no comment on reaction to the change-over in Portugal itself, as this book is concerned with Portugal only insofar as events and policies there affect Mozambique.

Shortly before Spínola's resignation, much publicity was given to the racial disturbances that took place in Lourenço Marques and other towns in Mozambique. Such disturbances are inevitable when a privileged section of a community seeks to maintain its position at all costs, and another section fears that the freedom it has been promised may yet be withheld. Further, when two sides have been locked in armed conflict for ten years, and animosity has been deliberately fostered, it is hardly surprising that friction should arise when they are suddenly required to look upon each other as allies. In spite of the September riots, and less serious disorders that took place occasionally during the remainder of 1974, it has been both astonishing and admirable to see the way the leaders of Frelimo have kept their heads, demonstrating to the world their political maturity and sense of responsibility. In international affairs, too, Frelimo leaders have shown a similar prudence and responsibility.

Portugal's rule over many centuries in Africa has been characterized by the exploitation of the inhabitants. The people of the new Mozambique will be extremely jealous of their new-won independence; and will be unlikely to exchange one form of external oppression for another, in whatever guise it may appear. Mozambique is to reach full independence on 25 June 1975, exactly thirteen years after the foundation of Frelimo, and almost eleven years after the beginning of the armed struggle against the Portuguese régime. There is, of course, a danger that after this date there will be a backlash from reactionary forces within the country and outside, but the rulers of independent Mozambique will, without doubt, be well prepared for such an eventuality.

And what of Messumba? Strangely enough, the Mission once again became a Zona Neutra, where, after the ceasefire, both sides were able to make initial contact with each other. At first, naturally, there was mutual suspicion; but with the missionaries' help, the change-over in the lakeshore area was accomplished without undue difficulty.

By November, landmines and booby-traps had been removed and there was no hindrance to the Mission resuming its work in the outstations. Manda-Mbuzi, Chicale, Ngoo, Mpochi and many others were once again visited by our clergy, often accompanied by Frelimo personnel who, today, know the places so much better than anyone else. In a letter I received from Messumba towards the end of 1974, my correspondent wrote: 'During the last few days, I have been making some visits either to the Frelimo base or to our old church buildings, and always there have been several children to be baptized. The Frelimo people have been very good and do see the value of what we are trying to do.'

From time to time I get news of the people mentioned in this book. Of the Juma family, Carlos, the eldest son, died as a direct result of the disciplinary treatment (starvation) he received in Machava prison; but, four and a half years later, his youngest brother, Pedro, barely a teenager when I first arrived at Messumba, was appointed the first Frelimo Governor of Lourenço Marques. Yet another brother, Matias, one of the first batch of students we sent to the Escola Técnica in Vila Cabral, works for Frelimo in Tanzania. Matias Chissancho, who also went to the Escola Técnica, is today in a position of responsibility at the base at Metangula. The feeling at Messumba, and no doubt throughout Mozambique, could be summed up in a sentence from Reggie's Christmas letter to me: 'We thank God who has answered our prayers for the liberation of our country.'

This book is dedicated to the people of the new Mozambique, and to the memory of those who suffered and died in its attainment.

25 February 1975

Roads and Railways used by author

Mozambique international boundaries

0 50 100 150
Scale in miles

Map 1.

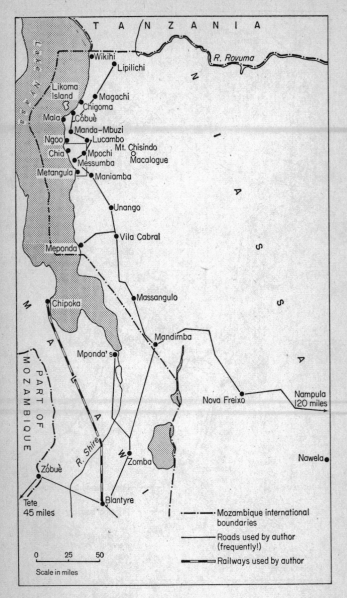

Map 2

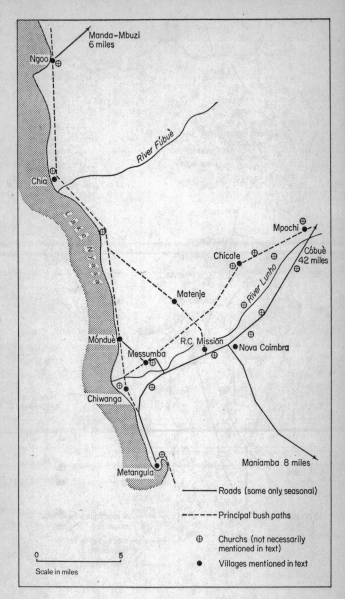

Manda-Mbuzi
6 miles

Ngoo

River Fúbuè

Chia

Lake Nyasa

Mpochi

Chicale

Cóbuè
42 miles

River Lunho

Matenje

Móndue

R.C. Mission

Nova Coimbra

Messumba

Chiwanga

Maniamba 8 miles

Metangula

——— Roads (some only, seasonal)

– – – – Principal bush paths

⊕ Churchs (not necessarily
mentioned in text)

● Villages mentioned in text

0   5

Scale in miles

Map 3